# WOMEN IN THE ORTHODOX TRADITION

# WOMEN IN THE ORTHODOX TRADITION

FEMINISM, THEOLOGY, AND EQUALITY

---

ASHLEY MARIE PURPURA

University of Notre Dame Press
Notre Dame, Indiana

Copyright © 2025 by the University of Notre Dame
University of Notre Dame Press
Notre Dame, Indiana 46556
undpress.nd.edu

All Rights Reserved

Published in the United States of America

Library of Congress Control Number: 2024947143

ISBN: 978-0-268-20922-3 (Hardback)
ISBN: 978-0-268-20925-4 (WebPDF)
ISBN: 978-0-268-20924-7 (Epub3)

GPSR Compliance Inquiries:
Lightning Source France, 1 Av. Johannes Gutenberg, 78310 Maurepas, France
compliance@lightningsource.fr   |   Phone: +33 1 30 49 23 42

# CONTENTS

| | Acknowledgments | vii |
|---|---|---|
| | Introduction: Toward an Orthodox Feminist Theological Engagement with Tradition | 1 |
| ONE | Acknowledging Tradition's Gendered Limitations | 29 |
| TWO | Commemorating the Patriarchal Woman | 61 |
| THREE | Spiritual Values and Gender Equality | 91 |
| FOUR | Theology and Women's Full Humanity | 117 |
| FIVE | Approaches for Unsaying Patriarchal Androcentrism | 139 |
| SIX | Resources for Advocating for Women in Tradition | 169 |
| | Conclusion | 193 |
| | Notes | 205 |
| | Index | 265 |

## ACKNOWLEDGMENTS

This book is foremost for and indebted to the Orthodox women past and present in my religious and academic life who continually inspire and challenge me by their theological witness and diverse ways of living tradition. It is a labor of love and many years in the making. Within its pages are insights and examples that I presented in earlier formats at various conferences and discussed over tea with my scholarly friends. I am grateful for the interlocutors and feedback I had in those settings to begin to explore these ideas. In 2020–21, I was supported by an NEH Faculty Fellowship in Orthodox Christian Studies from Fordham University's Orthodox Christian Studies Center, which allowed me precious time to focus on research and writing chapter drafts. An appointment as a research associate in the Women's Studies in Religion Program at Harvard Divinity School in 2023–24 offered additional revision time and supportive and intellectually rich conversation partners for preparing the final manuscript for publication. I am immensely thankful for the anonymous reviewers' careful readings and helpful suggestions. Their questions and observations have shaped this book into something much better. I offer my appreciation to Emily King and the whole team at the University of Notre Dame Press who have made this book a reality. Last, and forever important, I thank my family for their daily prayers, examples, love, and support.

# Introduction

## Toward an Orthodox Feminist Theological Engagement with Tradition

Amid many various cultural contexts, levels of local participation, and individual perceptions, Orthodox Christian ritual practices and pastoral approaches reflect patriarchy as normative and even at times divinely reflective. As a global and historical norm, Orthodox Christianity does not admit women to the priesthood or episcopacy, refers to its leaders as "patriarchs" who oversee "patriarchates," and relies on a "patristic" tradition for much of its theological development and interpretation.[1] In these and other structural ways, Orthodox Christianity privileges patriarchal and androcentric (and mostly clerical and often monastic) voices and perspectives as if they were universal. By "androcentric," I mean the centering of male and men's perspectives and preferences over those of others (in this case, women), and by "patriarchal," I refer to an inequitable power dynamic that privileges men's leadership and control (particularly of women). In one contemporary example, Orthodox Christian hierarchs met in 2016 at the Holy and Great Council and issued a statement rejecting discrimination based on sex and affirming the "equal dignity of all people."[2] The fact that the signatories of the statement were de facto exclusively male did not seem to Orthodox leaders to contradict this statement. Exclusion in this instance was not recognized by the hierarchs as attesting to a type of gender-based inequality, even though to many women and men it was.[3] This example demonstrates that exclusively male clerical authority to speak for and to the whole church often ignores or dismisses its own reinforcement of patriarchy as representing and participating in exclusionary and oppressive power dynamics. Narratives and hymns praising the equality of female saints, high levels of church attendance by women, historically powerful female monastic leaders, women beneficiaries, and sainted empresses, alongside theological discourses appealing to the equality of the sexes in spiritual life, appear to affirm the Council's statement. Indeed, Orthodox tradition features numerous prominent female saints and historical figures who shaped the course of Orthodoxy (Mary the Theotokos, above all).[4] Women are *almost* everywhere in the church. Yet, despite attestations of gender equality by prominent figures within Orthodox Christianity, the representation of women within the tradition—both as a religion and as the collective sources of religious memory—is patriarchally limited. I say "patriarchally limited" here because it is not just that the focus of tradition has been shaped disproportionately by men (and therefore androcentrism), but this androcentrism reinforces the religious leadership of men to speak for and determine the ways women can be recognized as Orthodox within Orthodoxy.

Orthodox Christianity thus has a tradition of claiming equality even as it maintains patriarchy. This poses a challenge for addressing issues related to women's equality because the sources, practices, and precedents that might inform an Orthodox response are disproportionately patriarchal. Orthodox tradition is not neutral for women. It privileges men, or at the very least male control and leadership of the church. But what is tradition, and why does it matter for Orthodox Christians? Tradition, broadly understood within Orthodoxy, is the witness of God at work in the church in time.[5] More concretely, this refers to historical sources, teachings, and practices handed down by each generation that are recognized by the church as valuable for expressing and cultivating Orthodoxy. This includes but is not limited to scriptures, doctrinal and canonical texts, teachings of saints and historically influential theologians (patristics), liturgical texts and hymns, ascetic and embodied practices, rites and sacraments, iconography and sacred arts, the holy orders, and the lives of the saints, both lived and as recorded in hagiographies. I say that tradition is not limited to these genres because Orthodox Christians regard tradition as "living." It is living in that it is an ongoing source of revelation for how the faithful might learn from the past to inform understandings of God, and human life in communion with God, in the present.[6] Tradition is both written and recorded but also experienced in the lives, bodies, and practices of Orthodox believers. Within Orthodoxy, tradition carries significant authority in developing new theological expressions by maintaining continuity with the already accepted teachings of the past. Tradition, as representing a witness to what the church acknowledges to be holy and conducive to holiness, is thus compelling to invoke in arguing for how the church should be understood in the past, present, and future.

Inasmuch as it is invoked as the source of authority to claim continuity with the revelation of God in human lives of the past, tradition is also contested for how Orthodox Christians refer to it to shape their lives and ecclesial communities in the present. This is particularly the case regarding religious interpretations of gender, where continuity with tradition affects women's opportunities and equality. The significance of being a woman is culturally and historically diverse in ways that are often eclipsed in attempts to defend an unbroken Orthodox tradition and religious heritage. For example, a common rebuttal to the question of ordaining women to the priesthood is that it is not and has never been part of our tradition, without acknowledging the different social circumstances and gender constructions that precluded its previous possibility and that are no longer generally normative. Admittedly, any application of, or appeal to, tradition to elucidate contemporary issues that are understood and contextualized differently in the premodern world is a hermeneutical and theological challenge. Issues related to women are particularly challenging because of the historical and contemporary androcentric nature of Orthodox tradition. As I show in the next chapter, most of the sources appealed to as tradition and what counts authoritatively as "tradition" in the present are disproportionately influenced and determined by men. Even when tradition is presented as being a source of understanding for all, it leaves women at an often-unacknowledged disadvantage. Consequently, the usual Orthodox method of referring to its tradition to formulate responses to the issues of the present is always going to produce a result that continues to privilege men unless it addresses its own patriarchal androcentrism first. This book is an attempt to identify and address the patriarchal androcentrism of Orthodox tradition as theologically problematic and to offer constructive resources for undoing its limits within Orthodoxy.

## RATIONALE

The sources and practices of Orthodoxy perpetuated and endorsed across generations as spiritually beneficial and divinely inspired present partial and problematic religious constructions of women. Well-educated men, often ordained or monastic, overwhelmingly influence the textual sources and control the liturgical rites most significant for Orthodox Christianity. In one resurrection hymn sung cyclically in Orthros before Sunday Divine Liturgy, for instance, Mary Magdalene is affirmed as a "herald" of the resurrection but only after attributing her mistaking of Jesus for the gardener (John 20:15) to the worldliness and inferiority of her gender, saying, "her thinking was still mundane, as a weak woman that she was."[7] Such negative gender constructions are theologically problematic because Orthodox believe there should be a correlation between what is believed (*lex credendi*) and what is prayed (*lex orandi*).[8] Consequently, prayers that invoke limiting tropes about women (and other demographics for that matter) are theologically problematic because they show either that Orthodox are praying in words that they do not believe (e.g., women are inherently weak) or that they do believe. These partial androcentric representations of women deny women's full equality. Similar words and practices that subtly and overtly diminish the status of women may be disconnected from women's self-understanding and agency in their religious communities but are idealized in the liturgical context nevertheless.[9] Imagine a young girl who is told by family members and schoolteachers that she is strong, smart, and capable of achieving her dreams and that same girl loves church and learns to chant, only to be discouraged by encountering a gendered put-down in the words of a hymn that would be intolerable in any other context. How is she to make sense of such gender discrimination in her religious tradition? The commemoration of women in an androcentrically limited way, even if just reflective of historically normative attitudes, presents the patriarchal constructions of women as conducive to or reflective of Orthodoxy.[10] This is what I refer to in chapter 2 as the "patriarchal woman" of Orthodox tradition.

In more recent years, the androcentric trajectory of Orthodoxy has been maintained by an exclusively male hierarchy even as women continue to fill churches and use unofficial ecclesiastical positions to shape the traditions of their faith.[11] Although there have been numerous initiatives to restore the female diaconate, the ordination of women to this office has failed to be widely realized throughout global Orthodoxy.[12] The reason for this lack of action is complex but cannot be said to be unrelated to a type of latent misogyny and limited view of women's "roles" pervasive in Orthodox cultural and ecclesial contexts. The reasons for individual and communal positions regarding gender and the status of women within Orthodox Christian communities are socially entangled and cannot be limited to singular sources or simplistic religious interpretations. However, the possibilities for arguing for women's equality and opportunities within Orthodox Christianity will remain limited if the patriarchal roots of its historical past and present tradition are not addressed first. That is, any argument on behalf of women that draws on or appeals to tradition will always be constrained by the androcentrism of the past and its situation in a patriarchal religious system. This book responds to the tension between theological values of equality and the ecclesiastical maintenance of patriarchy. I suggest in the chapters that follow that the historical constraints of patriarchal androcentrism can be loosed by prioritizing a theological view of God united to all humanity and approaching tradition as a revelation and promotion of that theological confession.

Orthodox Christians past and present bring with them a plethora of perspectives and a diverse range of identities that simultaneously resist uniformity and polarization even within local parish communities. The historian Judith Bennett's observation that "patriarchy might be everywhere, but it is not everywhere the same" certainly resonates when one examines the breadth of Orthodox Christian communities across the world and even across a single town.[13] Regardless of the ways one might observe the patriarchal nature of the church, many Orthodox women exercise significant agency in their parishes, widely teach the faith, and devoutly practice in ways that may ignore, accept, transform, or meaningfully interpret any patriarchal androcentrism experienced in *their* Orthodoxy.[14] Yet even such authority and autonomy in women's religious identities and participation are still dependent on a certain degree of conformity to an ecclesiastical tradition that disproportionately privileges and empowers men. Women who perform their genders within the boundaries of patriarchal expectations may have significant influence, but it cannot be forgotten that this influence is still bound by expectations that if transgressed place women at a disadvantage.[15] Some women within Orthodox Christianity constantly negotiate their own "patriarchal bargain" whereby they give up some level of autonomy in order to gain authority through visible conformity.[16] Other Orthodox women may assume traditional and even subordinate roles in religious contexts but increasingly expect and participate in more egalitarian values in secular spaces. For some, this may present a type of troubling double identity, but others may find performing traditional gender roles the most empowering and meaningful expression of their religious identities.[17] Even if the majority of Orthodox women are perhaps untroubled by the gender dynamics of their faith or have impressive determination of their own religious lives, this does not undo the imbalance of power that is still gender-dependent. A 2017 Pew Research Center survey found:

> On balance, Orthodox women are more supportive of women's rights than are Orthodox men. In most countries, women are less likely than men to agree that a wife is obligated to obey her husband. And in several countries, women are less likely than men to agree that men have greater employment rights than women, especially when jobs are scarce. But women are not always more supportive of liberal positions regarding gender roles. In the majority of countries surveyed, women are about as likely as men to agree that they have a social responsibility to bear children. They also are as likely as men to agree that a traditional marriage, where women are primarily in charge of household tasks while men earn money, is ideal.[18]

Such findings suggest that women who identify as Orthodox Christian are perhaps more conservative (or at least contextually more supported in expressing conservative views) on gender issues than their nonreligious peers but also more differently minded on several issues of gender equality than the Orthodox men surveyed.[19] Although the lived experiences and numbers of religious Orthodox women may seem to contradict the notion that the Orthodox Church is patriarchal in any problematic or dominating way, the commemorative and liturgical sources of this tradition continue to privilege particular types of androcentric perspectives as universal, and the patriarchal control of the church persists with its resistance to women's ministerial inclusion and leadership.[20]

Some Orthodox women theologians and scholars express a feeling of futility and redundancy when their compelling arguments for increased opportunities for women in the church remain unaddressed. Kyriaki Karidoyanes-FitzGerald, for example, observes that for decades ecclesially invited women's meetings have ignored the suggestions they have solicited. She writes that women "seem to be regurgitating over and over again the same list of 'a theme and variations' for the application of *orthopraxia* [right practice] regarding the participation of women in the Orthodox Church. . . . To continue in this manner insults faithful Orthodox women and men; and furthermore, it is abusive."[21] Echoing the frustration Karidoyanes-Fitzgerald identifies, the Orthodox theologian Carrie Frederick Frost suggests there is a "silent schism" regarding gender, where women's concerns are not addressed by the men in power so they just leave the church.[22] This gives the appearance that ecclesial patriarchy is unproblematic because fewer dissenting voices remain in the church.

On sharing a brief explanation of this book with a male Orthodox colleague, I was surprised to hear him respond that he did not think the patriarchal heritage or structure of the church really had any detrimental impact on the lives of present-day women. The number of Orthodox women I have encountered personally, professionally, and in scholarship who express the exhaustion and futility of trying to explain precisely this to male priests and colleagues suggests otherwise. This type of frustration with not being heard, with being dismissed, resonates with the feminist scholar Sarah Ahmed's observations of women voicing institutional complaints only to be "heard as being tiresome" and as "distracting somebody from doing '*important* work elsewhere.'"[23] Invoking the feminist methodological corrective that women's experience matters, I want to share one additional personal anecdote to demonstrate the disconnect between women's concerns about being represented in their own tradition and men's dismissal of them. I recall as a graduate student at the end of a course on Orthodox theology remarking with some tentative frustration to the male professor that he did not assign or mention a single woman author in the course, only to be told that Orthodox women writers only write about women's issues and that this is a cliché not worth assigning. I appreciate that the professor did not want to essentialize women in women's issues, but in dismissing the women authors he was familiar with, he failed to recognize the other types of work or genres women were engaged in and to see them as theological. Such gatekeeping concerning who theologians might be and what theology looks like in Orthodox scholarship can be frustrating. Ahmed compellingly demonstrates, however, that *"frustration can be a feminist record."*[24] I would add that in the Orthodox context, such a record tells us something important about the social-religious construction of women; the constriction and freedom of their choices for engaging theologically; the perception of their institutional value; the power structures and patriarchal legacies they push up against; and the women's voices that are reflecting theologically on their own lives, talents, and thoughts as already divinely valued but finding dissonance within the church. The patriarchal structures and authorities within the church that ignore, speak over, and dismiss the contributions of women reveal its patriarchal privileging.

How then might one make sense of a tradition that claims and even overtly celebrates the potential for human equality in Christ, yet structurally precludes its realization in the church? Why should Orthodox Christians reconsider critically the ongoing impact of patriarchy in the church when it has been established so long in Christianity historically? What resources are there within the tradition to see what the teachings of the church are in more affirming ways despite the weight of its androcentric patriarchal past and present? This book begins to address such questions by thinking through sources of Orthodox tradition from a perspective that appreciates the multivalent nature of gender within religious expression and finds the critiques of contemporary feminist theology and gender theory helpful for articulating Orthodox theology and its relation to its tradition more inclusively.

## ORTHODOX AND FEMINIST THOUGHT

Since the late twentieth century Orthodox leaders' responses to feminism primarily have been rejections of or justifications for why feminist critiques do not properly apply to Orthodox contexts. Some religious believers suggest that such an engagement is not only unnecessary but also antithetical or at least external to Orthodox "approaches" or "tradition" itself.[25] Others take pride in the fact that, in their view, Orthodoxy has escaped the theological challenges and divisive changes that feminism has prompted in other religious traditions.[26] Orthodox responses to feminism are enmeshed in broader cultural encounters and issues that many Orthodox see as unequivocally antithetical to Orthodoxy (i.e., abortion, sexual liberation, same-sex marriage, and an inversion of the traditional gender hierarchy).[27] In Russia, for instance, "traditional family values" have been promoted politically and by ecclesial institutions that privilege women's subordination in the domestic, maternal, and marital realms.[28] Likewise, in the United States, Orthodoxy's appeal as a new religious home for some converts is related to its perception as a type of haven for morally conservative thinking—not least on questions of gender.[29] In countries with significant Orthodox populations, issues relating to women's equality are approached conservatively and often tied to constructions of cultural identity more broadly. The Orthodox responses to issues of gender equality are often entangled with attempts to push back against the seeming hegemonic imposition of the values of the cultural "West" and preserve or reclaim an Orthodox identity against a perceived threat.[30] The discourse of the Russian Orthodox Church about feminism, gender equality, and sexual diversity exemplifies this conflation of conservative values with Orthodox identity. Yet the Orthodox church is increasingly shaped by women benefiting from greater gender parity in education, employment, control of one's own body and choices, and improved status in ways that concur with Orthodox values of women's equal dignity before God. In addition, even Orthodox religious contexts and symbols themselves have been powerfully invoked to make feminist statements within the church.[31]

From polarizing issues such as women's ordination to intractable views on sexuality and abortion, Orthodox Christianity and feminist thought may seem to be rather limited conversation partners.[32] For many Orthodox women, there are perceived differences in social values, historical-cultural developments that problematically and atheistically imposed feminism under communism, and various other perhaps stereotyped evaluations of feminism in "Western" culture and Christianity that make it appear incongruous with their Orthodox identities.[33] On the other hand, many secular feminists underestimate religion as a potential force for liberation and agency within women's lives, with the result that Orthodox who want to engage in feminism but are unwilling to do so in a way that abandons certain religious values may be viewed as not being sufficiently feminist.[34] Moreover, the range of diverse movements and intellectual developments for improving, naming, and more accurately understanding the diversely situated lives of women, and acknowledging the spaces where they have been misrepresented or erased, makes the term "feminist" a loaded category for signification.[35] Indeed, some find the term more exclusionary than useful because it can invoke certain gender essentialist views.[36] But just as there is not a singular uniform "feminism," not all feminist and Orthodox values are at odds.[37]

Although Orthodox Christianity may be a few "waves" behind in its feminist theological engagement, some feminist commitments can help negotiate and articulate the dynamic between religious claims to the equal humanity and spiritual potential of women and the patriarchal specters that seem to negate them. First, despite the scriptural account of the creation of "women" and other religious justifications and explanations for the naturalness of certain gendered behaviors, hierarchies, or gendered positions, interrogating gender in Orthodox Christianity through the normative understanding that gender is socially constructed and performative allows us to see the dynamic ways gender functions to communicate and cultivate religious ideals. From the critiques of Simone de Beauvoir to the insights of the more contemporary Judith Butler, we see that gender is socially and culturally constructed, such that it is through these constructions and contexts that women *learn* to be women, that sex and bodies are given particular significations, and that one is socialized to perform one's gender.[38] Religion is certainly one of these contexts that is entangled with the broader social and cultural gender values; it may reinforce, reject, or react to the gender norms that are elsewhere expected of those who participate in it. Orthodox tradition, with its long memory, is no exception, and even its seemingly stable concept of womanhood includes significant variations and tensions reacting to diverse social and cultural norms. Feminist historians attending to premodern Christianity offer helpful approaches for making sense of how women are included, omitted, and rhetorically constructed in religious sources.[39] The awareness of the constructedness and rhetorical use of gender offered by feminist and gender theorists allows us to examine examples of *how* the Orthodox tradition constructs womanhood and evaluate that construction in light of its theological claims. To call a woman "manly" in present English usage, for example, may conjure socially negative associations about a woman's appearance rather than compliment her brave spirit and emotional fortitude as it did in the androcentric privileging discourse of early Christianity (and as it is still employed in many Orthodox hymns to praise female saints). Gender, even in Orthodox thought, is not a stable concept but rather a category that has shifted across time, that varies across different cultural contexts, and that is deeply entangled with social power dynamics.

Second, gender does not happen in a vacuum, and what it means to be a man, a woman, or nonbinary in any particular context varies greatly. Theorists such as bell hooks, Audre Lorde, and Kimberlé Crenshaw draw attention to the diversity of experiences of being a woman and point out that who is conjured or counts as "woman" in any given context is inflected by other aspects of identity, such as race, ability, ethnicity, and class.[40] Attending to the realities of difference and the way that various structures and systems of power inflect one's experiences of identity disrupts a singular or essentializing definition of "woman." Not all women have the same experiences, desires, relationships, status, race, abilities, or bodies. There has been little consideration of the models of holiness that are presented through Orthodox commemorations and in spiritual teachings that do not sufficiently reflect the diversity of real lives.[41] This is a fact that is true for men as well, but it is exacerbated in the case of women because women's representation is less and is filtered through a subset of patriarchal mediators. One can certainly see within Orthodox tradition, however, women who are privileged for representing values and behaviors aligned with a patriarchal gaze and women who are altogether omitted or only negatively portrayed. Women who are silent, chaste, pious, humble, suffering, ascetic, or exemplary beyond male expectations of feminine holiness are privileged in patriarchally controlled tradition as saints, and those who imitate them in visible ways are welcomed in liturgical spaces as "good Orthodox women." On the other hand, the perhaps more relatable churchgoing mother with rambunctious children is labeled "too noisy and worldly" for sacred spaces and exiled to the "cry room," and the young teenager thoughtfully trying to feel confident and beautiful in her "Sunday best" is told she looks too provocative as she is harmfully sexualized in what should be a safe and incarnationally affirming sacred space. Thinking alongside feminist critique requires us to disrupt these partial spaces and discriminatory surface-based representations and strive for deeper inclusivity. I suggest in chapters 5 and 6, based on the belief of naming tradition as a way of recognizing the Holy Spirit at work in the church, that intentionally seeking this representational accuracy and inclusivity is theologically important.

From Luce Irigaray to Gayatri Chakravorty Spivak, feminist scholarship has invited a reconsideration of the subjectivity of women and how women's voices and identities are shaped and restricted by symbolic and social orders in which they are rendered subordinate, secondary, or subaltern by more dominant others.[42] Recognizing such insights and examining Orthodox tradition as a product of patriarchal discourse and power admits that Orthodoxy's patriarchalness protects itself from hearing and being disrupted by the range of voices and perspectives women might share that are currently unacknowledged or dismissed as external to Orthodoxy. Ahmed, for example, enjoins her readers in such circumstances to be a "feminist killjoy" and to "challenge the universal."[43] I adopt this critical approach of naming patriarchy as problematic instead of accepting with doctrinal or pious imperative the ecclesiastical status quo. Ahmed's secular critique of citational politics also seems to resonate with the type of critique one might bring to considering the dearth of women self-voiced and cited in Orthodox tradition.[44] That is, contemporary scholars and feminists recognize the politics at play in who authors choose to cite as authoritative and worthy of attention, who are gathered together as significant and worth listening to, and who are merely an addendum or are altogether omitted. Orthodox tradition is in its own way a type of ongoing citational practice, and it, along with its related scholarship, often suffers from an internal self-perpetuating restriction to certain authorities without considering the implications of who might be left out and what their voices might add. Despite celebrating Christ as one who himself is a gate-breaker, there is a lot of gatekeeping regarding conversations of gender and tradition within Orthodoxy.[45]

Some might say that there is no need for any type of constructive feminist engagement with Orthodox Christianity. They might admit that there are some unfortunate historical patristic remarks about women but argue that theologically there is no distinction between men and women, and women already have equality before God. I see this as a type of theological gaslighting to silence those who would argue that the living church could do better in witnessing to its theological claims.[46] It privileges theology and divorces it from lived human realities instead of seeing the incarnational problem of asserting the divine affirmation matters more than the human experience. Similarly, if one looks to the Orthodox patristic tradition, one might see authors who affirm women's spiritual equality, address women as esteemed peers, and advocate for improved social-domestic situations but elsewhere still betray misogynistic assumptions about women categorically.[47] Likewise, the opposite may be found within Orthodox tradition: men who are dismissive or suspicious of the earthly women they encounter but who lovingly venerate individual female saints. Equality may be claimed theologically, but the liturgical practices, commemorations, hymns, and conciliar gatherings of the church that are also supposed to reflect theology often say otherwise in their representation of women.

In the secular and contemporary contexts of the United States, the feminist philosopher Kate Manne has highlighted the disproportionate gender-based hostility and barriers women face, arguing for rethinking misogyny as something women experience rather than something men (and women) feel toward others.[48] This insight is helpful for methodologically shaping the critique offered in the pages that follow—for approaching a tradition of such well-intended Christian men who nevertheless produce texts and practices that many women may experience as theologically incongruous. Even if these patristic authors or church hierarchs do not have misogyny in their hearts, they still participate in and benefit from a social and cultural order that normalizes views hostile to women's advancement and that entitles men to speak authoritatively about and to the lives of women.

Thinking along with Manne also raises the question: Why and how does male entitlement function in particular contexts?[49] Within the

Orthodox tradition, one might question how norms and religious ideals entitle men to control women's bodies, appearance, liturgical participation, and access to religious knowledge; or how women might feel morally obligated to bend to androcentric ideals as a form of piety. Carol Gilligan and Naomi Snyder, for instance, have argued for the social-psychological construction of patriarchy as entangled with male desire and defensively thwarting an anticipated loss of self in a relationship substituted for a socially rewarded place in the patriarchal order. Such analysis prompts a critical examination of how Orthodox tradition might reject women as they are themselves and reward them for conforming to patriarchy in a way that invites the giving up of their own well-being.[50] Patriarchy in this sense affects women and men such that "the backlash against feminism can be seen not only to reflect men's fears that if women are liberated men will lose status and power or their honor; they may also reveal how women have served as the containers and concealers of needs that men have felt forced to disavow."[51] Patriarchy in its religious expressions cannot be separated from its broader culture and association with *power over* others, in particular, women. Even in all the ways one might note exceptions and spectrums of difference, in the words of Nancy Hirschmann, "patriarchy is premised on women's powerlessness and men's power."[52] Disrupting what it means to be a woman prompts rethinking also of deep-seated conceptions of what it means to be a man and how Christ within Orthodox theology offers a model of power that *liberates* and gives of itself to elevate the "other" rather than seeking to control or subjugate.

The centering of women in examining the patriarchal nature of Orthodox tradition opens new ways of reading and interpreting religious sources. If the church is intended to be universal (and Orthodox claim that it is "catholic," that is, universal, in every recitation of the Nicene-Constantinopolitan Creed), then exploring how certain types of androcentric views and practices are privileged and have an effect on the church is important. Of course, it should also be noted that Orthodox women may perpetuate and voluntarily participate in the religious ideals of womanhood found within Orthodox tradition in ways that empower them. However, as the feminist philosopher Manon Garcia rightly acknowledges, submission for women can be a practice of power and agency, yet it still fits within a socialized framework within which women are more vulnerable and pressured to submit.[53] Such entitlement and disproportionate expectations of submission, I argue in chapter 3, are theologically unjustified. But what might be the Orthodox response?

Although some Orthodox theologians have engaged feminism and several prominent Orthodox theologians have advocated for greater opportunities and equality for women in the church, only a few would identify themselves as feminist theologians, taking issue with either or both of the terms "feminist" and "theologian."[54] Nevertheless, Orthodox women's theological contributions from the twentieth century to the present identify issues in and approaches to developing theology uniquely shaped by the concerns and insights of women. The modern theological writings of Elisabeth Behr-Sigel (1907–2005), Myhrra Lot-Borodine (1882–1954), and Maria Skobstova (1881–1945) have received some attention.[55] Several volumes related to Orthodox women's participation in ecumenical dialogues and ecclesiastical-sponsored women's meetings give voice to particular concerns and theological reflections of Orthodox women from a range of professional backgrounds, perhaps most strikingly reflected on in Leonie Liveris's *Ancient Taboos and Gender Prejudices* and the essays in the edited volume, *Many Women Were Also There* . . . .[56] These volumes raise concerns and offer insights into women's liturgical restrictions, women's pastoral needs, restoration of the female diaconate, greater opportunities for women to influence hierarchical statements, and increased opportunities for theological education and ecclesiological involvement.[57] Liveris urges that "it is imperative for Orthodox women to break the silence on gender discrimination, challenge patriarchal prejudice, and question the culture and tradition of exclusion that denies them full participation in the life of the community and sacramental ministry of the Church."[58] Although the silence on the issues Liveris notes may be increasingly broken by women, their concerns too frequently remain unacknowledged. Other Orthodox women theologians such as Eva Catafygiotu Topping (1920–2011), Nonna Verna Harrison (1953–2022), and Valerie Karras have raised questions concerning the status of gender in theological anthropology and premodern sources, while Eleni Kasselouri-Hatzivassiliadi and Aikaternini Tsalampouni have constructively engaged with feminist critiques in biblical scholarship.[59] Recently, Frost has offered a theology of maternity and a vision for the Orthodox Church in the future that is more consistent theologically for women.[60] Kateřina Bauerová has brought the French feminist Hélène Cixous into dialogue with Maria Skobstova on motherhood.[61] Such projects pave the way for continued theological study by, about, and motivated by Orthodox women. In addition, several edited volumes have provided much-needed creative rethinking about the theological status of women and gender across Orthodox genres and historical contexts, especially about ecclesiastical participation.[62] Prominent male theologians also have significantly engaged in Orthodox theological reflections on gender and the status of women in the church, albeit with somewhat inconsistent feminist engagement.[63]

Beyond theology as a discipline, numerous women scholars of Orthodox Christianity and its related historical traditions and genres of spiritual expression serve as prominent contributors to shaping understandings of Orthodox women's lives, how religious and social constructs influence them, and how women, in turn, may have influenced these forms and the spaces where women display agency, authority, and significant presence within Orthodox religious sources.[64] Such historical, material, literary, ethnographic, and experiential findings are significant for understanding the rich particularities of women's lives and contributions to Orthodox tradition and theology. Even non-Orthodox theologians have brought gender and feminist analysis to their scholarship on Orthodoxy, or Orthodoxy into dialogue with their feminist theology, but constructive engagements with feminist thought produced by Orthodox women are still emergent.[65]

Numerous feminist theological insights shape this volume, sometimes foregrounded as interlocutors but especially to prompt the types of questions this book poses and make possible the critiques it offers. Such widely accepted feminist and gender theoretical insights about the constructedness of gender, the importance of representation, the detrimental effects of patriarchy on the lives of women, and the value of gender equality are not necessarily intrinsic to Orthodox thought, but it is only by thinking alongside such now normative, more secular insights that the analysis and constructive approaches of the following chapters are made possible.[66] The fundamental premise that theology must affirm women as fully human persons orients this book's conclusions. I agree with Rosemary Radford Ruether, who writes, "The crucial principle of feminist theology is the promotion of the full humanity of women. Whatever denies, diminishes, or distorts the full humanity of women is, therefore, appraised as not redemptive."[67] Likewise motivating is Mary Catherine Hilkert's questioning, "For feminists, the critical norm for praxis and theology is: What will foster the full humanity of all women, men, and children as well as the well-being of all creation?"[68] These positions draw our attention to evaluating theology not only by the degree to which it does not distort the full humanity of women, but also how much it fosters it and how, as Elisabeth Schüssler Fiorenza notes, it attends to "the experience of God's sustaining grace and liberating presence" for women.[69]

Orthodox Christianity, as I argue, has within its tradition both the troubling diminishment of women and the resources to foster women's full humanity and well-being. The relationship is complex and can be read as a contradiction but also has the potential to be recast with more intentionally inclusive commitments based on its theological heritage. Serene Jones insightfully reminds us that "feminist theologians know that purportedly comprehensive conceptual systems inevitably exclude things—and in many cases, those 'things' are related to women," a statement that could easily be applied to Orthodox theology. Simply ignoring issues of gender within Orthodox tradition does not resolve the theological tensions their presence raises. Similarly, one cannot just "add women" to tradition or theology and expect instant amelioration of a situation that has been structurally impoverished by excluding and controlling women's contributions for generations.[70] Jones continues, however, by writing that "theologians must tell the Christian story in a language and with images and doctrines that hold together as a whole" and "that avoids internal contradictions and demonstrates the mutually supportive character of its parts."[71] The story of Orthodox theology can be told in a way that acknowledges the patriarchal androcentrism that marks much of its tradition and begins to undo its constraints.

Orthodox theology can learn from earlier feminist theological developments in other traditions, especially relating to the sources and customs shared across Christianity. Catholic feminist theology, for instance, has centered on feminism in terms of "mutual relation/relationality, radical equality, and community in diversity." I agree that the method of the Christian feminist involves "criticism, recovery, and reconstruction" by critiquing "structures within Christianity that have historically been patriarchal, hierarchical, and damaging for women's full flourishing" and then seeking resources within the tradition that can be used to promote "inclusivity of mutuality, equality, and diversity."[72] Constructive feminist theologians such as Sarah Coakley, Shawn Copeland, and Elisabeth Johnson model how to forge theological ways forward within one's tradition even while critiquing it.[73] These theologians demonstrate ways to acknowledge the breaks and tensions in their tradition regarding gender while still resourcefully developing approaches to achieve greater theological consistency. Throughout this book, this method and approach is found useful to offer a feminist critique and response to aspects of Orthodox tradition. Issues such as the maleness of Jesus and calling God "Father"; male ecclesial leadership and theological dominance; a historically patriarchal religious leadership; what scripture has to say about male headship, women's roles, and the division of the sexes; and how the veneration of Mary relates to real women have been discussed at length by scholars of other traditions.[74] Orthodox reevaluation of its tradition in a way that attends to the androcentric construction of women in its sacred texts and customs can draw on these existing critiques and approaches in further considering sources and practices particular to Orthodox Christianity.

Women's issues *are* theological. Ignoring, undervaluing, or dehumanizing women is a theological problem because, among other things, it disrespects God's presence in half or more of the church. Theologically affirming women's full humanity and equality cannot be an extracurricular concern for a progressive minority but is centrally important for approaches to and understanding Orthodox theology as a whole.[75] Orthodox Christianity is globally diverse and has unique features and theological emphases compared to other religious traditions, so any dialogue with feminist critiques needs to reflect the particularities of its own voice.[76] For example, in this book I take up the Orthodox emphasis on divine-human communion by which Orthodox believe humans become increasing participants in divinity, referred to as *theosis*, divinization or deification. I also highlight particular liturgical, commemorative, theological, and spiritual-ascetic teachings that may exist to a certain degree in sister Christian churches through shared tradition but are centered more significantly in Orthodox Christian belief and practice.[77] In critically reassessing and responding to the construction of gender through religious sources, teachings, and practices, I also show that feminism and Orthodoxy are not dichotomous. Orthodox thinking along with gender and feminist insights permits certain observations and critiques that otherwise would be obscured. It is important for there to be uniquely Orthodox voices participating in diverse forms of feminist theological reflection—for credibility within Orthodox communities, for more nuanced attention to specifically Orthodox sources and theological priorities, and to explore how engaging with feminist critiques helps Orthodox see their own tradition in new ways, both its limitations and resources.[78] Feminist thought and theology also can be elucidated in new ways by Orthodoxy, in all its overt limitations and often-obscured potentiality. In the chapters that follow, I show that engaging Orthodox tradition with a feminist commitment to decentering androcentric and patriarchal privilege can foster mutually informed insights and approaches for a more inclusively affirming future.

Some Orthodox may object to the notion that feminist thought and theology has anything helpful to offer their own tradition or that there is any value for Orthodox to participate in this broader feminist theological conversation. However, I find that engaging with feminist critiques prompts Orthodox to evaluate the power dynamics and gender inequalities in their own tradition in a way that is theologically consistent with it. Reflecting on the critiques that might be offered to one's tradition can promote a type of penitence and humility that is deeply ingrained in the ascetic tradition. Orthodox ascetic examples prompt one to apply the critiques to oneself out of humility, examine how they might be true, and then make progress in repentance rather than become defensive. I suggest to those that disagree with the feminist premise or approach that engaging in this exercise can be helpful for strengthening one's faith as well. Acknowledging inequality and discrimination in the tradition does not mean that Orthodoxy is somehow damaged but rather provides an opportunity for further articulating the faith to a world that increasingly values equality. I will note that Orthodox history is full of examples of better ways to express the teachings of the church by being in conversation with the unorthodox. I do not suggest by this that Orthodox tradition will have or need some sort of triumphal defense against the liberal ideology of feminism (or that feminism is unorthodox). Instead, I suggest that by engaging with a feminist premise, Orthodox might be better able to articulate the ways they see the tradition as being on behalf of women and not as being a structure of patriarchal oppression. In so doing, they may come to a better appreciation of women's contributions and insights regarding their own faith and how they see themselves as inheritors of and contributors to tradition. Last, I want to observe that seeing how Orthodoxy is not either feminist or patriarchal engages in a type of apophatic theology that is deep within the theological tradition and helps us contemplate how the church is not limited or diminished by finite categories and assertions. It is always more.

Thinking alongside the aforementioned theoretical and theological insights can bring out new ways of seeing the structural, historical, and systemic imbalances of gender within Orthodox Christianity. Specifically, such engagement elucidates how gender is dynamically employed to communicate spiritual values and how religious values, sources, and practices perpetuate inequitable gender constructs and patriarchy as a mode of control. But critically engaging with Orthodox theology, tradition, and its gendered tensions can also prompt reconsideration of simplistic presumed dichotomies about gender and feminist engagements in traditionally patriarchal religions more broadly. Resources from within Orthodox Christian spirituality that I highlight in chapters 5 and 6 also offer to even the non-Orthodox scholar or practitioner models for honoring lived realities of human difference without external limitation or further marginalization, as well as religiously integrated approaches for opening up past and present religious systems marked by gender hierarchy.

While few might affirm the androcentrism of the past or present as unequivocally good or inherently Christian, I have yet to hear public arguments from Orthodox Christian scholars or leaders about the theological necessity of *unsaying* the normative patriarchal androcentrism that pervades the sources and many practices of the church. This book posits that such an unsaying is theologically warranted and can be done in a way that is surprisingly consistent with much of tradition, although, as I have indicated, some may claim that bringing feminist and gender theory into dialogue with traditional Orthodox sources is like asking, "What has Athens to do with Jerusalem?"[79] I contend that such a space of dialogue is essential not for externally dismantling Orthodox tradition and belief with feminist critique but rather for naming spaces where the tradition subverts or categorically subordinates women's full humanity. If one reads against the grain, we find Orthodox texts and liturgical acts that ostensibly claim gender equality but still betray patriarchal privilege.[80]

Thus, in this book, I analyze the patriarchal tradition's representation of women to bring to light tensions between religious claims about women's spiritual equality and discursive assumptions about the inferiority of women's humanity. Exploring this seeming contradiction illuminates the dynamic ways temporal norms are employed and disrupted to convey transcendent beliefs. By critically interrogating gendered rhetoric and androcentric religious norms, I argue for the theological necessity of unequivocally affirming women's humanity and offer approaches for rethinking "gender trouble" within Orthodox tradition.

## ORGANIZATION OF THE BOOK

The chapters that follow are organized to lead the reader through an exploration of the representation of women in the Orthodox tradition, how this representation has theological significance, and what theological approaches might be employed to promote greater equality and affirmation of women within it. I begin by drawing from prominent sources of Orthodox tradition to show that the patriarchal interpretation of the church and her experiences are perpetuated as normative and ideal in ways that largely omit the autonomous voices of women. Despite its often separate status within ecclesial contexts, patriarchy is not theologically neutral. Orthodox tradition is entangled with historical and systemic patriarchy in a way that is theologically problematic and upholds dehumanizing ideals about women as religiously normative.

In the second chapter, I examine common tropes marking the presence of women in Orthodox commemorative hagiographic and hymnic texts, liturgical contexts, and desert sayings. Based on their association with an atemporal and universalizing liturgical sphere as well as with a conception of the timelessness of holy teachings and sainted figures, the partial "patriarchal woman" presented in Orthodox tradition is seemingly sanctified. Where women are lauded as holy superiors to men, they are presented in ways that normalize androcentrism and the male control of the female. I note that even in instances where the boundaries of gender appear negated, women remain seconded particularly with respect to their humanity due to a history of embedded androcentric privilege. The normalized and pervasive presentation of women in the sources of

Orthodox tradition is partial, patriarchal, and equivocal on the state of women's humanity.

In the third chapter, I shift from what the tradition says about women to an examination of the Orthodox spiritual values of suffering, humility, and obedience that problematically render virtuous (even if inequitable) women's performance of their gender through a patriarchal gaze. Ascetic spiritual values have potentially greater detrimental effects on women who more often than men are socialized to be subject to others. Such values, I suggest, are not merely spiritually transformative but also have been problematically used to uphold patriarchal privilege over the well-being of women in ways that are theologically inconsistent. Spiritually providing ostensibly equal ascetic instructions for men and women ignores the incarnational reality of human existence and its diversity.

Having argued that various spiritual values and commemorative representations problematically privilege androcentrism in ways that undermine affirmations of women's full and human equality, in the fourth chapter, I demonstrate the *theological* necessity of prioritizing unequivocal affirmations of women's full humanity and equal personhood. Without these affirmations, the coherence of the incarnation, deification, icon veneration, and authority of tradition is called into question. By appealing to doctrinal consistency, I maintain that the intentional affirmation of women's full and equal humanity and a commitment to overcoming the limits of androcentric patriarchalism are theologically important.

Adopting a feminist theological perspective to move beyond mere critique, in the fifth chapter, I outline three preliminary theological approaches for creatively undoing the problems of patriarchy indicated in the preceding chapters. I suggest it is possible and theologically consistent to engage sources and values within Orthodox tradition in ways that intentionally acknowledge and begin to undo the limiting effects of their androcentrism. First, I suggest the Orthodox conception of power (and therefore patriarchy) should be grounded in Christological imitation as ultimately kenotic (i.e., self-emptying of privilege to elevate others). Then I show that the Orthodox theological tradition of apophasis, or unsaying assertive claims, should be applied to view tradition with more openness. Last, I reflect on the spiritual attitudes and teachings associated with hesychasm (the practice of silent prayer that prepares one for a mystical encounter with God, often as an experience of divine light) as a resource for reshaping how those in positions of privilege might invite and respond to the self-disclosure of ecclesially marginalized others. By extending these three teachings theologically (and simultaneously engaging in a type of feminist reclamation), I suggest Orthodox tradition has resources for undoing its patriarchal limitations and supporting women's equality.

While being similarly constructive, the sixth chapter shifts the focus from undoing the effects of patriarchal privilege to intentionally advocating for, theologically affirming, and reclaiming the fuller presence of women in tradition. I include three examples of how tradition can offer resources for advocating for women if its interpretation is anchored in privileging a Christological confession of Christ's divine-human unity that is on behalf of the marginalized. First, I propose adopting a commitment to preserving, defending, and honoring the divine image in oneself (and others) as a corrective to historical emphasis on suffering and subordination as sanctifying for women. Second, I highlight the hagiographic trope of exceptional women righteously subverting an expected gender hierarchy. Third, and intertwined with the previous two examples, drawing on the Orthodox celebration of the myrrh-bearing women as the first preachers of the resurrection, I emphasize the Paschal proclamation by and for the most marginalized. I conclude by emphasizing that the theological method suggested by the critique and response I offer demonstrates uniquely Orthodox possibilities for feminist theological engagement.

Throughout these chapters, I draw on gendered language, spiritual teachings, doctrinal beliefs, and sainted examples from texts and traditions still invoked in present-day Orthodox churches. Primarily, I consider the tradition, sources, theology, and practices supported and perpetuated by the leaders of the church rather than the more diverse and often subversive modes of lived religiosity among Orthodox women.[81] My conclusions are primarily anchored by evidence from hagiographic, liturgical, ascetic, patristic, and conciliar texts from within Orthodoxy's Greek (Byzantine) heritage and undoubtedly shaped by my own experience as a North American Orthodox laywoman. I draw on the Byzantine context because it is one that fundamentally shaped Orthodoxy in many global transmissions and through its imperial legacy had considerable influence in determining the theological formulations and foundations of Orthodox Christianity that are still proclaimed today. Consequently, it is the "Eastern" Orthodox tradition and theological context that I primarily engage.

However, it is my hope that this type of reflective analysis will contribute to comparable discussions that better address the particularities of sister churches in the Oriental Orthodox and Eastern Rite Catholic traditions. As an advocate of greater gender inclusivity in the church, I reject limiting definitions of feminism but hold commitments to improving the lives, opportunities, and equality of *all* women.[82] When I say "inclusivity" and speak of inclusion in the church, I do not mean it in the sense of bringing women or diverse others into an already exclusionary patriarchal structure without changing the status quo.[83] What I have in mind is rather a theological ideal of valuing the diversity of the church's many members as they exist uniquely and fully in Christ. Likewise, although my focus is the representation of women in Orthodox tradition, it is my hope this book may serve as a conversation point for the much-needed intersectional reflection on identities and peoples who have been marginalized through tradition. The distinction of people within the church based on gender is one of the most basic ways the church excludes (from the altar, the priesthood, etc.), for the most part without recognition of the compounding ways this external binary identification might affect people.[84]

Although the historically grounded texts, teachings, and practices I cite still may be found in present usage, they do not necessarily reflect widespread popularity. From my own anecdotal ecclesial experience, I know historical parts of the tradition, even if not prominent in their own time, can be used against women (even by women) in the present. The sources engaged do not automatically indicate their pervasiveness historically or ongoing usage against or on behalf of women. This is because I am less concerned with making the case that specific Orthodox Christians use particular texts, teachings, or figures to control women in various contexts and more concerned with exposing the insidiousness of an underlying patriarchal androcentrism for Orthodox theology. In my view, the latter case reveals the *systemic* effects of patriarchal androcentrism rather than just naming individual texts or teachings that can be dismissed as unfortunate misogynistic outliers of an otherwise unproblematic tradition. In this way, I approach tradition as most basically a historical witness of Orthodox thinking, practice, and spirituality that is still thought to be valuable to the Orthodox present. As I mentioned at the beginning of this introduction, tradition as an Orthodox concept is ambiguous: there are various contested meanings regarding how believers should think about what counts as "tradition."[85] Yet I use "tradition" less in the theological sense of how one should determine it and more pragmatically as referring to a collection of sources, practices, and beliefs that are generally acknowledged to be valuable in passing down the faith, as historical witnesses to Orthodox values and customs, and as what Orthodox Christians have produced in reflecting on their religious lives. Such a way of conceiving "tradition" attempts to balance the notion of tradition theologically as being the recognition of God at work in the church in time with the acknowledgment that such recognition is limited by human fallibility and bias.

In several chapters, I heavily rely on examples from hagiographies, hymns, and short spiritual stories or "sayings" because it is in these commemorative, rather than theologically discursive, genres that women are primarily presented and gendered tensions are most clearly exemplified. Sources that inform theology with authority within Orthodoxy include a range of genres and practices from tradition that reflect how previous generations have experienced, reflected on, and taught their faith. Hymns, liturgical rites, conciliar documents, patristic teachings, and hagiographies have significant influence and authority as sources for continued theological reflection. In addition, hagiographic and hymnographic sources are particularly significant in my analysis because they are often dehistoricized and departicularized through liturgical practice and communal commemoration—such that the gendered ideals they express appear universally confessed, sacralized through commemoration and prayer, and timelessly relevant (even if they were originally much more context bound). I reject the claim that theological texts do not say anything problematic about women and that it is just hagiographic texts or historical contexts that reflect inequalities that were normative in the times they were written. Such a line of thinking creates an overly narrow view of what counts as theology and reinforces a type of protective barrier around certain patristic authors and church teachings as exempt from critique. I prefer instead to privilege the incarnational reality of those Orthodox women who have experienced their tradition (theology at times included) as being patriarchal in a way that is problematic for affirming their equality.

I suggest it is not that Orthodox theology is a problem for women because of what it claims about God but that Orthodox theology as it has been reflected on through a range of spiritual genres and practices in tradition by various Orthodox leaders does not live up to and take seriously what it needs to affirm about women to be consistent with what it claims about God. To this end, in the last two chapters but also subtly throughout the book, I model what might be a type of Orthodox feminist theological approach to examine traditional sources not just in terms of what they meant historically but how they can be used to authorize the affirmation of women because this is consistent with a Christological confession of who and how Orthodox believe God to be in relation to humanity. In my engagement with historical sources, I acknowledge that they may be contextually limited, and I do not expect to find a hidden tradition of patristic premodern feminists. Rather, in reflecting on the sources and practices of tradition, I demonstrate that while the representations of women are limited, the teachings about encountering God can be used to reframe tradition and present approaches in a way that more consistently acknowledges all humans in the divine image with the potential for divine-human communion.

While certainly many Orthodox Christians have their own sources of knowledge and perhaps even subversive structures of religious authority, the written and liturgical traditions are authoritative in providing legitimacy and continuity with past and global Orthodox traditions. What is written, what is sanctified, and what is liturgically articulated in many ways is still indicative of what has been and what continues to be privileged in Christian traditions, even if not always widely heard or acknowledged by the laity. In these contexts, excluding, speaking over, misrepresenting, spiritually subjugating, and otherwise patriarchally limiting women's equality, freedom, and humanity undermine central theological claims and the authority of the sainted sayings of the Orthodox past. Even if they were not previously used in this way, I draw on sources that reflect Orthodox thinking that could be used either as a challenge to or as a resource for women's equality and full humanity. I also show that there are theological resources that may not have been privileged but that could be used on behalf of women's inclusion, autonomy, and equality. This is not to perpetuate a privileging of ideals over practices, theory over reality, or institutional over lived religion but to critically reevaluate and show the limits of the gender constructions institutionally, structurally, and systemically supported within Orthodox tradition—especially where they challenge foundational theological claims.

In conclusion, the patriarchal androcentrism I critique in this book is not just something that affects women. It is deeply connected to the privileging of celibacy and devaluing of the flesh and sexuality that are applied to men and women in many sources of Orthodox tradition. Yet the scope adopted in this book focuses on women because the weight of these ascetic values is compounded for women through their various experiences with the social and religiously constructed category "woman." Admittedly, this is only one piece in a much broader conversation about Orthodoxy and feminism and gender and historically patriarchal religion, and I encourage the reader to consider how the particularities and variations that emerge from the perspectives that follow might find parallels or discontinuities in the lives, contexts, religious traditions, and identities of more diverse others.

**ONE**

# Acknowledging Tradition's Gendered Limitations

Orthodoxy is in many ways dependent on patriarchy and integrates seemingly unavoidable patriarchal privileges in its religious beliefs, communities, history, and practices. The Byzantine scholar and self-identified Orthodox feminist Eva Catafygiotu Topping frankly observes, "Androcentrism, patriarchal prejudice, and pride lie imbedded in Orthodox tradition."[1] This is not something that can be undone by ordaining women or anachronistically imposing greater gender inclusivity on the genres of tradition. And because Orthodox tradition is and has been disproportionately controlled by men, it cannot be justly applied to resolve injustices encountered by women. In this chapter, I show that patriarchal androcentrism is entangled with the sources that have articulated the faith and communicated God to the faithful. Orthodox Christian tradition is not egalitarian when it comes to gender but rather is structurally and traditionally authoritative in ways that can exclude or disenfranchise the humanity and diversity of women.[2] Acknowledging the problems of patriarchy within the sources and practices of Orthodoxy need not result in a simplistic dismissal of the tradition that has given centuries of practitioners meaningful spiritual lives. Instead, it prompts a reassessment of the relationship between theology and tradition. Accordingly, in this chapter, I first introduce why tradition is important to consider in addressing issues of gender inequality within Orthodoxy. Next, I outline various dimensions of patriarchy to show that it is necessary to take patriarchy seriously within Orthodoxy even where it might be accepted as Orthodox and then show that tradition is patriarchal in ways that are problematic in terms of theology and women's full affirmation and equality.

## WHY ADDRESS TRADITION?

In Orthodox Christianity tradition holds significant authority, and what counts as tradition is disproportionately patriarchally determined. As I mentioned in the introduction, definitions vary, but "tradition" usually refers to the handing down of sources, teachings, and behaviors that are associated with Orthodoxy that witness retrospectively to the presence of the Holy Spirit in the church.[3] Orthodox tradition is not a static or merely historical collection of texts or a list of successive names. Tradition is not monolithic; it is variously determined and invoked throughout time and not without political agenda. As Oliver Herbel notes in his study of Orthodoxy in the United States, there is an element of change or instability in tradition in that it "has a content but is also constantly changing in response to new surroundings in a manner that seeks to maintain core structures or behaviors."[4] Reflecting similar dynamism, the influential Russian intellectual and theologian Sergius Bulgakov (1871–1944) observes that tradition is "the living memory of the Church" and that it "is a living power inherent in a living organism. In the stream of its life it bears along the past in all its forms so that the past is contained in the present and is the present."[5] Tradition in this sense is ongoing and continues to find expression within the church. It can include but is not limited to written texts such as scripture, canons, hagiography, prayer and liturgical books, pious sayings, icons, and architecture but also the lived component of holiness found and encountered in others and lived through religious practice.[6]

Orthodox theology is known through its tradition, just as God is known through his divine-human revelation in Jesus Christ in time.

Theology is revealed through the activity of the Holy Spirit at work in human lives that can be referred to and retold across generations. In tradition, we find Orthodox theology as it shapes particular historical people's thoughts, stories, practices, and ways of being. It is a continued Pentecost of the Holy Spirit at work in the church and a parallel to the divine incarnation in which each Christian can "put on Christ" (Galatians 3:27), as the divine Logos put on humanity. In tradition, God is again believed to be revealed in time through the communion of humanity with divinity that takes place in the lives of Orthodox Christians. Because Christians believe God transcends and is in time in the human faithful and in the incarnation, tradition and theology cannot be neatly parsed because they inform each other.[7] Orthodox theology and spiritual-ascetic teachings acknowledge that the work of the Holy Spirit is entangled in human lives who are temporally and culturally situated and still limited by sinfulness (by which I mean the extent to which humans do not love the way God loves). Thus theology can be known through the historically particular witnesses of tradition, but our conception of tradition is always somewhat distorted to the extent that we are not yet Christ-like. Tradition as the Orthodox record of God at work in the church includes temporal and human limits. I suggest, however, that Orthodox Christians should seek to overcome or unsay such limits rather than reinforce them as definitive of Orthodoxy.

It is consistent, therefore, to approach tradition as that which witnesses to the divine revelation known foremost in Christ and that which promotes the participation of Christians in the life of Christ.[8] Women are part of this divine revelation and divine participation. Orthodox Christians believe God is united to and for humanity, and this includes women. While most Orthodox might agree that this point is universally accepted, the construction of women in the sources and practices of Orthodox tradition does not unanimously support this claim. To omit, dismiss, or contrive women's witness in tradition is a theological distortion, just as to justify a theology that does not necessitate equal inclusion of women would be a denial of the tradition where we already find God at work in the lives of women. The words of the Orthodox scholar Valerie Karras could easily be applied as an internal critique of the church and its tradition: "If human society does not allow all human persons to express uniquely and distinctively the work of the Spirit, of uncreated grace, then it is impeding humanity's fulfilment of God's purpose and plan."[9] Consequently, I offer a critique of the pervasive tradition of patriarchy as a limiting aspect of tradition and one that sets up barriers to cultivating and confessing the possibilities of divine-human unity for the *whole* church equally.

An honest critical assessment of the ways Orthodox tradition is patriarchal is necessary for developing any type of constructive Orthodox feminist theological approach and, perhaps more importantly within Orthodoxy, more capaciously reflecting on God's presence in humanity (including the lives of women) and expressing what that presence means for all of humanity (women included). This assessment involves rejecting the dominance of the elite institutional religious narrative of Orthodoxy that claims equality or complementarianism while maintaining patriarchy.[10] The patriarchal androcentrism of Christianity historically has been critiqued from within other Christian denominations.[11] While some of what follows might be well-trod ground for readers familiar with feminist theological critiques from other Christian traditions, I ask patience with this overview, which is necessary groundwork for naming the way patriarchy restrictively functions within the particular contexts of Orthodox tradition. Orthodox Christianity has never produced a volume comparable to Mary Daly's *The Church and the Second Sex*, although many of Daly's critiques of her own Catholic tradition can be applied to Orthodoxy as well.[12] As feminist theorists and theologians have argued, patriarchy, no matter how entangled in religious values and gender-transcendent teachings, nevertheless perpetuates gender inequality and therefore warrants critique. For Orthodox Christians (who may or may not identify as feminists), this emphasis on equality might appear in tension with other spiritual values such as humility. However, the ways patriarchal androcentrism limits equality in Orthodox tradition are not just problems for women but also more significantly limit the human understanding and acknowledgment of God's work in the world. Thus it is necessary to honestly identify the patriarchal barriers within Orthodoxy to realize equality for women and the equally numerous and transformative ways God is at work in their lives and on their behalf.

One of those barriers is the construction and deployment of tradition itself. Topping remarks that tradition "with a capital 'T'" is "based on the prejudiced premise that woman is first in the order of sin and second in the order of creation. Translated into concrete terms, this means that woman is more sinful than and inferior to man. Consequently, in both church and society she must willingly accept silence, submission, and subordination as her proper place."[13] Despite the numerous women within Orthodox tradition (both as historical genres and praxis, as well as present living participants), it has been used to control and subjugate women. Even where women might affirm they are happy with the patriarchal religious context and tradition, it must be acknowledged that this attitude is one that is validated through a religious power dynamic in which they have less official power (this does not mean, however, that more traditional women do not have robust ways of exercising agency within a patriarchal framework). As many Orthodox women may attest, tradition is important for religious self-understanding, for connecting them with a meaningful religious (and often cultural) heritage, and for promoting a range of beliefs and practices that many find aligned with their spiritual goals. However, I would add that many Orthodox Christians, men and women, refer to tradition without fully realizing its latent and theologically significant potential for liberation.

Women are present in this tradition, but their voices are not represented with an equal weight if at all, and when they do appear, they are often filtered through male ideas about women (even holy women). For example, the desert ascetic St. Mary of Egypt is prominently commemorated as an exemplar of repentance from a life of lust during Great Lent. Her full hagiography is read as part of one of the liturgical services wherein her voice is recorded as recounting a life of sexual profligacy before fleeing to the desert in penitence. The hymns and the liturgical participants take Mary's words as her own without considering that they are in a narrative retold by a male priest-monk to a men's monastery to inspire the monks to greater humility (as if to say, "If a sexually sinful *woman* could be holy what is your excuse?," which assumes that women are naturally less capable of holiness and that uncontrolled sexual desire is one of the worst sins imaginable). In present usage, the hagiography is retold in a liturgical context that is still patriarchally controlled.[14] Mary's words, life, and record are thus an example of a prominent woman saint in tradition as seen and presented through an androcentric gaze. Of course, this critique can be leveled at nearly all historical writing, but the written sources of tradition inform the discerning *phronema*, or Orthodox mind, of the church. Consequently, accepting what was affirmed in the past as inspired shapes understandings of the church as unchanging in its core principles.[15] What Orthodox Christians acknowledge and appeal to as this "mind" of the church, and subsequently how they understand and approach tradition, is through a normalized, disproportionately androcentric (and often clerical or monastic) patriarchal lens. Although this is in part because of the decontextualization of particular sources in their application to the present, it is also because tradition itself and the practice of referring to it and passing it on are regarded as theological practice. That is, theology is believed to be known by participating in tradition, which is disproportionately patriarchal. This makes it very difficult to offer more egalitarian and inclusive arguments from within the tradition that appear to some to be sufficiently Orthodox (or alternately, sufficiently feminist).

Consequently, the pages that follow display the insight that can be gained when one questions the seemingly sacred status quo. For some, this analysis of tradition may model why and how Orthodox tradition is problematically patriarchal in ways that have been ignored. For others, it might elucidate problematic systems of thought that cannot be easily undone because they are deeply enmeshed with a religious identity many women find life-giving and authentic. Although my discussion is particularly concerned with the ways patriarchy troubles the tradition for women, I hope it also highlights the importance of attending to structures, language, religious values, sexuality, and authority that have intersectionally "othered" many persons (even men) or at least their representation and participation in the sources and practices of tradition more broadly.[16]

## WHY ADDRESS PATRIARCHY?

Historically and liturgically, Orthodox tradition is patriarchally androcentric. By this I mean it privileges men and the male as normative religious determiners of what constitutes the most formative aspects of Orthodoxy in ways that exclude or diminish women. Institutionally, the Orthodox Church functions hierarchically through the consensus of regional bishops (usually referred to as synods) and is therefore largely shaped and led by men. As a religious tradition, Orthodox Christianity is patriarchal in a public self-owned way: it traces its apostolicity through a lineage of "patriarchs" and divides itself into historical-geographic "patriarchates." Orthodox tradition is patriarchal in a historical perspective, and the conception of tradition as a spiritual ideal is for the most part determined patriarchally. Consequently, the boundaries of what is Orthodox and what counts as tradition are shaped by official patriarchally issued documents, a patriarchally overseen priestly leadership, patriarchally approved liturgical sources and practices, and historically patriarchal interpretations of the church and her experiences that remain influential. In a tradition that calls upon God as "Father," that embraces an exclusively male ordained priesthood, and that is fundamentally shaped by a patristic tradition in its theological beliefs and priorities, the privileging of male symbols and voices in determining the "official" and normative narrative of Orthodox Christianity is arguably celebrated.[17]

Some Orthodox Christians might distinguish between the problem of patriarchy in the secular sense of power over women and the Orthodox experience of the patriarchs, functioning within patriarchates and belonging to a church with an exclusively male priestly leadership and disproportionate patristic heritage. That is, some might see gender inequality in society as a problem but either ignore or dismiss it in religious contexts. Religious patriarchy may be conceived in a completely different sense from secular structures of gender inequality. For instance, an Orthodox woman might see her gender-based exclusion from a professional meeting that only included the voices, presence, and contributions of men as an unjust form of discrimination, but she might not similarly see her gender-based exclusion from an ecclesial conference that she was academically qualified to attend as discrimination. Being within the tradition requires a certain degree of acceptance of the "wisdom of the church" for the way things are, which then shapes the types of questions and critiques that can be raised while remaining within Orthodoxy. Orthodox Christians continue to refer to the patriarchal tradition as part of their theological method to respond to even contemporary issues, which results in a perpetuation of accepting a certain degree of patriarchy as prerequisite for doing theology in a manner that is recognized as Orthodox.

Within its expressions and sources, Orthodox Christianity may be encountered as patriarchal in a way that is at dissonance with the theological values it affirms and the attempts (honest, I think) at celebrating and elevating women as spiritual equals and even superiors. One only has to enter an Orthodox church and see the icon of Mary "more spacious than the heavens" featured on the apse, see the women filling the church, and hear the numerous hymns and feasts praising the holy deeds of women to acknowledge that Orthodox Christianity—as patriarchal as it may be—celebrates holy women, is practiced and valued by women, and is regarded as deeply unproblematic in all of its "patriarchalness" for many Orthodox women. Despite the numerous images of women filling the Orthodox church, the honor given to female saints, and the prominence of the Theotokos, it is still the case that these are women existing in a man's religious world.[18] For some women the church is a space where they perform a type of double identity, disjointed awareness, or even "himpathy" toward their religious sources and authorities.[19] In their churches, some Orthodox might excuse or ignore a gender-exclusive system, something that would be rejected as unacceptable and discriminatory in nonreligious contexts.[20] Others have publicly repeatedly expressed disappointment with the patriarchy and gender-based inequality they experience in the church only to have it dismissed by the men who are in positions of authority to change it.[21] Ecclesial hierarchs, even when sympathetic to women's concerns, may refuse to enact changes such as restoring the female diaconate with the excuse that to do so would cause further schism in the church.[22] However, maintaining the status quo in this way diminishes the concerns of women and itself exemplifies patriarchy—the privileging of the concerns of men and their power over the needs of women.

As much as some Orthodox believers might want to claim that a religious and priestly patriarchy does not reflect gender exclusion or reinforce problematic cultures of misogyny, that is just not the case. Nancy Hirschmann explains that feminism requires a type of "double vision" that acknowledges the cultural and contextual conditions that lead to such systems as patriarchy and also acknowledges that "some groups of people systematically and structurally have more power to participate in constructing than do others."[23] The result of such inequality is that it is "often more difficult for women to define themselves within a masculinist epistemology, language, and discourse" and that "this greater difficulty means that such individuals have less freedom than do members of the dominant social groups.[24]

Orthodox tradition leaves little room for the autonomous voices and offerings of women and others who might not conform to patriarchal expectations of gender performance within the church. That is not to say that women are not influential but only that their contributions historically have been filtered through the voices of male authors or maintained as part of the "tradition" by male religious leaders. Ultimately, women are dependent on male religious authorities for full liturgical participation. In terms of significantly shaping the practices and beliefs of Orthodoxy, with few exceptions women's influence and authority are hidden, secondary, or taken for granted in support of more visible male leadership and androcentric public religious articulation. For example, there are numerous women who in various parishes serve as the unofficial teachers, keepers of tradition, and maintainers of the church. These women might offer regular informal instruction, counsel, and correction to those who enter the church on how to practice and understand Orthodoxy. Beyond a physical presence in parishes, priest's wives and laywomen also have considerable online influence through blogs, social media, and support groups related to being an Orthodox woman.[25] Yet these young, midlife, and "old church women," even while perhaps having more unofficial authority at the parish level than the priest, are not included in most official ecclesial decisions.[26]

Despite all the historical-cultural norms one could use to explain why patriarchy has such prominence in Orthodox tradition, it is not excusable as an "an accident, nor an intermittent aberration in an otherwise benevolent system."[27] Within the history of Christianity, specifically, Orthodox tradition, I apply the words of the historian Blossom Stefaniw: "Knowledge *of women* is structured by patriarchal institutions. Counter-knowledge is inhibited or discarded by those same structures."[28] Gender-based religious patriarchy that claims it supports gender equality is not an example of "Orthodox as paradox" or the theological antinomy that marks other aspects of Orthodox theology.[29] Knowledge of women and their possibilities for responding to that knowledge are conditioned and constrained patriarchally. However "benevolent," inadvertent, or historically implicit patriarchal structures in Orthodox Christianity may seem, they have a limiting effect on the presentation and participation of women in the tradition by privileging an androcentric expression and determination of Orthodoxy as universal. Its deep historical and theologically interpreted hierarchical structure, as well as its responses to surrounding religious and cultural influences, shaped how the early and even present-day church presents itself as rightly ordered and organized in a way that cultivates virtue, even as it may inadvertently damage women. The persistence of patriarchy reflects choices—as subtle or overt as they might be—about control, order, privilege, acceptance, and power. These choices are worth theologically interrogating because they should reflect what Orthodox believe to be conducive to cultivating a life of divine communion and increasing divine likeness.[30] Such theological consistency, however, is not always present in the deep marks of patriarchy on Orthodox tradition.[31]

Patriarchy as a culture that values masculinity, men, and manliness over women, and as an objective fact attested by numbers (in terms of leadership offices, representation, etc.) is present in the Orthodox tradition. The patriarchal control of the tradition implicitly empowers some acts and persons and disenfranchises others. In some areas of Orthodoxy, namely, the clerical hierarchy but also many sources of tradition, there is a religious prescription of "women's submission to men" in a way that "grants power to men and systematically disadvantages women *as women*" and is upheld ideologically and structurally, to paraphrase Manon Garcia's conceptualization of patriarchy.[32] I am always struck that when a hierarch needs a translator for some international gathering, it may be (and in my observation, often is) a woman who is chosen. Translators may stand in front of the church and speak in these otherwise all-male gatherings, yet the words they offer cannot be their own; rather they must pass on the meaning of what the more authoritative man has said. No one seems to wonder what this woman standing in front of the church or in a room of male bishops might offer if *her own* words were invited and affirmed among the hierarchs.

In multiple practices, commemorations, and authoritative textual sources, Orthodox tradition renders women at a "relative disadvantage vis-à-vis men."[33] After joyfully returning to in-person church services after weeks of streaming them online during the COVID-19 pandemic, I recall my then five-year-old daughter lamenting that she could no longer see what was happening at the altar because, unlike her brothers, she was not allowed to serve behind the iconostasis and no longer had the camera view of the priest's actions during Divine Liturgy. She was excluded based on her gender, and even as a child, she felt that her ability to participate in and learn about *her* faith was limited in more ways than her brothers because she is a girl. Implicit misogyny structurally reinforced through patriarchal exclusivity and male leadership is deeply ingrained in the values and religious institution of the Orthodox Church. If one takes Kate Manne's explanation that misogyny should be understood "as more about the hostility girls and women *face*, as opposed to the hostility men *feel* deep down in their hearts" and acknowledge that even within Orthodoxy "a girl or woman is facing disproportionately or distinctively gendered hostile treatment because she is *a woman in a man's world*—that is, a woman in a historically patriarchal society," then the harm religious patriarchy can carry (even when seeming to work or speak on women's behalf) becomes more recognizable.[34]

Even though many might not perceive gender-based hostility in an Orthodox context (or at least those that stay and remain Orthodox and thus identify as with the tradition), Manne's definition of misogyny is helpful to think about the environment that women encounter and the symbols that confront them as being self-negating, dehumanizing, or just erasing rather than some sort of intentional male malevolence. As Manne notes, "Misogyny may be a purely structural phenomenon, perpetuated by social institutions, policies, and broader cultural mores."[35] Patriarchy, although not synonymous with misogyny, especially in Orthodox contexts, is nevertheless implicit in perpetuating the latter, because Orthodox patriarchy does not undo its own privilege in order to advocate for women's respect and equality (a kenotic behavior that I suggest in chapter 5 is Christologically imitative). In historically Orthodox majority countries, there are often broader patriarchal social values and practices reinforced by the church that affect the lives of women in terms of access to education, medical care, reproductive options, safety, financial independence, and opportunities for professional advancement. Structurally privileging men in tradition, liturgy, and leadership is not unrelated to the feelings and attitudes people express about and toward women in nonreligious contexts. Systems of patriarchy even in religious contexts reflect and perpetuate values about who matters and how they should be treated. Theologically within Orthodoxy, everyone should be valued as a person created and loved by God, and everyone should be honored as bearers of God's image.

## IN WHAT WAYS IS ORTHODOXY'S TRADITION PATRIARCHAL?

### Liturgical Privileging of Masculinity

While feminist theologians in other Christian churches have called for more inclusive language when referring to God, beyond the scripturally based trinitarian formula, this has not widely been the case in Orthodoxy. The God encountered most frequently within Orthodoxy is masculinized even if above gender altogether and even if the Orthodox tradition includes resources for addressing God in feminine terms. Kathleen McVey rightly notes that authors in Syriac Orthodox traditions historically highlighted the maternal aspects of the trinitarian God, to expand beyond the well-established observation that the Holy Spirit is a feminine noun in Syriac.[36] Similarly, Susan Ashbrook Harvey convincingly argues, that it is not just the Spirit that takes on feminine characteristics, but the whole Trinity in Syriac poetic praise, with nothing unique about the Spirit's noun feminization.[37] In the Greek-speaking dominant culture of Byzantium, God is also depicted in ways that defy a strict masculine father image. Symeon the New Theologian (d. 1022), for example, makes ample use of the image of suckling at God's breast, based on 1 Corinthians 3:1–2.[38] Christ is figured in maternal imagery as well in various biblical passages that do not go unnoticed by patristic homilists and commentators.[39] When female images of God do appear in scripture or theology, however, they are almost always bridal or maternal, which runs the risk of gender essentialization or reducing women's identities to these particular types and the patriarchal associations conjured by them.[40] These poetic and symbolic images, however, do celebrate God beyond the male, but they have not found resonances in liturgical forms or the naming of God.[41] The Catholic feminist theologian Janet Martin Soskice cautions us that changing the gender of the words *Father* and *Son* could result in a difference of meaning and understanding of divine relationship—something that would be theologically problematic.[42] Consequently, the God that most Orthodox encounter as they follow along in written prayers or liturgical services is gendered masculine, even though there is potential for incorporating feminine language and ungendered language for God within the broader sources of tradition.

Despite its more varied and poetic heritage, the liturgical address of God exclusively with masculine names does not help undo the theological problems posed by privileging androcentrism and patriarchy. Indeed, the visual and ecclesial privileging of men and patriarchy is sometimes upheld along a divine gender correlation between God and the priesthood. Even if one might redefine what that divine masculinity looks like, there is still an encounter with God who is Father and Son and whose circumcision is celebrated as a feast day. That is, even if one wholeheartedly affirms queer theologian Linn Tonstad's observation that "divine masculinity never takes a single, determinative, proper form," there is still something presumed *more* "proper" about men and masculinity in Orthodox tradition than women inherently have access to.[43] The reimagining of what masculinity and maleness become in Christ in terms of undoing privileged social categories or associations with oppressive power is not highlighted as translatable as are other aspects of the condescension of the incarnation. The fact that Christ reveals a new nondominating mode of masculinity, one that takes on a gender-crossing ascetic form in later Christian tradition, wherein the ideal man is humble, filled with mourning (for sins and the world), desexualized, and occupied with nurturing care of the souls of others, does not necessarily benefit the opportunities available to women.[44]

Within Orthodoxy, the scriptural precedent for Orthodox liturgy, along with the iconographic affirmation of the incarnation of the divine Logos as Jesus Christ, gives a normative and timeless affirmation of the male body that does not have a female counterpart. Some non-Orthodox feminist theologians have argued for drawing on the personified wisdom of God, Sophia, as a way of reclaiming a divine feminine. However, this argument has been predominantly disconnected from the Orthodox conception of Sophia, which is developed in nineteenth-century Russian Orthodox sophiology.[45] The development of Sophia—essentially, divine activity in the world—in the thought of nineteenth- and early twentieth-century Russian theologians such as Vladimir Solov'ev and Sergius Bulgakov may yet prove to be a resource for an Orthodox way of naming the divine feminine and promoting a more gender-inclusive mode of theology.[46] Despite its gendered pronoun, however, Sophia is inconsistently gendered as feminine among those who write about it, and when it is feminized it is often presented in the service of complementarianism and gender essentialist views. In addition, sophiology is controversial because it has been accused of trinitarian confusion and panentheism, and Sophia does not have any gendered commemorative or significant liturgical expression.[47] The conception of divine wisdom and activity as Sophia does not equate or offer an equal counterpart to the male language marking Orthodox prayers, dogma, and belief. It may provide some paths forward for additional reflection on ways of speaking of God that subvert the effects of patriarchal privilege, but what those paths might look like has yet to be fully developed by an Orthodox woman.[48]

While Jesus's body was dogmatically affirmed as being fully and normatively human, in Orthodox piety, Mary's body was transformed from the norms of human women. Her lifelong virginity and "purity" stand to dehumanize her in terms of blood and penetration while affirming her nurturing and life-giving qualities of nursing and birth giving.[49] Despite the impressive piety that emerges throughout Orthodox history to honor Mary as Theotokos, or God-bearer, and the commemoration of her militant "saving" qualities that deliver believers from earthly calamities, heresy, and armed invaders, she remains nevertheless a human graced by God's transfiguring presence. She is not a female equal counterpart to God (even if in some devotion she might appear more important than God).[50] Her humanity in liturgy and patristic commentaries is rendered somewhat unrelatable to women to the extent that she is elevated and also paradoxically de-gendered in being interpreted as a symbol of all humanity.[51] While she does offer a robust feminine divinized presence and example, Mary is both particularized and universalized in a way that does not necessarily undo the privileging of maleness that occurs in worshipping God incarnate as a man. The visibility of God as man liturgically has elevated manhood and its associated attributes in ways that seconds womanhood in Mary. Daly's widely echoed observation that "if God is male then male is God" certainly finds resonances in Orthodox contexts alongside a celebrated Orthodox Athanasian formulation that God "was incarnate that we might be made god."[52] It is assumed women are included in the *anthropos*/humanity incarnated by the divine Logos described by Athanasius, but to Daly's point, there is little in the liturgical and commemorative tradition that affirms this without some sort of hesitation on the status of women's humanity.

## Patriarchal Precedent in Scriptural Tradition

The Bible within Orthodox Christianity, even with its fundamental Christocentric orientation and reading, exists as a historical product that contains within it images of male privilege, idealized patriarchy, and women's subordination.[53] How these restrictions and ideals are interpreted and expressed in the Orthodox communities that receive, study, and abide by them are various, but having scripture as a defining and creedal source of authority for the religious community embeds in it a degree of patriarchy. There are no known female authors in the scriptural canon, and given its various milieus of compilation, it reflects multiple historical gendered hierarchies and even the subversion of those hierarchies to convey meaning. This poses a challenge not just for Orthodox women, but all contemporary people who have to determine how to retain the spiritual significance and meaning of their Scriptures while acknowledging that they contain historical ideas about gender that are problematic.

The critical study of the influence of patriarchy on gender within the biblical text has been robustly discussed in the writings of biblical scholars and feminist theologians of other Christian traditions.[54] Among Orthodox biblical scholars and commentators, constructive engagement with such critiques is generally limited to a handful of women biblical scholars, who react to and receive the observations of these other non-Orthodox scholars with varying degrees of acceptance and usefulness.[55] Orthodox women biblical scholars have addressed issues of patriarchy within the Bible and, like many others, have attempted to read the Bible as primarily liberating in the context of its historical norms.[56] Yet the text itself remains a patriarchal production.

Hermeneutics aside, the scriptural text itself has significant authority within Orthodox liturgy ritually. The gospel book is an object of procession and veneration that is typically held and read aloud by a deacon or a priest. Particular biblical passages are read throughout the year and during liturgical rites, and scriptural verses and allusions give voice to various prayers and hymns that fill the Orthodox vernacular as a sign of holiness and biblical conformity.[57] In some jurisdictions it is common for women to read or chant the Epistle or Old Testament readings; in others, however, it is rare to see a woman read from the Bible on behalf of her parish. Similarly, in a few parishes there are various laymen and laywomen blessed as catechists and homilists; however, it is far from the norm to hear a woman preach in an Orthodox church. In these ways, men's words, reading, interpreting, and presenting the Scriptures are normalized with authoritative associations that women lack.

Internalized Historical Patriarchy Encountered as Timeless

Historically, male authors had more access to education, literacy, positions for theological writing, and opportunities for being privileged within recorded ecclesial tradition.[58] To critique Orthodox tradition for being patriarchal is in some ways just an honest assessment of historical records in general. Patriarchy certainly existed at the onset of Christianity, but it did not remain unchanged throughout diverse cultures and times. Despite instances where one could draw on the radical equality of the New Testament, the tension that is offered in Pauline literature reflects similar tension in the patristic tradition. Everyone is free and united in Christ, and Jesus's teachings seem to inaugurate a new era of social boundary crossing, yet preferences for hierarchy, order, and community control hold such egalitarian ideals in check.[59] Male familial and property leadership following a tradition of paterfamilias continued with new significance in Christianized contexts, extending male responsibility for the actions of others into the monastery, episcopacy, and influential Christian homes.[60] In the early church, gender expectations were constructed against "pagan" and "heterodox" practices to establish the church as distinctly good and with the conversion of the Roman Empire, more influential.[61] The values of the dominant culture regarding gender in many ways became the values of the church, yet theologically it maintained celebrated possibilities for the upheaval and inversion of social expectations to reveal the miraculous. Patriarchy in this way, from early Christianity, was normalized, yet held the possibility of holy subversion in sources and practices that are recalled as authorities for Orthodoxy in the present day. This is not to causally explain that patriarchy exists today due to patristic adoption of Greco-Roman ideals but to indicate that inasmuch as Orthodox tradition is regarded by some as timeless, it is also an ongoing production of socially entangled cultural and religious values and the negotiation of constantly shifting historical situations. Patriarchy is taught, negotiated, questioned, and changed through the choices made and the stories told by Orthodox believers, who, like the early church "fathers," are culturally influenced in how they make their Orthodoxy legible. Patriarchy may be a historically justifiable facet of Christianity, but it also reflects choices to privilege androcentrism that continue to the present.

In addition, within Orthodox thought and practice, the patristic and desert fathers are not just encountered historically where any gender-based disparities might be ameliorated by contextualization. Instead, the authors of many sources of Orthodox tradition are commemorated and prayed to as saints, lending even their problematic writings significant influence for those who refer to them. Likewise with hagiography and ascetic texts, a pious sensibility tends to be that if these forms of instruction, suffering, and mortification were good enough for the church hundreds of years ago, they still can teach holiness today. This means that Orthodox believers continue to encounter these figures and sources with authority in their *spiritual present*. For instance, even if Orthodox do not personally know a present-day quote of a priest telling a wife that she is obligated to have sex with her husband to keep a harmonious household, they have saints saying it. John Chrysostom (d. 407) explains in his homily on 1 Corinthians 7 that women "are responsible for their husband's licentiousness and the broken homes that result" if they "refuse their husbands" without prior mutual arrangement for abstinence.[62] This explanation and the scripture it is based on serve as an example of how tradition might present believers with sainted voices endorsing patriarchal, androcentric, and, at times, misogynistic views. The words of scripture, patristic teachings, and examples of saints are not just historicized in Orthodox spirituality but also encountered as alive in Christ. Sainted figures remain as *living* authorities that Orthodox believers turn to for spiritual counsel and often take their written words (historically situated or not) as valuable for informing their responses to their own present-day concerns. The degree to which spiritual sayings, patristic teachings, canons, or sainted stories are contextualized in catechism or preaching varies. In liturgical commemoration, hymns, and many believers' spiritual lives, however, the interpretation and application of the sources of tradition are often offered without critical analysis or historical context.[63] In this way, such decontextualized sources in which women had very little voice serve as part of the public narrative and personal application of Orthodoxy by which Orthodox Christians understand their goals, values, selves, and faith through a normative patriarchal framework.

Implicit Patriarchal Bias in the Patristic Tradition

Primary commentary on how Orthodox Christians should interpret scripture and understand their faith can be found in the writings of the church fathers. Much of Orthodox tradition is named "patristic" and draws on writings from such famed premodern "fathers" as Athanasius, John Chrysostom, Cyril of Alexandria, the Cappadocians, John Climacus, Maximus the Confessor, Isaac of Nineveh, John of Damascus, Theodore the Studite, Symeon the New Theologian, and Gregory Palamas, to name a few. Within what one might term the "patristic tradition," which Orthodox see as an ongoing project of theological witness even into the modern age, the numbers of well-known women theologians and female saints are quite disproportional to those of men, even in the past few years. Although Orthodox Christians regard the age of patristics as ongoing, the early Christian and medieval (or Byzantine) "fathers" remain more widespread in popularity, and their association with holding definitive positions during times of doctrinal controversy lends them great authority. Regardless of the efforts to draw attention to the few matristic authors and desert mothers, most extant theological writings that have fundamentally influenced Orthodox tradition are authored by or attributed to men. On occasion one might hear "fathers and mothers" of the church invoked, but if one were to compare lists, it is clear that a few desert mothers and writings in the name of a sainted woman (likely written by a man) do not compensate for a compendium of male theological authorities.[64] This is especially the case because women's writings and sayings need a level of conformity with androcentric ideals to be preserved and handed down.[65]

Even in women's monastic centers where women had opportunities and perhaps the education to write, the record of women's compositions are few, aside from establishing the monastic order of the particular monastery or writing the life of a fellow female saint (and these are mostly anonymous). Even the most notable ninth-century woman hymnographer,

Kassia, is rather exceptional in terms of her presence and voice in the tradition. As such, she runs the risk of being held up as a token to argue that the tradition is not patriarchal. One named author, whose hymns are intoned but a few times a year, does not correct a gender imbalance that otherwise dominates.[66] For the most part, women's sayings or writings are deemphasized compared to the patristic writings found in compendiums of ascetic wisdom, biblical interpretations, homilies, and spiritual treatises (aside from monastic *typikons*, or rules for women's monasteries), so that texts written by women remain unknown and underreferenced even if extant.[67] Unlike the rich corpus of women's mystical writings found in medieval Catholicism, there is practically no premodern writing by Orthodox women visionaries, even if there are a few hagiographic accounts of women having mystical experiences. This lack of texts recognized as authored by women speaking as authorities to their own religious experiences normalizes androcentric texts as having a type of universal authority for scriptural interpretation and religious guidance.

Patriarchal Conciliar Dominance

Patristic authors have most fundamentally shaped the theological formulation of the church by being bishops and other clerics invited to attend ecumenical councils or otherwise pastorally defend and define Orthodox belief—something that, aside from perhaps imperial or technical administrative exceptions, women did not and do not have the same level of access to. There are numerous liturgical commemorations throughout the year of the "Holy Fathers" of various ecumenical councils that emphasize the doctrinal contributions of sainted men and the belief that God has established them as "luminous stars upon the earth" to guide "all to the true Faith."[68] As any recent synod or Orthodox conciliar meeting demonstrates, this is very much still the case, even if a few women theologians or scholars might be consulted behind the scenes. Women are unable to say as male hierarchs do, "It seems good to us and to the Holy Spirit," an impressive statement that conciliar documents proclaim on behalf of the whole church but that women are de facto excluded from similarly proclaiming.[69]

Conciliar documents and historical canons that privilege men's contributions do not just impact dogmatic formulation but also shape pastoral and liturgical practices. Orthodox canon law with its associated commentaries, addresses several issues involving women, without providing women an authoritative way to participate in its formulation, application, or interpretation. Within the collection of Orthodox canons, there are teachings governing such issues as women's ordination, marriage, sexual behaviors, dress, tonsure, menstruation, maternity, and liturgical participation.[70] Some of the canons display a Christian rewriting of social gender norms in contrast to the context in which they were written, and sometimes reinforcing them through religious justifications.[71] However, the relevance and application of canon law for present-day women is very much up to individual spiritual directors (usually men).[72] In addition, the whole genre sets up the canon as a type of normative religious ideal that one needs a priestly blessing to adapt to one's own situation—again subordinating women to the interpretations of men. Perhaps more significantly, the canonical tradition honors men authoritatively stating consensus on issues that affect women without women's participation in the process.

Patristic Interpretations of Gender

Prominent male patristic theologians sometimes reflected in letters, pastoral homilies, theological treatises, and poems on the human sexed and gendered states. This means that texts that might be referred to as reflecting the religious understanding of the significance of gender or sex difference in tradition are primarily written by men or perpetuate views that privilege men. Patristic authors did not just come up with patriarchy as a Christian ideal. Perhaps I am an optimist, but I do not think that the majority of Orthodox clerics or men in general are *intentional* misogynists, and those mostly sainted authors who have contributed enduringly influential writings to the church I take as striving within the norms and constraining language of their times to improve the lives of women and affirm their spiritual equality. Despite the same relationship to the divine image that might be presumed from Genesis 1:27, patristic authors had varying ideas about women, their spiritual capacity, and their abilities to image the divine that reflect different contexts.[73] They likely did not intentionally choose to consider women inferior or weak compared to men or choose on the basis of religion to install male leadership of Christian families and churches. Yet they accepted what they were taught and brought Christian values to the gender order and understandings of their day—at times rupturing or sanctifying social expectations.[74] Privileged patristic authorities such as Athanasius, the fourth-century Cappadocians (Gregory of Nyssa, Basil of Caesarea, and Gregory of Nazianzus), Maximus the Confessor, John of Damascus, and Gregory Palamas articulated their faith amid theological controversies by drawing on non-Christian concepts and language from classical philosophy.[75] Thus, even while Orthodox can appreciate the nuances rendered possible by patristic thinking alongside the insights of Aristotle and Plato in developing understandings and terms for articulating trinitarian and Christological beliefs, they must also acknowledge the persistent legacy of ancient views of gender in Orthodox tradition. Aristotle's belief that women were incomplete and deformed men and should be ruled over by men, Hippocrates's and Galen's now-comical misunderstandings of the female anatomy that portrayed women's bodies as weak, insufficient, and dangerous to themselves and others, and Plato's affirmation of women's inferior soul and capacity for virtue in comparison to men—all reflect cultural values about women presumed by later educated Christian men.[76]

In fairness to the patristic authors who do refer to women, there is often an attempt to mediate (rather than adopt in practice) the religious ideal of Galatians 3:28 in which there is no longer "male and female" in Christ with the experience of living in a patriarchal society. However, affirmation of women's equality in Christ does not then translate to this-worldly human gender equality because the authors are constrained by the androcentric assumptions of their own contexts. As Behr-Sigel points out, even as women were included historically as equal spiritual members in the ecclesial Body of Christ, "the men who directed the Church did not escape from the contamination of the accepted ideas of their time, ideas which were transmitted by male-centered cultures and perpetuated a certain scorn for and fear of women."[77] Maximus the Confessor, for instance, famously talks of male and female as principles rather than persons but has in mind a type of androprimacy, which is the privileging of the masculine and the male above the feminine and the female.[78] The patristic positions and phrasings regarding gender and sexuality, the state of women with relation to men, and issues related to marriage and reproduction are still influential in shaping Orthodox views on gender and sexuality today without their historical limits always being fully acknowledged.[79] Women's interpretations of their own experiences and bodies are largely absent.

Patristic Accounts of Women

Beyond theological formulation, within the patristic tradition are hagiographies, ascetical instructions, and short, spiritually didactic narratives and sayings. Most of the known authors of these texts are men, or the texts were preserved and circulated through the facilitation or approval of influential (often clerical) men, perhaps with the exception of texts developed in women's monasteries.[80] Granted, many traditional Orthodox texts are anonymous or feature prominent female protagonists or foils for male spiritual progress, but the way they do so is shaped by androcentric assumptions (perhaps shared by women) regarding women. Gregory of Nyssa, for instance, lauds his sainted mother, saying, "A woman was the starting-point of our story, if indeed one may call her a woman, for I do not know whether it is appropriate to call someone a woman who was by nature woman, but who, in fact, was far above nature."[81] In his attempt to elevate his mother and demonstrate her holiness above nature, Gregory implicitly erases her womanhood and equates woman with the lower and baser "nature." I analyze such constructions of women through a patriarchal lens in the next chapter, but for now, it is enough to observe that the patristic attempts to point out the equality or superiority of women's holiness as transcending their being women are often problematic because they erase the possibility of a holy woman remaining a fully human woman.[82] Although there is also a temptation for all holy depictions to elevate the subject beyond the human to the angelic, the heavenly, or the spiritual, as I show in the next chapter, women are presumed to be in need of greater transformation because they are women.

Even where men write about holy women and praise them as equals or superiors, these saints' stories are regulated and perpetuated through patriarchal control and situated in androcentric discourse.[83] Holy women, or at least the telling of their lives, are conveyed in ways that are (or were) appealing and acceptable to male clerical and monastic authorities.[84] The male audience, voice, and depiction of holy women is the norm by which female exemplars are communicated to the church. It is worth noting also that hagiography as a genre includes texts of various levels of sophistication with varying ecclesiological and political agendas.[85] These texts are far from neutral; they serve as popular entertainment, edification, and literary genres relying on patterns, types, and preconceived expectations to deliver their message in a particular context.[86] The result is that the models of holiness presented as worthy of emulation are limited by patriarchal preferences and modes of recognition reflective of multiple influences, motivations, contexts, and literary sources.[87]

Although there are records of several patristic authors' interactions with holy women that evidence feelings of collegiality and equality, the language mediating these experiences remains patriarchal. That is, while some authors might take great pains to demonstrate gender equality, they do so by relying on the social assumption of a gender hierarchy. The writing of John Chrysostom to Olympia, deaconess, wealthy patron, and friend of the patriarch, whom Gregory of Nazianzus refers to as "a mirror of a Christian woman," serves as another example. While Chrysostom writes to Olympia as a peer and frequently notes her noble spiritual qualities, he displays misogyny in his critique of other virgin women who may walk or dress in a tempting way such that they might be better reckoned "among the women of harlotry." Thus, Chrysostom's respect for a particular woman does not negate his patriarchal views of women more generally.[88] As Behr-Sigel similarly summarizes, "Basil the Great saw in his sister Macrina his true spiritual master. Gregory of Nyssa was married, and St. John Chrysostom had the deaconess Olympia as his friend and confidant. Nonetheless, in his pastoral activities, St. John is often severely unfair toward the women of his time in that he accuses them of being responsible for the degradation of Christian mores."[89] Patristic authors' attempts to honor specific women reveal unquestioned patriarchal gender assumptions about women in general.

The Patristic (and Patriarchal) Mary

Of course, numerous patristic authors also write about and praise the Theotokos. Compared to some other Christian presentations of Mary, Mary's presentation in the Orthodox tradition is certainly one of prominence and authority.[90] Patristic homilies about the Theotokos make a woman's humanity essential theologically and certainly highlight the humanity of Mary being offered and used in the incarnation—but often in a way that it is then depersonalized. It is as if Mary is a divine vessel, no longer a distinct human being but rather a person whose identity has been subsumed in motherhood. John of Damascus's homily on the Nativity of the Theotokos, for example, says, "A womb in which the Uncontained dwelt and breasts of milk from which God, the little child Jesus, was nourished! Ever-virginal gateway of God. . . . Her whole being is the bridal chamber of the Spirit. . . . O Marvel above all marvels! A woman has become higher than the seraphim since God has been seen 'made a little less than angels!'"[91] In addition to reinforcing the notion that women are lowly, to marvel that "a woman has become higher than the seraphim" is the type of praise that figures her as a container or a human material provider rather than a full human person, a type of praise that is not uncommon in other homilies about Mary and in her liturgical presentation in hymns and prayers. Yet the Christological debates go to great lengths to emphasize the full humanity of her divine Son. When Mary's personality is liturgically represented, for instance, in the laments of Holy Week, it is voiced through the authorship of male authors and through an androcentric gaze.[92]

Pious imagining around the personality of Mary in Orthodox Christianity is highly developed. She appears in various hymns, for example, as one who interrogates and challenges an archangel, as a militant defender of the faithful, and as one who faithfully laments at the cross.[93] She is set forth as a model of deification for all people, not just women. The doctrinal significance assigned to Mary's ever-virginity or role in the divine incarnation that is emphasized in the church, however, may be disconnected from the ways still-living Orthodox women might relate to Mary.[94] Moreover, Mary's hagiographic and apocryphal commemoration has not yet been fully unpacked as a resource for empowering other women and affirming their full humanity. Mary is presented in the patristic and commemorative tradition as a free, empowered woman who has authority over many men, but at the same time, her representation is filtered through clerical androcentric priorities. Despite the numerous ways women and men might relate to Mary in their own devotional lives, what is celebrated in the official liturgical and common ecclesial context and sources is likewise patriarchally controlled and determined. Even with Orthodoxy's rich tradition of celebrating the maternal, feminine, and potential for divinized humanity through the example of Mary, the

Russian punk protest group Pussy Riot's request that "Mary become a feminist" is still lingering in the air unfulfilled or perhaps in the eyes of some suitably rejected.[95] There is a type of doublespeak regarding Mary and nearly all saintly women in the Orthodox patristic and liturgical-commemorative tradition, a tension between articulating the heavenly and negating the earthly, in ways that confront women with ambivalence about their humanity.

### The Partiality of Priestly Patriarchy

Perhaps the most overt expression of patriarchy within Orthodox Christianity is the exclusively male institutional leadership of the church by "patriarchs." To the present day, the Orthodox Church persists with an exclusively male-ordained episcopacy. There is practically no record of women being priests or bishops within this tradition.[96] Historically, there are numerous reasons a female priesthood was considered an impossibility for Orthodox Christianity (social conditions, restrictions associated with menstruation and childbearing, patriarchal norms, etc.), yet the mere existence of the male leadership of the church has shaped it and continues to shape it in a way that privileges androcentric perspectives.[97] Topping responds to the common pacifying response to those that call for the ordination of women, "all Orthodox Christians are called to the 'royal priesthood' (1 Peter 2:9)" by saying that "within this inclusive priesthood, however, some are more royal than others. Although women, too, are created in the divine image and likeness (Genesis 1:28), we are still categorized as somehow less royal and priestly than our brothers—in a word, less divine."[98] As a consequence of the institutional exclusively male clerical hierarchy of the Orthodox Church, the important ways Orthodox recount the continuity and consensus of their faith tradition also diminishes the contributions of women. Orthodoxy is proclaimed as "the faith of our fathers" because it refers to the "holy fathers" who gathered in the ecumenical councils and traces its apostolicity through the consecration of male bishops.[99] The male clerical (and at its highest ranks, now celibate) administration of the church is part of this tradition of apostolic succession. Despite the presence of "equal to the apostles" female saints within this tradition (e.g., Mary Magdalene and the women first to proclaim the news of the resurrection), the episcopacy traces itself back through exclusively male figures appointed by Christ.[100] This lineage in many ways prioritizes and privileges the contributions of men such that the tradition takes on a disproportionately androcentric form, even if Orthodox would claim women equally within its apostolicity. The spiritual lineage of the church as it is commemorated invokes more than just a lineage of male bishops. It also includes councils and canons drafted by men, sainted patristic theologians (often male and monastic), hymnographers, and male spiritual-ascetic authors that outweigh the presence and importance of sainted women (the Theotokos excepted).[101] There are notable women among the sainted ranks, but they are significantly outnumbered and nevertheless exist within a commemorative and textual tradition dominated by men, so their expression and depiction are rather constrained by (even if subversively in reaction to) androcentric expectations and types.

The practical effect of an exclusively male institutional hierarchy is that women have less official voice compared to their clerical male counterparts. Women are categorically denied access to overtly lead and publicly represent the church.[102] Moreover, there has been very little overt calling for women priests within this tradition, with perhaps the most progressive view being one of acknowledging there may not be any theological reason why women could not be ordained, but only that there is no apparent theological, only perhaps pastoral reasons as to why they should be ordained.[103] Similar discourse surrounds the restoration of the female diaconate, an ordained women's ministry for which there is historical precedent in the Orthodox tradition. The question of the female diaconate has gained some momentum in recent years, albeit not without controversy and with admittedly little widespread impact to date.[104] The public face of Orthodox leaders and decision makers is thus very bearded and male. What Behr-Sigel noted some decades ago rings true today throughout much of the Orthodox world:

> Women's place has been assigned to her by nature and by tradition. And in fact, women have felt quite comfortable there, not feeling in the least oppressed or frustrated. At any rate, this is what we often hear from ecclesiastic circles and it is partly true, but only partly so. Besides, do not those who usually speak on this question, mostly men, most often forget to ask women for their opinions.[105]

Orthodox male leaders are quick to highlight women's contributions to the church in sainted exemplars and maternal roles, but I am not aware of any calling publicly for women to be included in their hierarchical ranks as a manifestation of respect for women and a call for their equality. More significantly, I have not observed a widespread movement among Orthodox leaders to speak against misogyny and advocate for women's social equality, within or outside of the church. While the degree to which the proclamations and words of hierarchs influence and shape the church practices, beliefs, and teachings can be debated, with a few imperial exceptions aside, the *formally recognized* opportunities for women to officially and publicly define Orthodoxy are fewer than those for men.[106]

One striking example of this affirmation of the value and contributions of women alongside implicit negation of women's participation in the ordained hierarchy is the meeting of the 2016 Holy and Great Council mentioned in the introduction, where male hierarchs gathered with only minimal consultation by female theologians and issued a statement rejecting discrimination based on sex, though it unapologetically had only male signatories.[107] Due to their exclusion from the ordained priestly and episcopal ranks, comparable numbers of women are denied normative participation, voice, and authority within the church. Theologically, this gender hierarchy, privileging, and exclusion gives women the "experience of being out of tune with others," which Ahmed names as one of the experiences of "being a feminist."[108]

There are, of course, practical pastoral implications of exclusively male leadership in Orthodox Christianity that have been documented well elsewhere and are mirrored in other traditionally patriarchal Christian denominations. Issues of abuse, domestic violence, sexual experiences, reproductive health, home visits to single women, and counseling about familial relationships are frequently cited as particularly difficult areas for a singularly sexed priesthood.[109] Gender-based abuses of clerical authority, discrimination against women in various aspects of parish life, and mismanagement of women's pastoral issues have been documented, but women remain with little recourse within the church to address the negative effects of patriarchal power on their lives because of their widespread exclusion from the ordained hierarchy.

The patriarchal orientation of the Orthodox Church continues to shape women's liturgical experiences and ministerial opportunities.

Aside from women's monasteries, women's participation in liturgical and parish life, like men's is contingent on the acceptance of the priest but in a way that also religiously reinforces gender-based power differences and makes women disproportionately vulnerable to religiously justified abuse.[110] Women's religious participation is contingent on a degree of patriarchal subordination in a way that often reinforces gender hierarchy. Even prayers and rites specifically addressing women and their experiences (i.e., those related to birth and miscarriage, marriage, or becoming a nun) are filtered through and subject to patriarchal authority.

The liturgy is part of the tradition in which what is done may be different from what is written but also in which atemporal affirmation is idealized and instructions for changes are handled primarily at the episcopal and parish levels (again removing liturgical control from most women).[111] Moreover, the liturgical context is one of adaptability and variation at the local level, where despite diocesan instructions the performance of certain hymns or the participation in a particular rite might be omitted or adapted by the priest. The rite of churching an infant and mother, for example, and the prayers related to child-bearing have much variability and are widely acknowledged as needing revision to be consistent with both biology and theology.[112] For example, some prayers that are performed when a new infant and its mother return to church after forty days (during which the mother is excluded from communion) call for purifying the mother from bodily "defilement" or "bodily and spiritual uncleanness," implying that the postpartum state is one of physical impurity that excludes the woman from liturgical participation.[113] Frost rightly observes that there are points of tension in affirming the embodied reality of mothers and places where what might be significant to many mothers, such as weaning, are left unacknowledged liturgically, while the androcentric concerns of "purity" after birth are emphasized.[114]

With exclusively male control over sacramental access, women have little recourse for disagreement or noncompliance, which may jeopardize their ecclesial participation in a way that is particularly gendered. In addition, the visual symbol of the priest, deacon, altar servers, and sometimes readers or chanters sets up a male ideal of administering the church to the women who may fill it.[115] This representational androcentrism makes it seem like men are more entitled to certain ecclesial spaces, ministries, and authority, even when there is no theological justification for privileging the male body, manliness, and masculinity in the church. Theology that emphasizes the maleness of Christ as a justification for an exclusively male priesthood has been rejected by most Orthodox scholars as theologically incongruous. Any argument that men are somehow more iconic of Christ diminishes the image of God also affirmed in women and elevates physical attributes as determiners of iconicity that are exclusionary and seemingly arbitrary; for example, the church does not require that all priests have brown hair or are of Jewish descent.[116] Thankfully, there are exceptions in women's monasteries and sometimes among priest's families, but in most cases a woman's access to the altar, for example, is more restricted or at least contingent than a man's.[117] The potential effects of the liturgical presentation of women and female symbols in icons, hymns, and rites alongside an exclusively male priesthood shapes the perception of women, their status, and their appropriate "roles" in the church along seemingly sacred lines.[118]

## Patriarchal Control of Women's Liturgical and Commemorative Representation

In addition to the overt ways Orthodox Christianity privileges male leadership and patriarchal thinking about women, its tradition has been marked by patriarchy in ways that control women's representation in the church. Most obviously, the church herself is referred to as Mother, sometimes Virgin Mother, Bride, and so on. The church is feminized and frequently maternal, sometimes in identification with the Theotokos, as the one who teaches the faith through her mysteries and tradition.[119] This prominent woman figure, however, is nevertheless subject to male patriarchal constructions of and assumptions about women, mothers, brides, and virgins and in this way has limited potential to break down the restrictions of patriarchy. It is as if the church is filled with women and is herself a woman (even as the "Body of Christ"), yet is governed, headed, and controlled by select men.

Women have been and are sites of divine power on earth and are enormously influential in handing down the teaching and practices of Orthodox Christianity, yet remain disproportionately controlled in a system of patriarchal androcentrism. I certainly do not want to diminish the contributions of women martyrs, apostles, abbesses, saints, teachers, deaconesses, chanters, laywomen, and theologians who have shaped the church but only note that these women are remarkable in part because they gained prominence in a system and linguistic culture in which their authority and ability was not presumed normative. Despite the many instances where pious devotion, miracles, and the saint's intervention herself has prompted the recognition of numerous female saints, aside from their participation in prayerfully celebrating the saint's commemoration, women's exclusion from equal participation in the clerical ranks limits their influence in shaping who and what is included in Orthodox tradition. Perhaps some of the numerous anonymous hagiographies and hymns included in Orthodox commemorations may have been written by women, but this remains unknown.[120] A few sainted empresses and exceedingly wealthy women patrons are perhaps notable exceptions to the dominating influence of men. These women through their imperial or social power were more able to directly shape the direction of the church. For example, sainted women are recognized in Orthodox tradition for directly influencing devotion to Mary as Theotokos, the veneration of icons, the conversion of Russia, and providing properties and means for male hierarchs and theologians to flourish.[121] Likewise, the aforementioned contributions of Kassia for hymnography and several women monastic hagiographers are important.[122] These few, yet exceedingly noteworthy exceptions, should not be taken as tokens to excuse the omission of more women in positions of authority, nor should they be mistakenly representative of a type of more widespread gender equality. Even with these prominent female influencers in Orthodox Christianity, the narrative that is told about them, the record of their involvement, and their commemoration in Orthodox hymns and calendars are determined and maintained to a certain privileged degree by privileged men.

In addition to the words and actions of the liturgical context, the iconographic program of a given prayer space may reinforce and communicate certain gender ideals. The presentation of the female body and position in most Orthodox icons expresses theological and androcentric concerns about portraying the figure in a light that is spiritually beneficial. The visual representation of women saints, biblical women, martyrs, royal patrons, and personifications of natural elements in feminine form often fill the liturgical space. While the icon of the Theotokos is typically behind the altar, women are traditionally more restricted from that space than are men.[123] The depiction of women saints is often presented along the left-hand side of the church, where historically women might pray apart from their male counterparts, and in some churches this gender division is still maintained, even if unofficially. Where and how women appear iconographically is mediated through primarily a male priestly control of sacred space. Nevertheless, icons do have the potential to be written by, commissioned, or sponsored by women, again lending areas of female influence for shaping the liturgical imagery. Frost optimistically notes iconographic shifts may be to come as more women become iconographers, and perhaps in future generations there will be greater diversity of women's bodies and experiences represented in liturgical spaces.[124]

In a tradition that claims spiritual equality of men and women and that all people are created in the image of God, how is it that patriarchy seems to exist with unquestioned sacred justification? The sanctification of patriarchy as a dominating structure within Orthodox tradition is, for the most part, implicit and by association. Granted, there are several notable texts that give the divine institution of a stratified order of the church and name hierarchy as a mode of divine communication.[125] Nevertheless, patriarchy is in many ways integral to Orthodox identity as a religious tradition and in some ways, such as apostolic lineage and continuity with patristic theology, determinative of it. Consequently, patriarchy is not something that can be easily excised from understandings of Orthodox Christianity. If one discounts the authority of the "holy fathers" because they were primarily male, there is little left in the textual content that has so richly developed Orthodox faith and its intellectual and liturgical traditions. Likewise, if one rejects calling God "Father," then one rejects what has been prayerfully handed down by women and men as divine revelation that conveys a particular type of relationality. And if believers reject the places where men speak for women and women's autonomous voices are represented, the Christian tradition is deconstructed nearly into oblivion.

Even though patriarchal privilege and a certain degree of androcentrism cannot be easily overcome, they can be reconsidered in terms of their significance for influencing modern Orthodox Christians. Indeed, for the average layperson patriarchal awareness and influence may be much removed from their experience of the church. Perhaps one may see a remarkable degree of liberating impetus among patristic authors in light of their social-historical constraints, or one might see that in the mind of a brilliant theologian there remains a humbling blind spot concerning the gendered humanity around him. While patriarchy certainly has controlled the contours and expressions of Orthodoxy and Orthodox tradition, especially in its authoritative liturgical, commemorative, ascetic-spiritual, and conciliar contexts, it is important to note that seeping through the seams of what might appear an overwhelmingly patriarchally determined tradition are instances of subversion, celebrated negation, and paradox. Yet, even in the historically established and, we hope, well-intentioned male headship of the church, there are consequences for the ways women are androcentrically mediated. Through liturgy and the sources of Orthodox tradition, the faithful receive and perpetuate messages about whose liturgical participation matters, whose theological thinking is important, and whose holiness sets the standard for what holiness looks like—and this is overwhelmingly androcentric and determined patriarchally. Patriarchal privilege in the church and tradition undercuts its confession and cultivation of women as equal participants in the divine life. The problem of patriarchy within Orthodox tradition is not singular but rather is indicated collectively by various manifestations of privileged androcentrism and the limitation of women to equally shape tradition.

**TWO**

# Commemorating the Patriarchal Woman

Having established that Orthodox tradition is intrinsically marked by patriarchy, what, then, are the features of Orthodoxy's discourse about women? I claimed in the previous chapter that women are disadvantaged by the pervasiveness of patriarchal androcentrism in Orthodox tradition but also noted that depictions of women occur throughout commemorative sources and spiritual texts. The construction of the "patriarchal woman" in tradition, therefore, is certainly not singular, yet it is marked by motifs and themes that preclude women's humanity as equal to men's. Gender does not function in just one way but rather presents us with a nexus of values interwoven with and dependent on audience expectations for conveying meaning. But, taken collectively, what does the "woman" constructed and perpetuated patriarchally look like?

Drawing on examples from the categories and genres remarked on in chapter 1, in this chapter, I show that the patriarchal tropes of Orthodox womanhood construct a dehumanized patriarchal woman as an ideal. Encountering limited, negative, or otherwise dehumanized views of women in a sacred context privileges those representations as associated with holiness and Orthodoxy. As Susan Ashbrook Harvey observes, within religious tradition, "the 'mere' rhetoric of female inferiority has ... yielded relentless conditions of physical, intellectual, social, and cultural oppression for women over the entire swath of Christian history."[1] What is said about women in the sources of tradition has an impact on the lives of women. Accordingly, the ways women are represented in these sources can be used to justify or excuse behaviors and attitudes toward women that subtly and overtly reinforce their patriarchal subordination. This is not to say that there is a widespread practice of bishops claiming that based on a particular saint's life or patristic saying, women should obey men categorically. Rather, I suggest that these representations in sources that express and perpetuate religious ideals can be used to dismiss the concerns about equality that real women raise and foster a culture where women's equality is widely represented but through a patriarchal lens. The issue worth critiquing theologically is not so much that specific examples of historical misogyny or patriarchal cultures exist in tradition but that because these patriarchal constructions of women have been incorporated in the commemorative and spiritual-catechetical tradition, they can license the perpetuation of patriarchal androcentrism as religiously normative in the present.

Although historical hagiographies and hymns about women may reflect the rhetorical norms of their times, as part of Orthodox commemorative tradition, they continue to be perpetuated as spiritually beneficial in present times, usually without context or qualification.[2] The historical religious depictions of women as the "manly woman" of virtue, the virginal modest maid, the lusty temptress, and the divine mother are well established.[3] What I am showing, however, is that recalling and invoking these tropes in sacred settings is problematic for affirming the equality and full humanity of women. The recalling of these tropes through association with saints' commemorations or the trope's presence in texts that are still regarded as spiritually beneficial makes these patriarchally truncated images appear as the normative and ideal Orthodox views about women.[4] The tropes and ideals I present in this chapter are certainly not the only ways women are depicted in Orthodox tradition; there are always exceptions, and there are other, perhaps less problematic modes of reading and interpreting the examples I provide, but these are not yet reflected within the dominant commemorative tradition of the Orthodox Church.[5] Representing women through an androcentric gaze is problematic because it appears sanctified as an ideal and practice of the past and the present.[6]

The depictions of female saints within Orthodox hagiography, hymns, and even iconography must be evaluated critically because these sources are often invoked to defend the church from not perpetuating gender inequality. Orthodox tradition, according to one view, does not promote gender inequality because it commemorates strong, smart, exceptional, or prominent female saints.[7] But most of the texts written about these holy women reflect the priorities of men. Commemoration of saintly women in the Orthodox Church affirms the potential for spiritual equality between the sexes, but the recognition of women's humanity as equal to men's and fundamentally already sanctified and redeemed is less apparent. Even though there are sainted women in the highest heavenly positions of the church who serve for women and men as models of unbounded holiness, gender may be experienced restrictively as an inequitable social reality that is reinforced through liturgical, catechetical, spiritual, pastoral, and commemorative traditions.

The patriarchal representations of women are not just historical literary tropes or liturgical misunderstandings in their religious usage. Even subtly, they affirm and inscribe ideas about women and who and how they should be in the tradition. Invoking the words of Simone de Beauvoir, the historical and commemorative tropes about women inform religiously how "one [is] made a woman" and prompt a questioning, via Judith Butler, of the idealized ways "woman" is performed and constructed in the commemorative and liturgical traditions of Orthodox Christianity.[8] The questions of gender's relation to ontology, the naturalness of gender essentialism, and the relevance of complementarian gender "roles" are not answered with consensus among Orthodox scholars and practitioners.[9] Therefore, it is important to consider critically the ideals of Orthodox womanhood represented by textual religious sources of tradition and the problematic ways they are entangled with perpetuating patriarchal androcentrism as Orthodox.

## THE PARTIAL PATRIARCHAL WOMAN

In this section, I show several ways that the representation of women is limited because it is controlled by authoritative men. Orthodox tradition in its varied historical and cultural accumulation reflects varieties of voices, authorities, and intended audiences. Its portrayal of women is likewise diverse, yet the ways women's full humanity is represented and affirmed is only given voice in fractured modes because of the influence of its patriarchal androcentric context. Well-established historical tropes, ecclesially inscribed "roles," and religiously reinforced cultural gender expectations depict women in Orthodox sources through a patriarchal gaze that implicitly diminishes the equality of their humanity. The possibility of women's spiritual equality is affirmed, but their gender and humanity are held more ambiguously. Such inconsistency should give Orthodox Christians pause to reconsider how they rely on and invoke tradition. Women might appear powerful in their hagiographic depictions or liturgical commemorations, but there is often the potential for these figures (like the Theotokos) to be invoked and interpreted in ways that nonetheless privilege patriarchal power over living human women. Orthodox believers, however, may also draw on these same figures and depictions in unofficial or subversively empowering interpretations. In recent decades, scholarship in a range of disciplines has highlighted how women's piety, religious lives, and self-narrations may disregard or reinterpret what is "official" in more meaningful and even more pervasive ways.[10] Nevertheless, the Orthodox depictions of women in traditional genres warrant interrogation because, as the previous chapter demonstrated, the textual and liturgical sources of tradition have significant influence as determiners of Orthodoxy.

Admittedly, much could be said about the limited representation of men and masculinity in the commemorative tradition as well, about men being represented in similarly restricted and perhaps artificial ways. The authors privileged in Orthodox tradition are not representative of all or even most men. The limited expressions of manhood represented and idealized within tradition certainly are worth further consideration, but even in their limited conceptions, the "man" and the "male" have generally been regarded as universal norms privileged in tradition.[11] Even in various classes and social religious positions, being a man has more often than not (imperial exceptions aside) resulted in having greater access to officially determining and influencing their presentation and participation in Orthodox tradition. This does not mean that men are not left out or rendered partial in their presentation according to race, ability, sexuality, class, and so on but that such explorations must be reserved for discussion elsewhere.[12] Even where androcentrism gives way to greater inclusivity, "androprimacy" as an ontological assumption remains.[13]

Within Orthodoxy, even when someone might assert gender equality or a type of complementarianism, what is represented in many of the commemorative and liturgical sources of the tradition is not some sort of equalizing narrative but rather a series of liturgical, textual, and commemorative expressions that inscribe male entitlement over women in a religiously authoritative tradition.[14] Part of Orthodox tradition's patriarchalness is manifested as men speaking for and on behalf of women, thus implicitly devaluing women's unique voices. This includes a type of traditionally reinforced "mansplaining" that is maintained regarding women's experiences and representation. In the crowning prayers of the marriage rite, for example, the bride is prayed over in terms that express communal hopes for her assimilation to being a supportive, submissive, and fruitful wife. One prayer says, "Lord our God ... grant unto this woman to be in all things subject unto the man, and to this Your servant to be at the head of the woman that they live according to Your Will." At the end of the same service the groom is dismissed with the words, "Go your way in peace, performing in righteousness the commandments of God," while the bride is urged to be "glad in your husband, keeping the paths of the Law, for so God is well pleased."[15] The woman's experience in marriage and the hopes for her are sacramentally articulated to uphold patriarchy as something divinely desired. As with these marriage prayers, women's holiness is legible, scripted, and reproduced within and in response to patriarchal expectations—expectations in which one can see androcentrism eclipsing the full and equal humanity of women. If one thinks along with Kate Manne's critique of male entitlement, then one might interrogate how it is that men are entitled to speak for tradition, to speak for theology, and to appear self-named in Orthodoxy and rethink the mechanisms by which tradition teaches Orthodox Christians that men can speak for women, that women's bodies and demeanors are a spiritual problem for men, and that women should be subordinate to men.

Orthodox tradition not only scripts women's behaviors, but also their attitudes by presenting ideals about women, the female body, and women's associations in patriarchal religious contexts. Women now, as in history, engage, adopt, and resist such scripts to various degrees, but their association with Orthodox holiness is patriarchally presented. As Manne notes for modern women in secular contexts:

> Patriarchal ideology enlists a long list of mechanisms in service of this goal (a positive acceptance of subordination)—including women's internalization of the relevant social norms, narratives about women's distinctive proclivities and preferences, and valorizing depictions of the relevant forms of care work as personally rewarding, socially necessary, morally valuable, "cool," "natural," or healthy (as long as women perform them).[16]

We could easily substitute for our purposes that these types of messages are sent in historical and religious sources about how women should act and internalize particular forms of spiritual care that then order other responsibilities and behaviors. If subordination is internalized as holy humility, it is difficult to argue against women's submission with religious justification. Manne observes:

> Women's adherence to the relevant social roles . . . is supposed to look as natural or freely chosen as possible. . . . On the whole, however, this seamless appearance is almost inevitably deceptive, since more or less subtly hostile, threatening, and punitive norm-enforcement mechanisms will be standing at the ready, or operating in the background should these "soft" forms of social power prove insufficient for upholding them.[17]

Certainly in the Orthodox religious context, the punitive measures that function "softly" might be shame at not living up to or at least striving for or acknowledging as ideal the image of women set before them in religious sources. More punitive measures theologically are the knowledge that this somehow makes one regarded as un-Orthodox, unholy, and uncommitted to one's spiritual life and more overtly subject to hierarchically inflicted penances or liturgical exclusion, online or verbal harassment, and the exclusion from a community that may be central to one's life. Orthodox women scholars who publicly critique or question aspects of Orthodoxy are subject to this type of gender-based response. In considering the following historical examples and accounts of women from within the

Orthodox tradition, I invite the reader to think alongside Manne about how women fit within a man's mind and the patriarchal order, about what is done to enforce the patriarchy, and about how the values and sources maintained as Orthodox are oriented to upholding androcentric spiritual progress, values, and privilege (even if by inscribing certain behaviors on women, such as how to be subversive in a religiously ideal way). The examples in this chapter and the ones that follow serve to make visible the way patriarchy functions to control women and uphold its own power within tradition as acceptable and Orthodox.

Liturgical rites and spaces, including the dominance of the hierarchical ranks by exclusively male clergy, also create dependence of women on men and an unequal power dynamic that limits women's full representation within tradition. As Donna Rizk-Asdourian observes in the similarly patriarchal Oriental Orthodox contexts, "Women in some communities are expected to be *submissive* to the Church and *dismissive* about equality and positions of ecclesial authority."[18] The liturgical context celebrates a union of earthly and heavenly realities that appears to privilege earthly distinctions of the body over heavenly realities of union overcoming division and renders the ecclesiastical hierarchy a structure of gender-based oppression instead of one of increasing divine participation and therefore liberation. Of course, the whole church depends on the priesthood for the sacraments, but as I showed in the previous chapter, the exclusively male priesthood inequitably genders this dependence.[19] It is yet another instance within the church "tradition" where women are situated as in need of male mediation for spiritual participation and "good standing in the church" in a way that men do not encounter in a female counterpart. Even if one has a great spiritual mother, appeals to female saints, and has a domestic religious life structured around female instruction and leadership, participation in the liturgical life of the church necessitates female dependence on male mediation. Women are thus disadvantaged in the liturgical space even if their numbers surpass those of laymen or the clergy, because they are oriented to authoritative primary male actors leading or overseeing the service. Women are comparably disenfranchised from the liturgical space and restricted from accessing certain parts of it, which contributes to a construction of Orthodox womanhood as being gratefully dependent on the greater agency and authority of a man. No matter a woman's holiness, her activity within the liturgical space is gender restricted. In being ministered to sacramentally primarily by men, women enter the sacred space under qualification: they must be properly covered and appear sufficiently obedient, for example. It is not just the liturgical portrayal of women in textual sources that is problematic but also the ongoing living liturgical reality portrayed at each divine service where a gender order is inscribed as sacred and subtly or overtly celebrated in patriarchal leadership by an exclusively male ordained priesthood. Church leaders and even women parishioners tell women that they have equality and should look to the Theotokos or female saints as models in the church, that all gifts matter, or that the perception of women being excluded from ordained ministry is exacerbated by an overclericalization of the church in general. The fact remains, however, that although women have access to some things based on their gender, men have more consistent access to more things based on gender (the altar, the priesthood, chanting/reading during services, public decision-making roles, etc.). Orthodox tradition is often reflected, interpreted, and reproduced liturgically, and in this context women's possibilities are performatively constructed as more restricted than men's.

## WHAT IDEALS OF ORTHODOX WOMANHOOD FROM TRADITION ARE PROBLEMATIC?

### An Empty Claim of Equality

Orthodox leaders and sources from antiquity to the present claim there is fundamental equality between men and women. Certainly, no modern Orthodox theologian says overtly that women are not fully human or that they cannot be spiritually equal to men, and most would balk at the assertion that women are dehumanized through the patriarchal tradition and sanctified in a problematic way. Indeed, it is almost a trope of discussions had by men to claim the equality of the sexes, even when those *in* the conversation are only men. Such gender equality is frequently framed in terms of dignity, spiritual capacity, and being in the divine image.[20] Historically, Orthodox authors often make efforts to demonstrate the spiritual equality of women and even the ability of women to surpass men despite an inequitable sociocultural context or presumed physical inferiority. In proposing and defending this ideal of religious gender equality (or even women's superiority), male authors often resort to essentialism and idealism, which are still modes of depersonalization.[21]

In historical hagiographies of women saints, for example, some authors state at the outset that women can be holy too or that it is valuable to read about the lives of holy women. Stating this justification presumes a normative environment where it is assumed that women are not capable of comparable holiness and that their lives would be otherwise dismissed by the audience. The hagiographer of Mary the Younger (d. 903), for instance, explains:

> Only men are called to compete in secular contests and prove their bodily strength. The arena of virtue, however, is open to women no less than to men, and God the prize-giver generously grants the rewards and victory crowns to both sexes equally. . . . Here [i.e., in the arena of virtue] women are not sent away while men are accepted. . . . On the contrary, all sexes, offices, ages, and walks of life are called to this good fight. . . . So also with the blessed Mary, the wonder of our generation, who is the subject of our discourse. Although she was a woman, although she was married and bore children, nothing hindered her in any way from finding favor with God: neither <female> weakness of nature, nor the annoyances of wedlock, nor the needs and cares of child-rearing. To the contrary, it was these things which <God> gave her the occasion to find favor with and thus proved that those who believe and claim that such things form an obstacle to virtue are foolish and create pretexts for sins.[22]

The presumption reinforced in this preface is that Mary is remarkable for overcoming human assumptions and for her womanly social situation in a way that is holy, which in the context of this story is generosity and the patient endurance of brutal intimate partner violence. Mary's gender and its expression as a married mother are highlighted as not being obstacles to virtue. And yet the hagiographer privileges the norm by saying, "Although . . . ," indicating the dominant view of the audience—that a woman cannot be married, have children, and be holy. Mary the Younger's hagiographer claims that "crowns" of victory are given by God to both sexes equally, but his rhetoric suggests that his Christian audience is not fully convinced of this. The humanity of women then is subtly reinforced as being weaker and more prone to problematic attachments and therefore it is more remarkable that women can be transfigured in holiness. Although men and women may be divinely rewarded equally, the assumption reiterated in such a preface is that women have to do more to overcome their weak nature and the social conditions to demonstrate virtue. This is an implicit assumption that continues into contemporary contexts as well.

Authors within this historical Orthodox tradition are caught in a mode of expression, religious idealism, and patriarchal determination of reality that negates women speaking for themselves and exercising free self-giving personhood in the same way men do, or more precisely, in the way Orthodox believe Christ does.[23] The claim of equality between men and women is hollow because there is an underlying assumption and reality of difference that is lived and experienced as exclusion and inequality. In the circa fourteenth-century hagiography of Horaiozele of Constantinople, for instance, the author similarly demonstrates this tension.

> "In Christ," says Paul, the mouth of Christ, "there is no male and female." I believe that this surely illustrates that one (sex) is not inferior to the other, neither in the comprehension of higher divine truths, nor in their profession of faith, nor in their staunch and unyielding opposition to their adversaries. Thus Paul spoke, and he taught the female sex, in particular, by encouragement, by elevating them for contests in the name of God, and by anointing them for deeds of prowess.

But later the author recounts that Horaiozele replies to her male persecutor, "Are you not ashamed, raging one, that a woman has defeated you, or rather, utterly overpowered you, because you were unable to change my belief?"[24] These words reflect a presumption of gender inequality, that women are less capable compared to men so that it is surprising (or, in this instance shameful) that one might surpass a man, even amid the claim to spiritual equality. Like the preface to Mary the Younger's hagiography, this text reinforces the presumption of a gender hierarchy to show the female saint's holiness. Claiming women are equal to men spiritually while demonstrating this by relying on the assumption of their human inequality either sets an added step of sanctification for them (to first become like a human man on the path to holiness) or presumes it is surprising that a woman would be holy and thus subtly reinforces the idea that men are inherently superior.

The notion of male superiority as normative in late antiquity also finds expression in the voices of female saints. For example, a desert saying recounts that two male anchorites on coming upon Amma Sarah said to each other, "Let us take this old woman down a peg or two," and then they said to her, "See that your *logismos* [thinking] be not lifted up, amma, and you say to yourself: 'Here are the anchorites coming to me who am a woman.'" Amma Sarah said to them, "I am a woman by nature but not in logismos."[25] One of the few desert sayings attributed to a woman that Orthodox Christian tradition retains includes both a surpassing of expected gender as a limit through holiness and within that surpassing a subtle denigration of the category of women as something less than. The attempt to show women's holiness as equal to or surpassing men's based on this hierarchical conception of gender reinscribes assumptions of women as inherently submen and therefore subhuman. That also makes the women saints supermen or superhuman such that women's humanity or "nature," especially as it relates to the body, is devalued. Such embedded rhetorical gender tensions in hagiography undermine claims to women's equality and problematically devalue women's humanity. If women's humanity is devalued, then the incarnation itself is brought into question. To be salvific, divine unity to humanity in the person of Christ requires an affirmation of the fullness of a woman's humanity because it is from a woman that Christ receives his humanity.[26]

The very need for the hagiographer to state that women do indeed have personhood, equality, salvation, holiness, and so on is a subtle instance of a man speaking for a woman in a way that keeps women fixed as "outsiders" to their own tradition. In the *Life of Melania the Younger*, for example, the fifth-century martyr Melania meets with the empress, who proclaims about Melania to her servants and court, "She has rather even bridled nature itself and delivered herself to death daily, demonstrating to everyone by her very deeds that before God, woman is not surpassed by man in anything that pertains to virtue, if her decision is strong."[27] The praise of Melania hinges on the strength of her decision and in this way negates what is legible as virtue, and how it might be sought and attained is determined in a system built for men. The hagiography infers that women can be just as good as men before God if they try really hard—basically, as a man would. It also reinforces a type of bootstrap narrative for women, wherein the social, cultural, and religious barriers to recognizing Melania's sanctity are erased, and her attainment of equality is contingent instead on adopting a type of manly resolve.[28] While the spiritual capacity of holy women may be lauded even beyond that of men (which assumes that they start from a position below men), the theological norm that Ruether identifies as "the promotion of the full humanity of women" seems to be undermined by privileging androprimacy.[29]

An author may affirm the potential of women to achieve spiritual equality, yet also reflect values to the contrary regarding the equality of women's humanity.[30] Claiming women have equality while reinforcing the normativity of human inequality within spiritually didactive sources thus provides license for patriarchal gender values. Behr-Sigel rightly notes, "Through the centuries, the Church has in reality always proclaimed the Divine Word which sets out the fundamental equality of men and women before God." To the extent that this equality is not realized among humanity, it is part of the "cross" by which the church will be judged.[31] Even with rich hagiographic examples of spiritually equal and empowered women, there needs to be acknowledgment that these sources reflect and have the potential to reinforce patriarchal androcentrism. To the extent that they do, their claims to equality for women remain empty.

Negation of Womanhood as Holy

Orthodox tradition includes tropes and rites that arguably restrict women by prioritizing androcentric representations. This does not, however, reflect a "separate but equal" construction of gender. Gender essentialism is not inherently Orthodox, and to expect historical patriarchal sources to treat gender in fixed or stable ways is as much an anachronism as invoking the tropes examined in the previous section as universally indicative of contemporary women.[32] Instead, there is a certain set of male attributes privileged for men and women, with the result that to the degree women attain this ideal, they can become honorary men, and to the degree that men deviate from it, they become more "womanly."[33] Consequently, in premodern Orthodox religious texts from the Byzantine tradition, expectations of particular genders are inverted, negated, and rhetorically engaged to convey the transformative potential of divine power for the spiritual benefit of those who hear (or in some cases, sing) them. Martyr accounts, for instance, may valorize the woman suffering violence, specifically the female martyr who is rendered more pitiable and therefore more admirable based on gendered expectations of bodily weakness, frailty of mind, and virginal or pious innocence. In contrast, a male martyr may have a different and less impactful effect as, for example, a soldier who is already prepared for physical violence, bravery, courage, and endurance. The different expectations make women more useful for conveying the significance of divine power as it turns someone who is not expected to be bold, smart, or brave exactly that (even more than their male cohorts). The negation of women in "womanly" terms in such martyrdom accounts and hagiographies serves to reveal divine power and inspire the reader but is predicated on the negation of a woman being holy as a woman. Language and examples from hymns and hagiographies featuring women demonstrate that women have the potential to manifest divine likeness, but due to privileging androcentrism, this likeness unfortunately seems to be expressed at the expense of affirming their identities and experiences as women.[34] Thus, gender functions in many Orthodox commemorative texts, not as something ontologically fixed, but rather as a set of assumptions that can be transcended in holiness. In the lives of most women, however, this is not necessarily the case; existing as a woman socially and religiously may categorically restrict one from certain sacred spaces or hierarchical offices—no matter how holy. Although being spiritually unlimited by one's sex or gender is significant for affirming the freedom made available through a life in Christ, commemorating women for transcending womanhood can render the women themselves negated, overidealized, or in some other way devalued in their humanity.

The historical trope of women's holiness being expressed by donning "manly" attributes is well established, yet how that functions in the creation of an ideal of women saints still commemorated in the present reinforces a gender hierarchy.[35] Women may be able to become holy, but, as with the examples of Melania and Mary the Younger, they may do so only by putting aside their womanliness (attributes such as weakness, worldliness, and uncontrolled emotions) and adopting the performance of the more preferable masculine gender. Both in attributes of virtue and the body itself, the "manly woman" is a hagiographic trope repeated in hymns and commemorations. By continuing to sing and celebrate the sanctity of women in the likeness of men, Orthodox Christians perhaps unwittingly continue to reinforce notions of women's inherent inferiority to men. The humanity of women is sidelined, erased, and negated to reveal the presence of divine power—which also problematically is dependent on the assumption that divine power and women *as women* are mutually exclusive.

Saintly women who hid themselves in male monasteries and lived as eunuchs highlight the logical end of associating holiness with a certain type of manhood.[36] Luce Irigaray's observation appears to ring true in Orthodox Christian sources: "The most human and the most divine goal woman can conceive is to become man."[37] Yet this gender imbalance has received little critique within Orthodox theology. Several scholars have made compelling cases for reading female saints who choose to live as monks, sometimes in a men's monastery, as transgender, but within Orthodox commemorations, these saints remain counted among women.[38] There are several celebrated saints in this category whose lives, while distinct, share a general narrative of concealment of femininity through manly presentation to avoid unwanted circumstances (usually marriage, abuse, or parental separation), excelling in a monastic setting even beyond their male peers, discovery (often not until their death), and inspiring others to greater spirituality or working miracles.[39] For example, Matrona of Perge's hagiographer explains about the sixth-century saint that "holy Matrona . . . displayed the traits of holy men in the midst of monastic men and mastered the feats of accomplished solitaries."[40] Such gender transitions leading to ultimate gender transcendence imply that adoption of the male gender has to do with spiritual achievement and superiority rather than mere social presentation. The hagiographers celebrate these female saints for attaining holiness beyond their womanly gender—and convey the saints' holiness precisely by demonstrating that their holiness does not fit within the social constraints of and religious assumptions associated with women. Linn Tonstad's conception of "the affective life of binaries" as gender norms that "do not lose their power by being inverted, transgressed, or crossed [but] . . . are the very means by which they maintain their power" resonates in the gender-negating dynamics involved in communicating women's holiness.[41] In using transgression of gender expectations as a marker of sanctity, Orthodox commemorative rhetoric reinscribes patriarchal gender hierarchy and inequitable gender assumptions as normative.

The manly is prioritized and often aligned with the heavenly. The womanly, apart from the virginal-maternal, is not, and, of course, the virginal and the maternal are both feminized states often historically controlled and idealized patriarchally. In her seventh-century hagiography, the desert ascetic Mary of Egypt is not initially recognized by the priest-monk Zosimas as human and then is later thought to be a holy man, so that these two states—the angelic and the manly—are conflated and invoked with pious comparative potential. Mary is not recognizable as a woman because she is so ascetically holy.[42] Similarly, about Melania the Younger it is said, "she had been detached from the female nature and had acquired a masculine disposition, or rather, a heavenly one," thus conflating masculinity and spiritual advancement.[43] In the life of the fourth-century ascetic Pelagia of Antioch, the erasure of the woman into a divine creature is described nevertheless in masculine expression. When the bishop Iakobos goes to visit the presumed eunuch Pelagios, the author, the tenth-century Symeon Metaphrastes, writes:

> When she came out, he saw Pelagia—and he knew neither who she was, nor, even if someone had forewarned him, would he have been able to recognize her at all or surmise who she was from her appearance; for her skin color had been transformed, her eyes had become hollow, and everything about her had been altered and changed because of her abstinence; indeed no one else in Jerusalem, when seeing her, suspected that he was looking at a woman. . . . Iakobos, as if receiving the blessing from a man, stood bewildered at the sight of her abstinence.[44]

Pelagia is transformed from a woman to a man through asceticism. The concept of a holy woman still appearing womanly, perhaps with a soft, round, alluring, or otherwise unsubdued body runs counter to the Christian ascetical norm. The flesh mortified must then appear "manly." Women's humanity, their human bodies, is thus presented as rejected or at the very least subordinated to the masculinization of the ascetic male body and the strength and control of male virtue. In praising women saints and even demonstrating them to be superior to pious men, hagiographers also implicitly diminish and erase the woman's humanity. A female saint is in this way most easily rendered holy by describing her as no longer recognizably a woman.

Even when the female protagonist is not configured as manly, there is a rejection of normative womanly attributes akin to holiness. As Harvey has noted, holy women are always "exceptional."[45] Sainted women are overwhelmingly beautiful, intelligent, noble, beneficent women who resist or altogether reject marriage and wealth in favor of asceticism and charity; women who were tempted or fallen and then leave the world in extreme penitence; martyrs who offer witty unwavering defenses of their faith; the occasional empress turned ascetic; women who narrowly escape rape by divine intervention; and the nun or ascetic who surpasses those around her, often family members or men, in piety. Of course, many hagiographies weave a tapestry of overlapping and intersecting tropes, but few do not include at least one of these themes in some form, and these tropes leave out *most* women. What of the women who were tortured and raped without any divine intervention or immediate righteously constructed self-destruction? What of the poor, disabled, or physically unattractive women? What of the women who live in unremarkable domesticity or labor daily with great love or prayerful faithfulness? The absence of these types perpetuates a limiting androcentric gaze on women's holiness without attending to what might be most beneficial for actual women (and men) to hear about as models of sanctity. I am not saying that the extant female saints are not found useful and empowering by many women but that their incorporation in the commemorative cycle and liturgical space is dependent on accepting dominant androcentric views. Mary of Egypt's annual liturgical commemorations, for example, continue to model a gendered type of shame-based spiritual schooling, with the implicit assumption that there is nothing more sinful than a woman who like Mary of Egypt enjoys sex. Historical hagiographies are still the basis for the retelling of women saints' lives in collected volumes, *synaxaria* (records of saints to be commemorated each day), and daily readings and recommended as beneficial spiritual study.[46] So while one may think these tropes and problems are restricted to the presentation of women in historical texts, they continue to be taught (although with varied frequency and reception) as models of holiness among Orthodox Christians. I suspect subversive hearings, reinterpretations, and pious reimagining by women are common but have not prominently entered the mainstream narrative of holiness because they disrupt the patriarchal presentation of women and because women are excluded from many authoritative positions allowing them to teach these interpretations.

There also exists the trope of overidealizing women to the point of nearly erasing their humanity. Many examples of this type of commemoration can be identified, but the most prominent is the Orthodox veneration of Mary the Theotokos. The Protoevangelium of James as well as numerous hymns and homilies tell of the Theotokos being in "purity" even after birth, and some include the notion that Mary did not experience pain while giving birth.[47] Mary is praised by Orthodox as one who, "without corruption" (ἀδιαφθόρως), gave birth to God. This incorruptibility can refer both to virginal purity and, perhaps more broadly, to the integrity of her whole humanity in its Christological offering.[48] While the dogmatic importance of Christ's divine fatherhood and full unblemished humanity is clear, this praise removes Mary from the experience of any other living woman's conception and childbearing experience.[49] As theologians from other Christian denominations have asked for decades, what might be the significance of the Marian ideal for "real women"?[50] For Orthodox, Mary has a great deal of significance for men and women, but her humanity is so diminished in expressing the "Mother of God" incarnational affirmations that one wonders what is left for her to offer in the incarnation: Was she ever fully human to begin with?[51] Mary is theologically placed above the angels and human nature, but such concerns perhaps are unbalanced by androcentric concerns in ways that truncate her humanity and relatability as a woman.[52] Aside from Mary, the lives of saints are replete with representations of noble, beautiful, youthful, and intelligent women saints who are desired by men and valued for their patriarchally conformed piety. This leaves still-living women with a lacuna: women whose lives are not retold or commemorated because they were marginalized beyond the purview of the clerical and monastic ideals that shaped what Orthodox womanhood should look like. But representation matters, especially in a church filled with both written and living icons and in which reflecting on the images Orthodox see before them is regarded as spiritually formative.[53]

Most men do not experience such a gender-based negation or overly idealized transformation of attributes; or where one might say they do, for example, by meekness, humility, and tears, there is not the same degree of transformation. They are not praised as "womanly." Men are transfigured into Christ-likeness, but women are transfigured into a state of holiness that yet appears incomplete or incompatible with the lived realities of their gendered existence. Women are expected to adopt such virtues as humility and meekness as well, but these expectations are already culturally and socially imposed, so the legibility of these attributes as Christ-like requires an additional degree of expression or is otherwise taken for granted. For a woman, to be Christ-like is to become the ideal submissive feminine woman while also expressing manly control and boldness that denies their "womanliness." In some ways this is helpful because it shows that holiness is beyond a particular cisgender expression but also problematic because it privileges androcentric values about what women's sanctity might look like over how it might actually appear more diversely.

Women as Inherently Problematic

In many hagiographies, spiritual narratives, and even liturgical rites and spaces, women are sometimes presented as naturally problematic and liminal. Women are depicted as overly emotional, as the source of temptation and prone to lust, as worldly and noisy, and as distracted by maternal attachment, among other negative traits.[54] Accordingly, there are also depictions of women that do not present the woman's holiness but protect men's holiness from women. One example is from the desert sayings attributed to Abba Arsenius. After a noblewoman comes to visit him, he says to her, "Do you not realize you are a woman and cannot go just anywhere? Or is it so that on returning to Rome you can say to other women: I have seen Arsenius? Then they will turn the sea into a thoroughfare with women coming to see me," and then dismisses her, saying he will pray God takes remembrance of her from his heart. Later, when she falls sick, the bishop explains, "'Do you not realize that you are a woman, and that it is through women that the enemy wars against the Saints? That is the explanation of the old man's words; but as for your soul, he will pray for it continually.' At this, her spirit was healed and she returned home joyfully."[55] Although the woman ultimately rejoices that the saint will indeed pray for her, the story is predicated on a woman being humbled by a male saint based on assumptions about and rebukes of her gender. Arsenius rebukes the woman because she has entered a space that is disrupted by her womanly presence; she is out of place. In a view presumably shared by the audience of this text, the woman lacks the agency and freedom based on her sex to "go just anywhere." Likewise, Arsenius rebukes the woman for a type of prideful gawking at him that will cause a flood of (presumably noisy, worldly, and spiritually insincere or foolish) women to come to disturb him. Perhaps ironically, it is women who are often the objects of the entitled "male gaze" outside of this monastic context, even though this text still invites its readers to stand with Arsenius to look disdainfully at the noblewoman. The bishop says to the noblewoman, "Do you not realize that you are a woman?," as if that should be enough to keep her from seeking out a holy man and as if that it is through her sex that "the enemy wars against the Saints." This conclusion, of course, is predicated on the unvoiced assumption that saints are men. Despite what one might assume is associated with the womanly, all the bishop says is that women lead people (men) away from holiness, simply based on being a woman (however that might be socially constructed).[56] There is a degree of assumed danger associated with women's presence; they are seen as potentially contaminating and tempting for holy men. More generally, it is also that women are rendered in such discourse as antithetical to the practices of holiness. Only by transfiguring their bodies through asceticism and making them no longer womanly is the danger overcome.[57]

Similarly, numerous hagiographies name women's natural dispositions related to maternal care, or emotions, as something that needs to be overcome or controlled in a "manly" fashion because they are problems for and different from those of men. The construction of women's emotions and feelings in this way not only negates their validity but also gives license to men to name how women should feel and behave in order to be holy. For example, when Mary the Younger mourns the death of her five-year-old son, the hagiographer praises her, saying that even though Mary's "heart was broken and torn asunder ... she kept to herself ... without ... displaying unseemly behavior." This assumes that Mary is not displaying the type of loud mourning expected of normal mothers and associated with femininity as lack of emotional control.[58] Mary is praised for having overcome what might be considered very natural for her sex and maternal state. Relatedly, married women saints are praised for only reluctantly being intimate with their husbands or are depicted as holy for trying to avoid marital intercourse.[59] Surely these saints' lives display a monastic preference for celibacy and asceticism, but they also perpetuate a mode of negating female desire for another human being, engaging in marital intercourse out of a sense of obligation or gendered obedience as holy, and problematically sanctifying nonconsensual sex within marriage. All these aspects idealize patriarchal control over women's bodies and experiences in multilayered ways. Women are told how to feel, how to abstain, and how to submit through such narrative retellings that idealize female saints via a patriarchal and primarily monastic lens.

Liturgical rites and spaces also perpetuate a religious ambivalence about the natural functions and goodness of women's bodies. Much of women's presentation in Orthodox spaces appears to be not about presenting women before God but concealing women from the eyes of men who stand before God. Historical practices are well established, and cultural traditions of separation of men and women in the liturgical spaces in some churches persist, but what is more common in current practice is the prohibition of women behind the altar during liturgical services (excepting women's monasteries), as I mentioned in the previous chapter. There are some instances of female altar servers or acolytes, and at the time of this writing one ordained deaconess, yet this remains geographically limited and very controversial among Orthodox.[60] Expectations of dress and covering, of modesty and concealment, are pressed on women in ways that are not for men.[61] Modesty is not universally emphasized as an external manifestation of interior humility before God but more often taught that women need to be responsible for distracting men who might be tempted by them. In many Orthodox communities, a woman is still considered involuntarily impure during a flow of menstrual or postpartum blood, even though this presence of blood is in accordance with how God created the female body.[62] Women's bodies even today have thus not escaped the historical shaming and responsibility for others' actions and thoughts that is found in tradition. Women's natural bodies appear in Orthodox tradition as problems; it seems as though it is only when they are ascetically emaciated, disfigured as martyrs, or disguised in manliness until after death that their uncovered bodies can convey holiness. What does this teach Orthodox Christians about caring for their bodies as temples of the Holy Spirit or about the goodness of their bodies as part of God's creation?[63]

## Women as Objects in Relation to Men

Women who feature in spiritual narratives, hagiographies, hymns, and spiritual letters exist in a religious world that is not primarily constructed for and by them. Instead, women are constructed in various religious genres as underdeveloped subjects whose presentation somehow furthers men's spirituality. In the sixth-/seventh-century century collection of spiritual tales by John Moschus known as the *Spiritual Meadow*, for example, there are numerous women presented this way. The Theotokos features as a powerful defender of Orthodoxy, and women appear as temptations and act as the solicitors of miraculous intervention. However, in nearly every story where women are present, the women function to reveal or further the holiness of a man. Moschos highlights the authority of these women to teach the monks humility by playing on the assumption that women are generally sources of temptation and monks are supposed to be virtuous. When this recurring plotline is inverted, for example, when a farmer's daughter successfully reasons with a monk not to rape her, it renders the female characters in surprisingly authoritative modes of agency to shape the spiritual lives of both the monks in the texts and those who hear it.[64] Yet the authority of the woman is in service to cultivating male humility rather than teaching widespread respect for women as spiritual teachers. Similarly, in one tale, a nun flees to the desert to live as an anchorite to avoid being the cause of a young man's sin, but after seventeen years, she is divinely revealed to a male ascetic. The story emphasizes that "by divine inspiration he [the male anchorite] knew all about her" and that the woman is unable to escape the man's discovery of her holiness. In this episode, the reader is told that God reveals to a man a previously hidden woman against her will, with the result that the male anchorite "glorified God."[65] While one might assume that he glorifies God about this woman's degree of holiness, one could also read this text as the man glorifying God for revealing to *him* a woman that had been hidden from others. The male monk is moved to prayer and thus enhances his spiritual life at the expense of revealing the hidden spiritual life of a woman against her will and ostensibly with God's help.

Even the varied commemoration of the Virgin Mary as militaristic protectress, Athonite abbess, or imperial heavenly queen celebrates Mary as upholding androcentric interpretations and priorities.[66] As I previously mentioned, in some festal hymns, Mary is reduced to a divine vessel, a womb, and offers "humanity," yet the depth of her personhood is left unexplored.[67] The sixth-century hymns of Romanos the Melodist regarding the Annunciation famously render Mary as an erotic virgin, giving her voice and a persona (much like other dialogue hymns) but through a male author.[68] As much divine inspiration as one may want to attribute to the poetic genius of Romanos, or other male hymnographers, it is nevertheless a tradition in which the woman is silenced and given voice only through the view and authorship of men. I am well aware that historically there is a dearth of women authors and there are few collections of hymns attributed to women writers, yet little is done to acknowledge *what this lacuna does* to the Orthodox perception of women in the church and the theological construction of gender.[69] It seems at least in some ways to reinforce the notion that men should be entitled to speak for women and their experiences in the church. Women's voices are not needed. This is a theological problem, because to render the voices of half the church unimportant reduces recognition of the possibility of the Holy Spirit at work in them. It diminishes the confession of divine-human unity for women.

## CONTROLLING THE PUBLIC PERFORMANCE OF WOMANLY IDENTITIES THROUGH TRADITION

Even amid the rejection of holy woman as woman, acknowledging the intrinsically problematic assumptions in representing women in Orthodox traditions, the liturgical life of the church includes engagement with womanly attributes and female characters as spiritually beneficial and liturgically appropriate. Specifically, in the hymnography of the church, some female voices are presented for all liturgical participants to sing and prayerfully dwell in—regardless of their sex or gender. Some examples are Kassia's hymn of the sinful woman, the Life of Mary of Egypt, and the Holy Friday hymns in the voice of the mournful Theotokos.[70] Women's identities are engaged to marvel at the incarnation, to mourn, to repent for sexual sinfulness, and to prepare one in a state of penitence. Such prominent examples give voice to an ostensibly female experience of birth-giving, mourning for one's child as a mother, wiping Jesus's feet, or turning to piety to flee sexualization. However, even these examples are controlled by a male hierarchy and often sung in the voices of male choirs or chanters. While, as I have argued elsewhere, this may negate a type of cisgender binary fixity in the liturgical space, it also provides further evidence of men dominating women's experiences and appropriating them for public use. Similarly, in the act of mourning and singing lamentation, the character and act are integrated but moderated through male liturgical performance and mediation. Maternal pondering on the incarnation is offered to all without any explanation or qualification on what such pondering might mean to actual child-bearers, those suffering child loss, those who desire but cannot bear children, those who are worn out by the children they have, or women who do not feel called to be mothers.[71] One might also wonder about the role of patriarchal concerns in shaping the expression of these women's voices in the liturgical context. Mary of Egypt's self-narration for example, which is then incorporated in the Lenten service cycle, has the spiritual-beneficial model of ascribing sinfulness to oneself to induce a state of penitential humility.[72] The public liturgical performance of recounting a woman's sexual enjoyment as the worst sin of all reinforces the belief that women are inherently more prone to sin than are men. One might think that genocide or some other life-taking atrocity would be a more relevant story for modeling repentance, yet the penitence of the fifth week of Lent is anchored in a woman's sexual misdeeds.[73] The spiritualization of women's experiences and expressions without offering other avenues for women's liturgical self-voiced expression presents patriarchal control falsely as universal and feminized.

## ANDROCENTRIC CONTROL OF WOMEN'S BODIES AND BODILY EXPERIENCES

In addition to these hymnographic commemorations of the female and womanly perspectives and postures through the male gaze, there is within Orthodox tradition the male *control* of female bodies and embodied experiences. The depiction of women in hagiographic narratives suggests that "tradition" presents women's bodies and bodily experiences in ways that are androcentrically oriented and patriarchally limited. For example, hagiographers interpret women's bodily suffering as beautiful in an androcentric mode that demonstrates control of emotions, both sensationalizing women's suffering and controlling its expression.[74] The *Passion of Tatiana*, for instance, says of the saint, "She uttered no cry of distress nor did she groan with pain as her flesh was cut into pieces so horrifically, but with courageous endurance and magnanimous strength, she resiliently offered the Savior a grateful doxology from the psalms of David. . . . She was . . . mercilessly hewn into pieces by the hands of the blood-sucking executioners."[75] Even though the persecutors in most martyrdom accounts are not Orthodox, the retelling of them from a patriarchal and androcentric perspective by Orthodox Christians does an additional form of violence to the women they depict by retelling their abuses without allowing for women to reflect authoritatively on the gendered aspects of their martyrdom. It denies the women agency and then denies women who receive these narratives the ability to reflect authoritatively on their own suffering and agency. Men control women by controlling the stories about them and how they are retold within a patriarchal commemorative context. From martyric and ascetic impulses toward transcendence and masculine transformation to ritualized idealizations of women's sexual and procreative capacities, the liturgical, hagiographic, and hymnic presentation of women's bodies and related experiences are mediated through a type of androcentric lens that obfuscates the realities of women and their human bodies. This type of patriarchal narration of women's experiences and bodies eclipses a fuller witness of the Holy Spirit at work in the church in ways that are perhaps messy and disruptive of expectations and categories that Orthodox Christian communities have come to value and privilege. An honorable retelling of a saint's story out of love and piety is seen as virtuous, yet it is a type of virtuous distortion of the truth, or seeing the end (communicating holiness) as trumping the means (a fictive narrative). These ends need to be revisited if communicating one model of holiness obscures and limits the perception of the holiness of others.

Although the history of Christianity is rife with ascetic impulses and theologies that control and shape, deny, and liberate the bodies of men, women, eunuchs, and others, the control of the body is primarily through androcentric texts and practices. Women, especially in monastic contexts, certainly also controlled the body in various and religiously significant ways but cannot be said to have done so independent of strong patriarchal approval. What is lacking, then, is not only documentation of women's lives and bodies and their own understandings of how they are holy but also *religious value placed on women deciding what to do with their bodies and what their embodied experiences mean for themselves.* Recognition and celebration of more and more diverse saints would be a start toward affirming women's freedom to act and understand their bodily states and activities for themselves. All meaning is contextual and refers to others, but in obscuring the experiences of women, the commemorative construction of women obscure the tradition overall. And in valuing texts about women's suffering, enduring, and heroic bodies, women's embodied experiences written almost exclusively by men or through an androcentric lens subtly perpetuate the theologically problematic notion that men have a religiously endorsed right to speak for and control women, including women's bodies. This undermines the autonomy of women to determine their own bodies, which has an incarnational impact, if, for instance, one thinks about the Virgin Mary's consent being important for the divine-human unity of Christ.[76]

## MODELING GENDERED TROPES: PROBLEMS FOR THE PRESENT

Because historical Orthodox gender constructions are situated in commemorative and catechetical contexts, even in contemporary moments where the surrounding social context perhaps is more egalitarian or inclusive, the tropes discussed above are reinforced. Orthodox women saints whose hagiographies, hymns, and *akolouthias* (commemorative services) have been written more recently sometimes still include gendered language and tropes about their marital status, purity, maternity, modesty, and relation to the men and clerics around them. For example, the life of St. Methodia of Kimolos (1861–1908) includes the hagiographic formula, "from a very young age she stood out by her piety, modesty, and love towards the Church," and it continues by explaining that she reluctantly marries, is widowed, and then becomes a reclusive nun.[77] Even in the retelling of the lives of more unconventional modern women saints such as Xenia of St. Petersburg (d. 1803) or Maria of Paris (d. 1945), subversion of patriarchal authority is accepted as indicative of their exceptional holiness rather than a widespread call for the equality of women among ordained men.[78] Maria of Paris is commemorated in hymns as a suffering martyr, but the hymns do not highlight other perhaps more significant activism, subversions of Nazi authority, or theological aspects of her saintliness. The very relatable aspects of her life as a divorced mother who suffered the loss of a young child or as a strongly opinionated intellectual and politically involved local leader are not included in the commemoration of her holiness. She is holy in these hymns because she was martyred, drawing on earlier hymn types as a "bride of Christ."[79] Xenia is praised for being "divinely wise" in her holy foolishness and for "rivaling the angels" and in some versions of her hymns avoids the gendered tropes attributed to most women saints.[80] Yet she is not praised as a woman but is holy in the way her life no longer resembled that of a woman but rather as an angel and holy fool. Where there exist nonecclesial records of the lives of these and more recent women saints, the patriarchal selectiveness by which they are commemorated is evident.

The ways in which women are presented in tales and commemorations of holiness thus become part of the Orthodox discourse and thinking about women. The subjects of times past are called forward into the present and the future with uncritically engaged images of women in limited and male-dominated presentations. In many ways, the project of hagiography in a patriarchal religious and historical context is problematic in that it speaks for women and imagines the voices of women and then holds up these beloved figures and narratives as sacred exemplars. Such commemorative narratives and hymns need to be read open through historical contextualization and recognition of rhetorical tropes so that one might see the holy person beyond commemoration contoured by patriarchal concerns.[81]

Beyond the tropes that are recalled in expressing what holiness looks like based on the ways women were praised in the past, contemporary recognition of female saints maintains a familiar vernacular regarding women that perpetuates male entitlement to women's holiness. The process of recognizing new saints in Orthodox Christianity may begin with localized popular veneration of an individual known to be holy, but formal canonization and liturgical commemoration ultimately depends on the bishops. Women saints are thus only fully recognized as saints by male hierarchs, and there is a clericalization of power that is gendered and renders women's holiness always subject to male authority.[82] This is true of male holiness as well, yet men are and can be among the ranks of hierarchs who are authorized to formalize the recognition of sanctity. Because women are not ordained priests and historically have been subordinated socially, there is an implicit limiting of the types of holiness women are recognized for having that would warrant canonization. In this way, women are not just disenfranchised from articulating and recognizing what holiness looks like for other women publicly but also subtly inscribed with a diminished capacity for recognizing a greater variety of holiness on behalf of the church.[83]

Women's holiness is limited and concealed from recognition by maintaining an androcentric tradition that confers on men the right to determine how women's religiosity should appear and how women should appear in religious contexts. Women are determined and named by men without having a space to name themselves and determine the bounds of their identities. Without women having a voice and an equitable share in authority to have that voice heard and spoken, a fundamental expression of their humanity in the image and likeness of God is jeopardized and limited. Men are more entitled in the tradition to shape Orthodoxy because of the gendered hierarchy and priesthood but also because of the normative social gender hierarchy that privileges men, a hierarchy that is mirrored and sanctified in places of theological and liturgical authority.[84] This way of naming holiness and women by men within the tradition functions as a type of spiritual and gendered interpellation. Who can address women such that women respond and identify themselves as the ones addressed or invoked? There is a patriarchal authority that calls for women's acknowledgment and submission in identifying with the images of women that tradition sets forth.[85] What a text in Orthodox tradition means is not just what it says, but the authority it gives to speak for another, to name their experience and subjectivity, in terms of interpellation, response, and attunement. Women lack this authority in Orthodox tradition, as even in their articulations they must be attuned to androcentric and patriarchally established religious norms.

Women appear within the patriarchal tradition as patriarchal constructions. Women are represented as tropes, types, "others," without voice, autonomy, and full humanity. Both historically and in more recent discourse, women saints and the Theotokos are set up as tokens of equality where widespread change for living women is negated. The everyday activities of many women who long for an example of a "monk who finds God while cooking a meal with one child clamoring for a drink, another who needs a bottom wiped, and a baby throwing up over his shoulder," although sanctifying, are ignored and diminished.[86] There are exceptions to historical patriarchal tropes and instances where they are overly generalized, but they still dominate the view of women represented in the commemorative tradition. Women, in being a part of Orthodox tradition are disproportionately subject to a privileged androcentric orientation and patriarchal oversight. Any type of "add women" solution to androcentric assumptions of holiness does not work because it still relies disproportionately on the authority and privilege of male authors to invite the audience to recognize the holiness and value of women.[87] The religious construction of "women" in tradition is problematic because men are fundamentally the determiners and controllers of what is named as authoritative; men are the default referent, the namable, the expressible, the norm, the full, the human, and women remain other, second, exceptional, and partial. This poses difficulty for drawing on tradition to develop a theology of gender and to claim the equality of women based on Orthodox tradition.

The tradition also presents itself as authoritatively speaking for and over the experiences and voices of real women, who are unvoiced themselves. As they are diversely constructed in different genres and periods, women remain surprisingly patriarchal, that is, subject and subordinate to male (often clerical) determination for their existence, in the tradition. To the extent that tradition is held as sacred, this partiality and limitation is a significant problem. Women who do not conform, who were left out of the narrative as subversive or worse yet, as unremarkable because they were ordinary women, leave a blind spot in tradition. Tradition is problematically conceived if the voices of women are replaced by the narratives of men about women and the writings of women are conformed to tropes and assumptions dominated by authoritative men. The partial and dominating discourse about women without women's voices or with their voices mediated through an otherwise androcentric tradition poses lingering problems for women, and what the tradition teaches about women, for those who value women as full and equal human persons. To construct women religiously in terms that privilege androcentric and patriarchal concerns, especially in genres that are invoked as spiritually beneficial and commemorative of holiness, entangles these constructions with religious belief and praxis. To restrict or artificially imagine the humanity of women likewise undermines the fullness of the divine incarnation and obscures the unique diverse divine image created by God in each human person in favor of a more easily controlled, interpreted, and replicated "type."

THREE

# Spiritual Values and Gender Equality

The previous two chapters have shown that the patriarchal and androcentric dominance in Orthodox tradition qualifies its affirmations of women's equality, humanity, and spiritual potential. In this chapter, I examine how normalized patriarchal and androcentric presumptions shape ostensibly nongendered spiritual teachings in ways that disadvantage women and their ability to critique the patriarchal status quo. Orthodox spiritual teachings privilege self-abasement over equality and an ongoing process of becoming more fully human over some sort of intrinsic equal humanity. These values and teachings make it difficult for Orthodox women to advocate for themselves and their equality with religious justification because it can easily be dismissed as pride. Those who critique the patriarchal aspects of the church or argue for greater equality are frequently caricatured by "traditional" men and women as not sufficiently submitting to the teachings of the church and the divine order.[1] Ascetic virtues related to denying oneself and the valorization of suffering as martyric, compounded with a theological anthropological premise that all persons are in the process of becoming more fully human (in the way God has called us to be), make it challenging to argue that the effects of patriarchal androcentrism presented in the first two chapters are in fact theologically problematic and need to be addressed.

Although becoming more fully human in Christ, or humble obedience, is not differentiated by gender in the sources of the tradition, its location in an androcentric and patriarchal context can reinforce gender hierarchy and inequitable abuses against women. That means that not only do certain spiritual teachings make it difficult to advocate for greater gender equality, but some also exacerbate inequality as a consequence of their androcentric premise while making it appear virtuous. After all, how can Orthodox theology argue for equality as an ideal that should be pursued in this life when the divine model of equality is held Christologically in tandem with the obedience of the Son to the Father unto death, voluntary self-sacrifice on behalf of another, and humbly allowing injustice to be done to oneself to realize a spiritual good?

Feminist and liberation theologians in other traditions have developed robust responses to this problem of Christological imitation in self-sacrificial obedience especially for marginalized communities, but a comparable Orthodox response is lacking.[2] Orthodox theology needs to articulate its teachings and tradition on this issue in order that the fundamental proclamation of God as love (1 John 4:16) can be known and affirmed by *all* the members of the church. Although I certainly reject the caricature that feminism and its critiques are wholly secular, pro-choice, "Western," and antithetical to Orthodoxy, there are spiritual values within Orthodox tradition that make women's arguments for equality, equal opportunity and access, and unequivocal recognition as fully human *seem* so. Orthodox Christianity sits within this tension where spiritual emphasis on humility, self-giving, obedience, submission, acceptance of suffering, silence, dutiful participation in a divinely ordained hierarchy, and a divinely instituted gender hierarchy all make women or others who might seek greater voice or equality in their religious lives seem un-Orthodox. But what is rarely taken into account is that such a construction of Orthodox ascetic teachings presume and privilege androcentric positionality and consequently disadvantage women by ignoring the ways their spiritual realities may already be experienced and constructed as subordinate. Obedience, humility, suffering, and self-giving are revealed perfectly in Christ. As such, these ideals are also tied to full freedom and full humanity, which Orthodox sources do not sufficiently affirm for women.

Therefore, even as humility and self-sacrifice can be spiritually beneficial, the conditions of freedom and full humanity that promote spiritual progress rather than cloak spiritual harm are not equitably applied to women—and are in some circumstances undermined.

Numerous sources from different historical moments could be used to provide evidence of spiritual values of subordinate suffering and human development through spiritual progress. In this chapter, I primarily draw on examples from medieval Greek (Byzantine) hagiography, the *Philokalia* of the Greek tradition, and premodern collections of ascetic desert sayings.[3] This is not intended to be exhaustive but rather to point to beloved and influential writings within Orthodox tradition by some of its spiritual elite and acknowledged expert saints.[4] It is important to note that most of these sayings and writings are primarily by premodern monastic male authors (a few desert mothers aside) and likely were originally intended for a monastic and ascetic audience.[5] However, monastic teachings and texts have significant authority among Orthodox because they reflect ideals that laity are often unable to attain or devote energy to.[6] As experts on prayer and spiritual life, these sources reflect values of spirituality that pervade and influence Orthodox tradition beyond the monastic communities. Spiritual elders to this day advise their spiritual children to carefully read and learn from these texts without providing historical context.[7] Moreover, the genre of sayings and counseling spiritual letters continues in present-day saints' writings.[8] These sources also reflect a collection of varied yet deep thinking on what is spiritually beneficial and how one can make spiritual progress that is viewed as authoritative.

## SUBORDINATE, SELF-GIVING, AND SUFFERING

As I explained in chapter 2, in many premodern Orthodox hagiographies of women saints, it is stated at the outset that listening to tales about holy women is spiritually beneficial because women can be holy too. Many of these very same narratives then celebrate the women saints' voluntary self-abasement, suffering, and obedience unto self-harm or even death.[9] This is not unique; these attributes are celebrated in male saints' lives as well. But what is ignored is that the women saints the authors and commemorative texts praise embrace modes of self-subjugation that women in patriarchal cultures are already socialized to impose on themselves. For decades, the disproportionate impact of androcentric spiritual values on women has been recognized as a gendered theological problem by theorists of other traditions, one that Valerie Saiving famously observed as the "feminine" sin in the "negation of the self."[10] Even as women and men might be conceived as equals, women have a harder time realizing that equality, bringing to mind the words of Patricia Hill Collins: "Even though men and women may both be born free, it seems that women will have a much harder time becoming free again, if ever, because male domination has so profoundly rigged the deck."[11] Orthodoxy is no exception to such an observation. Women, as we saw in the previous chapter, in Orthodox patriarchal constructions, because of their gender, are often expected to be inherently subordinate, physically suffering, and more aware of their lowliness in comparison to men. Then they are praised for and instructed to adopt spiritual ascetic virtues of more self-denial, suffering, lowliness, silence, obedience, and humility—virtues that can further subjugate them to patriarchal control instead of helping them realize their freedom and equality in Christ. To me, at least, this appears as a type of incoherent theological doublespeak: Women, you are liberated and equal in Christ, but to witness to this divine liberation and equality, you should accept being treated unequally and not exercise your freedom but rather further conform yourself to patriarchal expectations. Women are affirmed as equal partakers of the divine life but with inequality in this life either ignored or valorized.[12] Stories and sayings promoting the spiritual benefits of suffering, humility, and obedience reinforce values that have been used to do violence to women and rest on the presumption that women should be doubly humble, long-suffering, and obedient based on their "female nature."[13]

Suffering and Sanctification

Even though Orthodox prayers and liturgical texts relate to God overwhelmingly as merciful, compassionate, and loving, there are numerous examples in ascetic and hagiographic texts of valorizing suffering as redemptive, spiritually beneficial to produce other virtues such as humility, and divinely imitative on the basis of the patient long suffering of Christ himself. The hagiographies of Mary the Younger and of other ninth- and tenth-century "pious housewife" saints provide examples of women being valorized for suffering in ways that idealize patient suffering as characteristic of being holy. Although patient suffering is idealized for both men and women, the experience of this suffering is compounded by gendered expectations and power dynamics. Mary is a married woman with children, but the hagiographer explains she is still able to find favor with God.[14] While this may seem a wonderful example of a philanthropic and pious wife and mother finding holiness in the mundane, what the author also refers to is domestic violence that led to Mary's death at the hands of her resentful and jealous husband. The presentation of Mary's holiness is entangled with the gender-based violence done to her and her patient acceptance of it. Likewise, another hagiography tells us that the husband of Thomaïs of Lesbos "used to strike the noble <Thomaïs> frequently, mocking greatly and sneering <at her>. But she remained steadfast, like an iron tower that is not at all shaken even when being savagely attacked, meditating constantly on the words of the Gospel," and then instructs the hearer to "turn your mind to the divine life of the blessed martyr . . . since she also received many beatings, and was scourged unbearably for the sake of the divine revelations of our Lord. . . . [S]he bore the blows with good grace, like a martyr rejoicing in Christ." This woman, more directly than Mary the Younger, is praised for a martyric marriage, for suffering intimate partner violence, and for "rejoicing" and bearing "the blows with good grace."[15] Thomaïs is praised for being steadfast and emotionally controlled while being physically and verbally assaulted. This type of righteous acceptance of suffering can be read as Thomaïs claiming agency in her faith to subvert the power of her husband's abuse even while submitting to it.[16] As powerful as these examples may be, for those in unavoidable situations of suffering, they do not show that God would want Thomaïs or Mary to leave, defend themselves, and ultimately not suffer if possible. Thomaïs's ultimate liberation comes only at her death. Thus, this example, like many others, shows women how to suffer in a way that is spiritually productive but not how to righteously resist and change the external conditions that give rise to their suffering in the first place. Although the same could be said for men, there is an additional axis of power based on gender difference that places women at a disadvantage for seeing themselves empowered in their faith to advocate for their lives and for others to recognize them as worth advocating for, especially in inequitably gendered conditions that have been normalized as sanctifying or divinely ordered in Christian tradition (marriage, for example).[17]

Considering Anna Mercedes's reevaluation of theologies of kenosis, or self-emptying, helps us acknowledge the significant ways women such as Thomaïs can still draw on submission and self-giving as forms of subversion and resistance. Mercedes shows that women and others who are in precarious situations may voluntarily adopt kenotic attitudes and behaviors as a way to respond to adverse conditions to maintain significant agency and preserve a sense of self.[18] Mercedes explains that although "self-giving may appear as the loss of power, kenotic outpouring may also ... bear a mighty current ... resisting oppression ... and redefining subjection."[19] This way of acknowledging the slippage of power dynamics within relationships where "power that is kenotic generates and regenerates itself in motion," rather than being a "static quality that could be the possession of any one group," helps us see women in subjugating circumstances as both victim and empowered agent (a dynamic that applies to the suffering Christ, I might add).[20] That is to say, those in situations of suffering may find modes of agency, self-realization, and meaningful survival in their ostensible submission and reframe their suffering as a divinely imitative offering of self. For example, the well-known story of St. Sophia and her three young martyred daughters, Faith, Hope, and Love, involves an eagerness to suffer in persistence of the faith and the reconfiguring of unspeakable torments as joyful offerings of love to Christ.[21] This redefinition of suffering as a type of welcome gift is a common trope of martyr's commemorations but also might make sense of otherwise senseless violence in a way that preserves the personhood of the one suffering on their own terms, even if idealizing it in ways that can perpetuate abuse and violence as spiritually productive. Suffering is constructed in many sources of Orthodox tradition as an act of love and a mode by which one comes to love God and know God's love.[22] There are many ways in which such thinking can be problematic, especially for those who are abused by "loved ones" and in the name of "love." I hope that most Christians would agree that the conditions that give rise to such kenotic subversions of the martyr saints should not be idealized or intentionally sought. Orthodox spiritual texts, however, often idealize opportunities for making spiritual progress at the expense of the self or personal safety without the balancing confession that because God loves her, God does not want the saint to suffer.

While many modern translators and commentators are quick to note that the hagiographic depictions of spousal violence as sanctifying are exceptions and should not be taken as an unproblematic ideal, there are nevertheless pastoral instructions that reflect the sentiment that women should endure rather than avoid suffering as a type of piety and marital faithfulness.[23] It is not enough to say that these few isolated historical hagiographic examples do not have an impact on the present when the values that support and are expressed in them still find expression in the spiritual counsel given to women. From personal accounts, I know of women who have been counseled in confession to bear the abuse of their marriages as a path to sanctity. I know of women who have been told to keep their assaults quiet in order to not destroy the reputations of men, sometimes priests.[24] I know of women who have turned to their tradition to find solace in their violent households and have encountered the above-mentioned saints' lives. For some it is empowering to know there might be spiritual meaning in their suffering and sainted fellow sufferers, but it does not show them that leaving an abusive relationship could also manifest holiness or that the church should advocate for their support, freedom, and safety because they know that God already does.

Some priests may draw the line at physical abuse, but women may be told to endure all manner of toxic and traumatizing relationships as a potentially sanctifying opportunity.[25] Verbal abuse in particular is something that is regarded in some spiritual sayings and saints' lives as something to be endured and applied internally, as if one deserves insults and more.[26] Beyond physical and sexual violence, there are areas of power differences, pressure, and coercion that dehumanize and belittle women, that may chip slowly away at their sense of self and sense of embodied humanity as being loved and united to God. These daily gendered burdens and normalized expectations are perhaps more insidious and pervasive, often internalized and without clear pastoral objection because there has yet to be a robustly defended theological rationale for advocating for the full and flourishing *humanity* of women in the way there has been an emphasis on their suffering.[27] Stories of abuse are historically problematic and not unrelated to the ways spiritual values continue to be used to keep women subject to vulnerability, control, and abuse.

Within Orthodox Christian tradition and spiritual teachings, affliction and suffering are presented as paths to holiness. It is not just enduring and patiently accepting suffering that is valued spiritually, but even seeking and rejoicing at suffering. Abba John Colobos was instructed by an elder, "Go and beseech God for the battle to come upon you, likewise the affliction and the humility you had before because it is by means of battles that the soul makes progress."[28] This saying suggests that one should not only embrace affliction when it comes but also seek out suffering and opportunities for spiritual warfare if life appears too easy. A saying of Peter of Damascus similarly urges that "as he [the spiritual person] advances through this humility towards divine and unfailing love, he accepts sufferings as though he deserved them. Indeed, he thinks he deserves more suffering than he encounters," and thanking God for being "found worthy of knowing and enduring these things by the grace of God, he is filled with a strong longing for God."[29] According to this saying, one not only endures suffering but thinks oneself worthy of even greater suffering, and then considers the suffering as a divine gift for one's spiritual growth. This can certainly be problematic—to suffer abuse and think that God wants one to suffer, or that this is the sign of God's love and a divine gift. Ascetic as it might be, it can certainly open areas for abuse, and there is not currently a robustly developed spiritual value alternative or safeguard against this view. Such construction of humility before God and embracing one's lowliness, one's spiritual sinfulness, with a corrective divine punishment and perceiving opportunities for suffering as graces from God and signs of divine love are particularly theologically problematic for the already marginalized because they validate the conditions of suffering as desirable even when not voluntarily assumed. For any Christian conception of suffering to have a spiritual value and not inadvertently depict God as a sadist, it needs to presume a privileged free person (historically, a privileged man) as its subject—that is, one who is not already socially oppressed, enduring suffering, or otherwise subordinated in their freedom.

One of the few desert mothers, Amma Theodora, explains that suffering beneficially is connected to its voluntary assumption, saying, "Every adverse situation produces a reward for us if we are willing," and "We will be not able to inherit the Kingdom of Heaven other than through many afflictions and temptations."[30] Notably, this Amma provides an example of a woman speaking to uphold the patriarchal ascetic value of suffering but links it to voluntary acceptance with the phrase, "if we are willing." Again, this preserves the agency of the individual to reframe their circumstances to be spiritually meaningful even under conditions of significant constraint but also encourages the acceptance of adversity as the means of salvation. Such a teaching and similar teachings do not leave much space for those suffering injustice, pain, or abuse to speak out against their circumstances without being also viewed as less committed to their faith.

Makarios of Egypt explains likewise that "the greater and more grievous the suffering, the greater their [the martyrs'] glory and the more intimate their communion with God." If the goal of Orthodox life is divine communion, then such a teaching appears to frame suffering as the best path to pursue it. Indeed, there are many ascetic stories of voluntarily adopted hardships as evidence of saintliness. However, there are also saints who are recognized as holy for relieving the physical and emotional suffering of others and working to protect the powerless.[31] Perhaps that Christian teaching based on Christ's own example as a healer, liberator, and comforter could be prioritized within Orthodox counsel to temper the ascetic emphasis that pervades so much of tradition. Makarios continues, however, by saying that "those who love the Lord may be recognized by the fact that because of their hope in Him they bear every affliction that comes, not simply courageously but also wholeheartedly."[32] In this last saying, Makarios teaches that it is not merely enduring suffering that is virtuous but also embracing suffering as an act of love. Love, however, implies freedom as a precondition, such that the spiritual value of suffering out of love for God cannot be brought about by imposing or expecting suffering of another based on such aspects of identity as gender; it must be wholly voluntary. I do not want to negate the agency of the marginalized, but the conditions of freedom for more freely loving and willing to be consistent with Orthodox theology of deification should always be more increasingly sought. This is not something that can occur individually, where one person tries to improve their own conditions of freedom, but also must be the collective, intentional work of the church for the world as the living Body of Christ. However, such a socially oriented emphasis within Orthodox tradition is currently underrepresented.

Divine suffering is a revelation of love because it is freely taken on without a warrant or compulsion on behalf of another. The conditions of Christ's sacrifice and obedience include his status as a free, rational male with an autonomous will. (It is not that maleness is significant in and of itself but that it renders the humanity of Christ privileged in ways that a female Christ would not be in a similar historical context.) Christian theologians from within and outside Orthodoxy have offered reinterpretations of self-giving and Christ's own kenotic example to qualify the seemingly totalizing virtue of the suffering and negated self. Aristotle Papanikolaou explains that kenosis is "not primarily self-sacrifice, but a state of being that liberates eros, the desire to be in relation with the other," and that it is "a precondition for relations of love and freedom, the only context in which the self is truly given."[33] Kenosis in this way could be understood as an ethic of true self-realization and a practice that both facilitates and is dependent on freedom. The model of kenosis that Sarah Coakley describes as "power in vulnerability" reflects a *voluntary* vulnerability and empowerment through choosing humility.[34] Freedom, choice, and agency are key to rendering suffering spiritually meaningful—even if those are enacted under constraint. Likewise, Gabrielle Thomas draws on the writings of Gregory of Nyssa to argue against the Christian "valorization of vulnerability" if it also suggests that God desires human "pain and suffering."[35] That is, there are sources in the Christian theological and patristic tradition that set limits on what might be understood as acceptable conditions of lowliness or suffering, with the primary determiner being the premise that God is loving and therefore not one who wants humans to suffer. God is fully free, so God also desires human freedom. Vulnerability as openness to the other and even openness to God is possible and valuable without inflicting violence on oneself or configuring suffering as part of God's will for certain categories of people over others.

Unlike the Christological ideal, for humans, the suffering described in spiritual texts is always warranted, and for women, it is compounded in several ways. First, women are regarded as lower than men in the gender hierarchy, such that women saints are lauded for demonstrating manliness in enduring suffering—that is, women cannot just endure, but must first overcome their "nature" to suffer properly—with bravery, without undue emotion, and with control.[36] Second, no matter how much they endure purgative suffering, they remain in actuality women, they are still classed below men, and they are perceived to inherently have more faults and sinfulness to overcome.[37] And third, women are expected to suffer and be humble based on their gender, from the pain of childbirth to enduring marital "annoyances" (read unwanted and nonconsensual sex) and humility before laymen, priests, and so on.[38] The experience of suffering for one who lacks equal conditions of freedom in many of these stories, who is idealized for suffering and believe they deserve it, is intersectionally compounded for women who are culturally and religiously socialized to already tolerate such things. Thus, inequality and abuse can be ignored or even idealized based on Orthodox spiritual teachings as opportunities for holiness or spiritual benefit.[39] Even where women enact agency to accept suffering as an act of divine love, their options for surviving and flourishing in those circumstances often constrain their exercise of full freedom. To ignore, normalize, or valorize suffering for a particular group or individual whose freedom is already circumstantially constrained is inconsistent with the ways that Orthodox Christians relate to God in the words and practices of liturgy. Christ's passion is affirmed as voluntary, God's love is confessed as ineffable and boundless, God's Son is sent for the salvation of the human race, free will is gifted in God, and God's mercy is invoked in nearly every Orthodox prayer.[40]

Subordination and Obedience

Subordination as a religious ideal can compel one to compliance, by sanctifying putting one's own will aside for the sake of pious obedience to another.[41] Yet it is not just to a singular clairvoyant elder that obedience is presented as virtuous within Orthodox tradition. Obedience signifies denial of one's own will and judgment not only before someone who is recognized as spiritually more advanced (often referred to as an elder) but also before the teachings of the church collectively. But the teachings of the church and how they are intended are not universally agreed on—especially when they are developed and articulated through an androcentric ascetic-privileging lens. This poses a challenge for questioning the patriarchal aspects of tradition because such a lack of acceptance can be religiously configured as disobedience. The fifth-century sayings attributed to Mark the Ascetic include the advice that "unquestioning acceptance of tradition is helpful for a gentle person, for then he will not try God's patience or often fall into sin."[42] The implication in this saying is that the more spiritually advanced person may understand tradition with more nuance, but for the simple person, simple acceptance can be a spiritually safe path to follow.

Another anonymous desert saying similarly reflects this dynamic of unquestioning submission to tradition or an elder as a way of guaranteeing spiritual progress: "If somebody has trust in another and gives himself in subjection to that person, he need not heed the commandments of God, but concede all his wishes to his father, and God will not reproach him, for God seeks nothing so much from novices as suffering through obedience."[43] Obedience is thus represented as a preeminent virtue. With obedience, however, often comes religious abuses of power and authoritarianism. In addition what is valued in a monastic-ascetic context is often mistaken as a transferrable ideal whereby one thinks not for oneself but gives oneself and the whole will over to the direction of a "spiritual father," even at the expense of other commandments. Symeon the New Theologian, for example, has in mind a true spiritual father when he writes, "The demons rejoice when a person argues with his spiritual father, but angels marvel at him when he humbles himself to the point of death. For then he performs God's work making himself like the Son of God who was obedient to his Father unto death, the death on the cross."[44] Humility and obedience even to the point of death are valued in Christological imitation, yet boundaries are easily blurred, and the foresight and pure intention of a spiritual leader can never fully reflect divine perfection. Although there are certainly writings (even by Symeon himself) about the qualifications for a worthy spiritual leader generally, the cautious evaluation of religious instruction and guidance for protecting oneself from abusive circumstances once one is already under another's spiritual direction is not significantly represented in the sources of Orthodox tradition. Obviously, men and women are called to humility and mutual obedience in divine imitation, but the consequences for women who do not render themselves humble and obedient can be more severe because they transgress both gendered and spiritual expectations. Moreover, being pressured to make oneself humble and obedient to conform to gendered expectation is not the same as pursuing such virtues freely in divine imitation.

Orthodox spirituality teaches that obedience to a spiritual elder is lauded when it is complete and unquestioning, even when the instruction goes against rational logic. The desert ascetic John Colobos's elder planted dry wood and told John to water it until it bore fruit, and after three years it miraculously did, at which time the elder said, "Take and eat some fruit of obedience."[45] This type of obedience is predicated on the assumption that the one to whom obedience is given is spiritually more advanced, has the novice's best interest at heart, knows how to instruct spiritually, and gives a seemingly ridiculous task for spiritual benefit. There is a hierarchy of spiritual superiority, and for women this hierarchy is compounded by gender. Would it have taken longer for a woman to produce the fruit of obedience because it is assumed to be more grievous if she is disobedient? To my knowledge, there are no desert stories of holy mothers putting men under obedience in such a way that requires them to do the nonsensical purely for the sake of obedience. What is idealized here is men who are not already assumed to be obedient learning to do a nonsensical task merely because it is desired by the elder to demonstrate their humble submission to him, a pattern of behavior no doubt well known to many women across time without flowering logs.

The life of the ninth-century Theodora of Thessaloniki shows Theodora's abbess admonishing her for looking out for her own welfare and moving her sleeping mat from a wet spot without permission. For this, Theodora is sent by her abbess into the freezing rain for the night, and the hagiographer says admiringly, "What person now or in the past has ever known a woman to show such obedience and to wrestle in such contests?"[46] Theodora is a woman corrected by a woman, yet the ideals and the articulation are patriarchal. The hagiographer comments on the miraculous event in gendered terms and calls Theodora's obedience a "terrible sight, a woman, the soft and weakest vessel, thus spending the night in the open air."[47] Theodora's obedience is explained as remarkable because it demonstrates a degree of physical fortitude that is unexpected for a woman. This episode, however, teaches that it is wrong or at least disobedient to follow one's instincts in caring for oneself without permission from a superior. Such a level of control that puts another's health at risk is shown as the abbess intentionally takes the opportunity to "procure for her [Theodora] the crown of obedience."[48] Sainted exceptions aside, how many women are intentionally demeaned without recourse to a safeguard by those in superior positions of social and ecclesiastical power who think they are entitled to control others and rebuke them for trying to protect themselves or improve their circumstances?

The influence of men's monastic communities on creating, preserving, and teaching spiritual instruction (especially in times of social instability or religious threat) has led to androcentric monastic values being spread through Orthodox Christianity as a type of high ideal.[49] This affects the presentation of women and their concerns in Orthodox tradition and extends the influence of monastic texts applied in nonmonastic contexts as spiritually beneficial. It takes what is held as an ideal out of the idealized context and attempts to apply it under disparate conditions that are not similarly protected. For example, in a monastic context, unquestioning obedience to one's spiritual elder is described by most spiritual writers as virtuous.[50] However, in a marital context where the husband, for example, presumes a position of power and requires subordination of his wife based on gender, then obedience is not oriented necessarily by spiritual edification. In addition, the conditions governing the monastic and marital situations are significantly different that the value should be reconsidered. The same activity is not fully possible based on different conditions. The wife, for example, is not necessarily voluntarily subjugating herself to her husband who she recognizes to be spiritually more advanced; rather she may submit because this is the expected, learned, "Christian," and perhaps enforced behavior. The safeguards of full freedom and mutual recognition of and respect for the woman's full humanity might be missing. Obedience based on gender does not necessarily produce healthy spiritual fruit; it has the potential to harm women who are already at a disadvantage in scenarios of gendered power dynamics. Certainly, for most people entering a monastery involves voluntary obedience and subordination, but what of parallels in marriage? What of pastoral and parish life? What of women to fathers, younger women to older women, and laywomen to parish priests? Subordination and obedience to the church, an elder, and tradition thus challenge the realization of the feminist premise that women should have equality and people should work to end sexist oppression within the church.[51]

Obedience is not universally spiritually beneficial for communicating divinity to humanity and shaping humanity in divine likeness. It requires certain conditions of divine similitude such as free voluntary assumption and orientation to producing humans in communion with God—as opposed to coerced subordination under a human or divine will. As I discuss in chapter 6, there are examples from within Orthodox tradition of holy subversion and righteous disobedience. However, here it is sufficient to reiterate that the cooperation between the human and divine wills modeled in Christ is one of voluntary and synergistic deification, not cloaking of domination or socially coercive submission in sacred terms. Obedience should be a voluntary assent of the human will to the divine will out of loving cooperation that results in the participative transformation of the human in divinity. Obedience cannot in Christ-like terms be owed based on gender or result in the further denigration of humanity.

Subordinating Humility

Like obedience, humility is interconnected with self-deprecation and should not be universally idealized for women, who Orthodox tradition already holds subordinate in expectations that lead them to a gendered vulnerability. In one desert saying, for example, Abba John explains approvingly of the biblical Joseph (Genesis 39:7–20) that, "because he kept silence, he sold himself by his humility. It is also his humility which set him up as chief in Egypt;" he could have defended himself, but due to the virtue of humility he did not.[52] Defending oneself is presented as antithetical to humility, such that any feminist project or women's personal defense of her rights, her body, her words can be dismissed as lacking in the preeminent value of embracing suffering as a form of Christologically imitative humility and condemned as prideful.[53] Although in most circumstances retribution for an insult or violence would be un-Christian, protecting oneself from serious harm is consistent with what Orthodox Christians pray for in every liturgy, even if it is not represented in sources of spiritual teaching as an ethical principle. For example, the whole congregation responds with "Lord have mercy" to the petition, "For our deliverance from all affliction, wrath, danger, and distress, let us pray to the Lord," in the Great Litany, expressing communal hopes in God's mercy to be delivered from various forms of suffering.[54] Similar to Abba John, however, Mark the Ascetic urges, "When harmed, insulted or persecuted by someone, do not think of the present but wait for the future, and you will find he [God] has brought you much good, not only in this life but also in the life to come."[55] Just as the patient endurance of suffering is blessed, so is the acceptance of suffering as a mode of embracing humility and cultivating holiness. Yet the theological inconsistencies of such values—that those who are subject to oppression must accept their lot and develop their humility spiritually with hope for a better afterlife—are manifold. God is not oppressive. Orthodox celebrate Christ as the Harrower of Hell and the one who tramples down death by death in the present. God is a loving liberator of humanity who gives up himself to free humanity from bondage. Spiritual liberation does not preclude the possibility (and indeed, the good) of being liberated from situations and structures of harm in this life.

Like obedience, humility as a preeminent Orthodox Christian value also falls on women differently; women are often enculturated to already have greater associations with bodily shame, sexualization of the body and its need for modesty, and a gendered value of submissiveness.[56] Such associations are compounded and differently inflected by categories such as race, ethnicity, dis/ability, age, class, and cultural situation.[57] The attributes of concern for others and self-deprecation that may be spiritually laudable as humility also reinforce negative stereotypes of women as problematic for men and inherently more prone to impurity and responsible for sinfulness. An Orthodox feminist theological view might be that women need to see themselves and others need to see them as deifiable as they are—not as men, but in their diverse bodies, in their gender attributes without essentialization, and in their uniqueness that does not conform to androcentric values. Orthodox need to be able to see God in women and to believe fully that women can point to their bodies and say, "This is God," just as Symeon the New Theologian claims about even the most taboo parts of the body (the womb and the penis) in his erotic mystical hymns.[58] There is not some part of the female body or of being a woman that makes one inherently less or unfit for being in communion with the sacred. As I demonstrate in subsequent chapters, if one believes that humanity bears the image of God, then to intentionally subject that divinely beloved and created image to abuse and distortion would be iconoclastic.[59] If one believes that such suffering polishes and perfects the image, it must be qualified by terms that make the potential for spiritual growth rather than devastation possible.

## NOT YET FULLY HUMAN

The second spiritual concept that challenges the realization of women as fully and equally human in Orthodox tradition and theology is that all humans in their spiritual lives are in the ascetic process of becoming fully human. Within many influential ascetic and hagiographic texts, full humanity is presented as a type of ongoing transformation in Christlikeness through the process of theosis. Theosis, or deification, has been the subject of patristic, Byzantine, and modern Orthodox theological reflection and development.[60] Although the concept of theosis has shifted across authors and history, the theological concept most basically means becoming increasingly like God (and in fact, "god" by grace) through participative divine communion.[61]

Theosis is often simply explained using the Athanasian terms that God "was incarnate that we might be made god," but within Orthodox tradition, there is also the theological belief that it is only through ongoing theosis that one becomes fully human (because it was Christ who restored fallen humanity to its fullness).[62] John Behr summarizes this deeply rooted theological trajectory: "Christ ... defines for us what it is to be God and what it is to be human, together and simultaneously, without confusion, change, division, or separation," and therefore it is to "Christ that we must look to understand not only what it is to be God but also what it is to be human."[63] Behr then draws attention to scriptural, patristic, and theological evidence from within the tradition to show that "rather than seeing ourselves as already human ... we are instead called to view all things in the light of Christ, such that there is one single creative-salvific economy of God, leading us from the sketch to the reality, from a breath to the spirit, from Adam to Christ, by sharing in the death of Christ, to be 'a living human being' ... the glory of God."[64] Behr's argument, as compelling as it is, rests on the human choice in baptism to die to Adam and share in the death of Christ to become a human being. That is, in response to the feminist critique that women are not regarded or treated as fully human, an Orthodox view could hold that no one aside from Christ is fully human.[65] This way of understanding, however, is then related to degrees of humanness through spiritual progress, that is, a hierarchy of divine participation and humanity. The spiritual life, specifically in texts authored by monastic leaders, is presented hierarchically as a type of ongoing process and progression through which one must work. Although not explicitly tied to a gender hierarchy, and even as I have argued elsewhere that it should not correlate to gender, Orthodox τάξης (order) based on creation, fall, and socialization ranks women second and below men in a hierarchy, with the Theotokos being the exception, as she is beyond hierarchy.[66] Women's starting point for participating in the becoming of humanity and the path to spiritual progress that renders us more fully human is always behind that of men. The result is that women have more to overcome, more distance to cover, before they might be regarded as fully human or at the very least, in response to Behr's conclusion, being human in the same degree that men are. It is a matter of inequity even when spiritual equality is claimed. This makes it seem as if God created humanity unequally and therefore as if Christ's incarnation as a man does not fully redeem women, or as if the image of God is less in women, which appears to fault God as an iconographer.

The notion in the theology of becoming more fully human in Christ is expressed as a type of synergy—voluntary cooperation with God.[67] Christ's death is unwarranted and voluntary; it is a gift of love because it is freely given. However, this emphasis on agency disadvantages many women because it ignores the structural barriers to having free, voluntary agency in one's life and spiritual behaviors. For instance, Maximus the Confessor explains that "by exercising this freedom of choice each soul either reaffirms its true nobility or through its actions deliberately embraces what is ignoble" and that if one is devoted in one's senses and actions to God, then "he has enhanced that sanctity which is his by nature, as created in the image of God, by adding to it the sanctity of the divine likeness that is attained through the exercise of his own free will."[68] The potential for becoming fully human rests with the human agent cooperating with the divine invitation and possibility. Accordingly, Gregory of Nyssa's *Life of Macrina* explains that Macrina was "by nature a woman, but who in fact, was far above nature," because she had "raised herself to the highest peak of human virtue through the pursuit of philosophy."[69] Again, this attitude that humans must transform themselves to be fully human does not account for the differences in individual gendered circumstances. For instance, it appears that women must first surpass their womanliness to then begin to transform their humanity in its fullness. Moreover, this way of thinking ignores the ways women are structurally and socially disadvantaged in making free choices and making progress through them—especially when, as I showed earlier in this chapter, subjection and submission to others is held in such high regard.

At least in contemporary Orthodox theology, theosis is not a gendered concept; men and women may attain divine likeness.[70] The freedom to choose the divine life and become fully human, Peter of Damascus claims, is not restricted by earthly and human conditions. He explains that if,

> by our free choice, we abandon our own wishes and thoughts and do what God wishes and thinks ... there is no object, no activity or place in the whole of creation that can prevent us from becoming what God from the beginning has wished us to be: that is to say, according to His image and likeness, gods by adoption through grace, dispassionate, just, good and wise, whether we are rich or poor, married or unmarried, in authority and free or under obedience and in bondage—in short, whatever our time, place or activity.[71]

Thus, while becoming fully human and deified is possible for women, laity, enslaved peoples, and so on, the tradition does little to account for the differing ways that humanity is anchored in positions of autonomy and privilege that make it more readily accessible for free (ascetic) men whose right to choose has not been taken away or controlled by another, who feel empowered in their choices, and who society deems acceptable and normative in their self-determination. Telling one who has been socialized to be submissive and subordinate that spiritual life rests in their choice and control would need to involve first assigning value to that individual's agency and empowering them to realize their choices in ways that can be recognized as having impact by others.

The belief that people are not yet fully human takes a particular toll on women, who have further to travel, so to speak, to become fully human based on "nature." We see this perhaps more prominently in contemporary contexts, especially with women of color, disabled women, queer women, and others who have been categorically dehumanized in ways that have been accepted or ignored by the church. Certain aspects of what hagiographers refer to as "womanly nature" and what patristic authors describe as intrinsic and natural to womanhood and femininity are often seen in ascetic and hagiographic texts as obstacles to divine becoming, rendering them less human. The Byzantine abbess Elisabeth the Wonderworker, for instance, is referred to in her hagiography as "transforming feminine frailty to manly resolution and, through self-discipline and painful ascetic practice, courageously overthrowing the ancient conqueror of our foremother Eve."[72] She is lauded for her choice to become more fully human by moving away from her gendered qualities and by pious will becoming manly in order to become more human. But women's desire to be recognized as fully human and treated as such is not a matter of their willing it so and performing "manliness" but of being recognized as equally human as women and treated as such by those in power around them.[73] Such recognition honors Christ's incarnation, because it is from woman that he took on his humanity and the divine image created within them.

Women's humanity is often restricted in androcentric conceptions of holiness that appear to diminish the ways humanity might participate in divinity and evidence divine likeness. For example, women witnessing their children sick or dying are often lauded for controlled or measured emotion, and maternal attachments are seen as distractions oppositional to spiritual progress. Of the sainted Athanasia (d. 860) it is said, "Even though the woman was God-loving, she was nevertheless tortured by maternal love and indeed, by the demands of nature."[74] Maternal love, nature, and the body here are presented as opposing higher spiritual aims instead of perhaps indicating a more authentic and equally holy way that Athanasia could become more fully human—through her love as a mother. This is not to say that women need to be mothers to be fully human or holy but rather to highlight that what humanity looks like in the divine image and how it might be attained is androcentric in much of Orthodox tradition in a way that dismisses and denigrates more diversely gendered alternatives. There are female saints, like St. Emmelia of Caesarea, who raise holy children (Sts. Basil, Gregory, Macrina, Theosebia, and Peter), but the emphasis in the commemoration of holy mothers is often on the sanctity of their children, again fulfilling an androcentric expectation of women as idealized domestic and sacrificial maternal figures.

How then can women be acknowledged to be fully and equally human if the assumption is that women need to become manly in holiness, that the gender hierarchy is reflected in some degree (at least in terms of the ecclesiastical leadership) in the spiritual hierarchy, and that humanity, in general, is not reflected on as being fully human and equal but as trying to return to a divinely created natural state and ever-increasing degrees of divine participation and divine likeness? Moreover, if everyone is progressing infinitely toward divine participation (or at least that is the spiritual aim), then there is rarely a point in time when one could claim categorically that men and women are fully and equally human, because not even two men are equal or fully human since all are still progressing toward divine-human communion. At the points where women are held up as spiritual equals or as superior to men, what has been covered in their spiritual progress presumes a lower starting point such that it relies on a fundamental inequality to name them as holy. In addition, equality, if viewed through an androcentric and androprimacy lens, is determined by conforming to the androcentric normative ideal. Thus, conformity to androcentric expectations might be mistaken as a measure of equality, when in fact it might obscure the differences in another that are significant in truly knowing the other as God loves and created them to be. Ignoring difference in favor of equality does violence to the specificity of a person's existence through which they have come to love and be loved. Maximus the Confessor highlights the importance of God's equal love for all and the equality of love of others that a spiritual person should come to possess.[75] When Maximus, like many in the Neoplatonic tradition before him, says, "In the multiplicity of beings there is diversity, dissimilarity, and difference. But in God, who is an absolute sense one and alone, there is only identity, simplicity and similarity," one has to wonder who is becoming like who in this process of deification.[76] If God is a god-man in Christ, then does that mean that women have to leave behind their gender? It nowhere appears the case that men become like women. As previous chapters have shown, this has an almost universal negative connotation historically—and in present Orthodox discourse.[77]

In many influential ascetic and hagiographic texts, full humanity is presented as a type of ongoing becoming, to which women may certainly attain divine likeness but with the assumption that based on their gender, they start at a lower point and are less likely to attain holiness. This presumed lowliness is particularly challenging because it is believed to be overcome, even by prominent Orthodox women theologians of the twentieth century, through voluntary self-sacrificing kenosis—connecting again to the values discussed above. Reflecting on the teaching of theosis as articulated in the writings of Behr-Sigel, Myrrha Lot-Borodine, and Skobtsova, Heleen Zorgdrager notes, "What is remarkable in the women's re-appropriation of the tradition is that (Christ's) *kenosis* is not merely presented as the *condition* for *theosis* (as in the classic formula of Athanasius) but that achieving *theosis* is *realized* primarily through the believer's practice of kenotic love."[78] Significant among these women theologians, however, is the emphasis not merely on kenosis as condescension and self-emptying, but its framing in a context of love. Love, as a free gift that cannot be coerced but only given, provides a mode by which kenotic emphasis of tradition and the ascetic presentation of suffering can be voluntarily interpreted. Even with this refocusing of kenosis as kenotic love, the expectations about who should act lovingly or want to voluntarily sacrifice themselves for the well-being of another are still entangled with gendered expectations. There are no different types of salvation for men and women, but understandings and expressions of theosis may still be gendered.[79]

## MARY AS A PARAGON OF SPIRITUAL VALUES?

Given the values of humility, obedience, and suffering and the belief in realizing full humanity in divine participation, the commemoration of the Theotokos is an especially interesting case to explore. She is an example of a woman who is recalled as holy even from her conception (for which there is a feast), is above all angelic ranks, and is regarded as the protecting abbess of Mount Athos, an exclusively male monastic peninsula. The celebration of Mary's holiness appears in liturgical texts, but aside from her role as the virginal Theotokos, her position is addressed through pious tradition in which there is some variation rather than a unified, systematic explanation. Although I posited in previous chapters that some aspects of her body and experiences are androcentrically constructed in commemoration, does she perhaps provide a counterargument to the claims I present?

Concerning the values of obedience and voluntary suffering, it is clear that Mary does not provide a counterexample but rather *the* ideal of human obedience, here embodied in a woman before God. Theologically, it is important to affirm that Mary voluntarily and freely (because God is not coercive and would provide her with a real alternative) offers her obedience to God in conceiving Christ.[80] Mary does suffer at the death of her son, but again, in that her conception and the birth of her son were voluntary and directly in relation to God, one can certainly claim an idealized form of righteous endurance and obedience before God. Even when Mary is suspected of adultery for her pregnancy, she does not suffer injustice or abuse at the hands of Joseph but rather is brought to be excused through angelic intervention.[81] Perhaps this episode tells us that God wants women to be liberated from situations of injustice. Suffering, humility, silence, and obedience are valued for all people, but the differences in situations of power are important. Such attributes are virtuous when one has power and voluntarily gives it up for the love of others, not as an oppressive power obligating and restricting the freedom of others to choose these virtues. As I explain in chapter 6, for the oppressed, it is consistent with Orthodox theology to seek liberation, to reject the oppression of the oppressed even if that includes the self, to recognize the self and others in the image and likeness of God when others refuse to do so, to defend the full humanity and empower it through obedience to God's liberating love first and foremost.

Concerning the second point of discussion in this chapter, that women are categorically below men and that all humans to the degree that they fall short of full theosis are not fully human, again there is a differentiation of circumstances because of Mary's direct divine involvement. Orthodox tradition holds that in the moment of Jesus's conception, Mary is "overshadowed" by the Holy Spirit and is purified and sanctified; she has God physically dwelling within her, so she would perhaps be the example of one who is fully human but also of one who continues in a life of asceticism (if one follows later Byzantine accounts of Mary's life after the ascension).[82] Mary does not start in a position of assumed lowliness, because the Christian introduction to her retrospectively assumes her holiness as Jesus's mother. A presumption of impurity or a tendency toward sin does not apply to Mary. Consequently, she does not counter this trope and challenge in ascetical teachings but rather provides the ideal of its application. She attains a position above the angelic hierarchy in her holiness and is fully human in her divine communion but in such a way that it does not apply to other women any more than it does to all men. The equality or super-equality and full humanity of Mary are contingent on her virginity and her role as Jesus's mother and Joachim and Anna's holy daughter. Indeed, she does model a fully human woman but one who had to be extraordinary in all ways and was deified in a feminine, childbearing role and remained sexually controlled through virginity for her entire earthly life. She raises the possibility of a woman being fully human, equal, and above a man, but again the conditions for her holiness are unique in all human history and a model of submission to a perfect divine agent that is not fully comparable to obedience and submission to a regular human person.

Emphasizing only the spiritual good of suffering, obedience, and humility in tradition makes it very difficult to call for change without seeming prideful, disobedient to the teachings of sainted elders, or insufficiently committed to better offering oneself to God. How Orthodox believe God is as revealed in the person of Jesus Christ, however, suggests there is room for developing teachings and practices that qualify these values and balance them in the confession of overwhelmingly perfect divine love. If Orthodox accept that Christ does not maliciously wish anyone, including women, to suffer, does not wish women as women to be obedient any more than men should be obedient, and does not desire obedience because gender and society use it to empower a certain class of men, then they should admit that Christ desires voluntary obedience and submission to God as an act of love in a way that may translate as obedience to others but that also may manifest as subversion and disobedience of earthly powers that are not divinely communicative and do not foster human dignity.[83] The conditions and pressures at play in the lives of holy women are rarely if ever described from the women's perspective. Although women are said in hagiographies and hymns to be equal to holy men, the ideal preeminently held in most of these sources is not equality but rather voluntary self-abasement and unquestioning obedience. For women (and certainly others), this could lead to religious justification being given for oppression, abuse, and suffering at the hands of others to whom they are already socially and religiously subjugated instead of promoting women's liberation from such dangers as a confession of the liberation that Christ has already granted them in the resurrection.

Women can demonstrate agency in ways that might be dismissed or overlooked even in instances of ostensible submission, yet such examples, while significant, should not substitute for better circumstances for women overall. Just because women can be agents and actively work toward their salvation in all types of horrific situations does not mean that these situations should be regarded as blessings and perpetuated, which at times Orthodox tradition seems to do. Asking to be recognized as fully in the divine image and fully human is not a complaint, a shirking of divine will, or a lack of patience but, as I argue in the next chapter, an acknowledgment of Christological truth. Some of the examples in this chapter have emphasized the conditions of freedom and voluntary choice in the pursuit of the virtues of self-giving, suffering, and lowliness for spiritual benefit. The values of voluntary suffering, obedience, humility, and becoming more fully human through divine participation only make sense in reference to Christ in whom they are perfectly revealed and known. Yet the power dynamics that govern freedom, agency, and choice in an androcentric religious context are complex and often drawn along gendered lines. The Orthodox tradition that emphasizes theosis as a precondition for realizing one's full humanity further complicates the representation of women's spiritual progress and possibilities within Orthodox commemorations.[84] The result is that in Orthodox tradition, values of equality and self-preservation are subordinated to values of humility and long-suffering, and the spiritual hierarchy toward theosis is entangled with the assumptions of an earthly gender hierarchy—both of which restrict arguments for women's equality and full humanity.

## FOUR

# Theology and Women's Full Humanity

Having surveyed the dominating patriarchal presence in Orthodox tradition, the androcentric shaping of women's bodies and experiences in commemorative genres, and the religious ideals that undermine claims for equality, I now turn to evaluate how such observations pose theological problems. As I have shown in previous chapters, some aspects of Orthodox tradition construct women in ways that diminish their humanity, perpetuate negative views about the female body, and obscure through a patriarchal gaze the diverse possibilities of God working in women's lives. Sainted authors may clearly *say* women are equal to men, but the commemorations and androcentric gendered expectations of women within Orthodox tradition undermine the realization of these claims for most women.

In this chapter, I show three areas of theological concern that emerge if the ambiguities and assumptions about women that patriarchal androcentrism carries within this tradition are not intentionally unsaid. I do this by prioritizing a starting point that is neither women's experience nor immanent claims about God but rather the incarnational imperative of divine-human unity. Such a starting point brings together feminist and Orthodox theological concerns to elucidate doctrinal issues such as

Christology and soteriology to shift the issue of women's equality from the external periphery of Orthodox consideration to a theologically significant center. The "otherness" of women, being "not man" and therefore perhaps not fully human, is problematic in its own right for women's redemption, but the theological problems of such a construction are not just women's issues. The traditional and sacralized depiction of women as "other" renders women's humanity diminished and subsequently jeopardizes significant theological claims of Orthodoxy. The patriarchal production of women, reflecting ambivalence about the fullness and equality of their humanity, is not just an instance of unfortunate cultural and social bias that has leaked into a purer Orthodoxy; it undercuts core theological claims of redemption for half of humanity and thus all of humanity. If Mary, a woman, is considered subhuman, then the incarnation loses its effect because divinity is united to a partial humanity, with the result that the true union of humanity and divinity remains problematically qualified. If one looks at the present-day patriarchal leadership of the church and the unfortunate gender-based abuses grounded in a presumed normativity of androcentric privilege, the real-world implications for the lives and well-being of women are evident. Even if one might say that the historical androcentrism of the tradition and exclusively male ordained leadership of the church do not harm women directly, they participate in and perpetuate the seconding of women as a normative, unquestioned, or even "Orthodox" value.

The three theological areas I address in this chapter are certainly not the only ones affected by the patriarchal androcentrism of Orthodox tradition. They are highlighted as examples of the theological importance of intentionally unsaying the presumptions about women that produce and reproduce inequality. I use the term "unsaying" in this chapter because it alludes to the prominent apophatic approach within Orthodox theology. Apophasis, or unsaying, is a mode familiar to Orthodox theology whereby one admits the partiality of one's claims and inability of assertively naming the subject.[1] As I show in the next chapter, the apophatic approach has potential for unsaying the problematic aspects of Orthodox tradition while still rendering it usable for the present. The three areas of theology that are my concern here demonstrate the need for such unsaying of the gendered partialities and equivocations patriarchal androcentrism presents in Orthodox tradition. First, if women are not fully and equally human in the same ways that men are, then most basic fundamental dogmatic claims about Christ's incarnation and human redemption are in jeopardy. Second, if women are fully equal and human but their representation as such has been artificial, restricted, or absent, then there is established a system of intentional poor iconography—and veneration of fictitiously embodied ideals instead of divinely created human persons—a transgressing of the Orthodox veneration of icons and again a rejection of the fullness of the incarnation. Third, if women are misrepresented and omitted from the tradition, then what is relied on as tradition authoritatively to guide the theology of the present is false. That is, it does not do justice to the work of the Holy Spirit in the lives of the faithful to maintain a conception of tradition that privileges patriarchal views when historical study and critical reflection identify omissions and misrepresentations.

Any way that Orthodox tradition is framed or invoked that omits or distorts the voices of women, rejects the work of the Holy Spirit, and presents an image of women, men, and God at work in humanity that is partial—prioritizing concerns about gender and power over theological confessions. In highlighting these issues, I demonstrate the theological importance of affirming directly the fundamental feminist claim that women are fully and equally human and the need to intentionally unsay aspects of tradition that reinforce a patriarchal partiality about women as a theological practice. I draw on patristic authors in Orthodox Christianity to support my claims. It is important to note honestly that none of these male authors is necessarily a closeted feminist, would see patriarchy or androcentrism as a problem, or would see the need to affirm women as fully human more clearly in the practices and teachings of Orthodoxy. The authors I cite are theological authorities, and I draw on them to show that what they articulated *about God* logically requires certain affirmations about women that appear equivocal in Orthodox tradition.

## INCARNATION

Orthodox Christians believe that Christ is fully divine and fully human. As Christ is without a human father, all his humanity must then come from his mother. This is a claim that is celebrated by numerous patristic writers and proclaimed in Orthodox homilies and hymns.[2] But as Christ's humanity comes from his mother, Mary then must be fully human to have something complete to offer in the incarnation of the divine Logos. Athanasius explains that God "prepared for himself in the Virgin the body as a temple, and made it his own."[3] Thus, affirming the full and honorable humanity of women is Christologically necessary to affirm the completeness of the incarnation. Any praxis or internalized belief that undermines this affirmation needs to be rejected as Christologically inconsistent. Cyril of Alexandria (d. 444) explains that in the incarnation God "was incarnate and made man; that is, taking flesh of the holy Virgin, and having made it his own from the womb, he subjected himself to birth for us, and came forth man from a woman, without casting off that which he has; but although he assumed flesh and blood, he remained what he was, God in essence and in truth."[4] To confess Orthodox Christology, one must also confess the full humanity and flesh of woman that was united and perfected in Christ. Even in the womb and in the act of birth, these spaces that later are liturgically associated with blood and impurity are the spaces that God chose to fill and from his human mother take on all of humanity.[5] For most Orthodox, this claim is not unusual or original; rather I am using an accepted dogmatic assertion to argue for an ethics of confessing the humanity of women with unhesitating consistency. To confess Mary as fully human, because Christ is, requires an ongoing confession in thought and practice among Orthodox that women have complete humanity in the divine image in the same way men do, with equal capacity to further realize its divine likeness. It is necessary to reject the implicit assumption of patriarchal androcentrism explored in the previous two chapters and state unequivocally that women do not have a subhuman starting point for deification compared to men or an innate spiritual or physical disadvantage for realizing divine likeness.

Symeon the New Theologian extends the incarnational logic of Mary's flesh being that which solely constitutes Christ's humanity to the Eucharist. When communicants partake of the body and blood of Christ, they should also understand that is the flesh taken from Mary. He explains:

> The same undefiled flesh which He accepted from the pure loins of Mary, the all-pure Theotokos, and with which He was given birth in

the body, He gives to us as food. And when we eat of it, when we eat worthily of His flesh, each one of us receives within himself the entirety of God made flesh, our Lord Jesus Christ, Son of God and son of the immaculate Virgin Mary, the very One Who sits at the right hand of God the Father.[6]

The body and blood that are consumed in communion are that which indeed belong to Christ, but without an earthly father, they are from none other than Mary. All of Christ's humanity comes from a woman. If that woman in some way had a diminished humanity, then Christ's incarnation would be incomplete. Symeon continues, "Since the flesh of the Lord is the flesh of the Theotokos—and by communing in this same deified flesh of the Lord, we both confess and believe that we partake of life everlasting."[7] The flesh of a woman assumed by Christ in his humanity is that which deifies and makes possible eucharistic participation. All communicants partake of the body and blood of Christ made possible through his taking such flesh of the Virgin to make his own. If she was in any way below or above humanity due to either the lowliness of her womanly nature or the loftiness of her holiness and purity, the fullness of the incarnation and efficacy of the Eucharist would be jeopardized.

The theological affirmation that Mary was fully human requires that this full humanity includes all the attributes of humanity that Christ assumed. That is, Mary must offer to Christ a human will and human energy, a human nature, a human body, all these human things that to pass on in fullness she must first possess. The canonically accepted Tome of St. Leo attests that "therefore in the entire and perfect nature of very man was born very God, whole in what was his, whole in what was ours" and that "we confess two wills and two operations, concurring most fitly in him for the salvation of the human race."[8] Where would Christ have received this human will and everything that was "ours" if not from his Mother, since he was without an earthly father? Accordingly, Orthodox need to affirm the fullness of Mary's humanity—even where it may go against or have gone against androcentric views of what and how women should be holy—to affirm the incarnation. Mary has a fully human will; therefore, women have a full human will and should be honored in exercising it freely. Mary's humanity that is offered to and united to divinity in the person of Christ, then, is not somehow removed from all women but affirms unequivocally the fullness of their humanity assumed in the person of Christ. For the incarnation to take place in a way that is redemptive and transformative for all of creation, Christ must take on full humanity, and Orthodox, like many other Christians, believe that he does.[9] On this point, Theodore the Studite (d. 826) states:

> If, whatever kind of being she is who gives birth, that which is born must be the same kind of being: since the mother of Christ is circumscribed, then Christ also is circumscribed, as her son, although He is God by nature. But if He is not circumscribed, then He does not have the same essence as His mother. Hence it would follow that His mother is not His mother—which is absurd.[10]

Mary must have full human essence to offer Christ in the incarnation, which requires the affirmation that women have full human essence in their humanity. There is not some other unsexed humanity, some flesh that is not provided first from a woman in the birth of Jesus. This obvious reminder serves to point out that the Orthodox have a Christological imperative to confess in all things that women possess complete humanity (even if individually someone might dehumanize themselves through sin or still not be fully human in their realization of theosis, as mentioned in the previous chapter). Commemorative traditions, rituals, or theological discourses that obscure or erase the full humanity of women, even implicitly, cannot be also said to consistently confess an Orthodox incarnation and Christology. Indeed, I am equating the feminist claim that women are fully and equally human persons with any claim to Orthodox Christology. One cannot have one without the other.

The inclusion of energy, soul, and will in the Christological debates, along with freedom, presumes that these attributes are intrinsic and natural to humanity.[11] All that constitutes humanity must be in Mary. That is, if one can say that Christ had these things in his human nature, then it would follow that the one who offered him his human nature had them without some sort of gendered impairment and that Christ did not discriminate in uniting himself to the humanity of a woman. Maximus the Confessor notes that "he [the Logos] took on himself our human nature in deed and in truth and united it to himself hypostatically—without change, alteration, diminution, or division; he maintained it inalterably, by its own essential principle and definition."[12] This would mean that it is doctrinally necessary to affirm that women also have freedom, energy, soul, and will as part of their human nature and that all these aspects were united to divinity in Christ.[13] As John of Damascus (d. 749) summarizes, "For the holy Virgin did not give birth to a mere man but to true God, and not to God simply, but to God made flesh. And He did not bring His body down from heaven and come through her as through a channel, but assumed from her a body consubstantial with us and subsisting in himself."[14] Any denial or diminishment of the will, mind, energy, and freedom of Mary would deny her humanity and deny the fullness of the incarnation. So when Orthodox Christians confess the humanity of Christ, they are also confessing Mary's humanity offered to him, including all the attributes and fullness that are present in Christ apart from sin. Therefore, it is necessary to unequivocally confess in liturgy, praxis, and interpersonal relations that women have full humanity in all of these attributes—or at least are not categorically diminished in their humanity in comparison to men.

Mary of course is often rendered the exception to her sex or gender and in some ways that distinguish her from women more broadly, but in the incarnation what she offers on behalf of all creation—as a woman —is her full humanity.[15] In the body formed from the flesh of a woman, the miracle of human salvation is made possible for all humans. Athanasius explains that Christ made the "body" his own in the incarnation and in so doing overcame corruption and death:

> From ours that which is like, since all were liable to the corruption of death, delivering it over to death on behalf of all, he offered it to the Father, doing this in his love for human beings, so that, on the one hand, with all dying in him the law concerning corruption in human beings might be undone (its power being fully expended in the lordly body and no longer having any ground against similar human beings), and, on the other hand, that as human beings had turned towards corruption he might turn them again to incorruptibility and give them life from death, by making the body his own and by the grace of the resurrection banishing death from them as straw from the fire.[16]

A woman's body becomes the mode by which God gives life to the world and restores the divine image in humanity. It is important in confessing the incarnational reality and soteriological claims of Orthodox theology to include an affirmation of women's humanity as being complete, not only completely redeemed in Christ, but the material means by which that redemption was made possible. It is not just humanity that Mary offers in abstract terms either: it is humanity born of the messiest and most taboo parts of a woman, the sexualized, the bloodied, the ritually impure. Most of these aspects are androcentrically removed from Mary in patristic homilies and liturgical hymns as a mode of piety.[17] However, that pious removal of Mary from all women reveals that the tradition holds that something about women's natural aspects of embodied existence and reproduction is unbecoming of God's mother. Orthodox Christians praise Mary above the angels and emphasize her unblemished purity before, during, and after childbirth. Yet the pious zeal with which Orthodox have rendered Mary may have eclipsed significant aspects worth celebrating as a Christological affirmation—that Mary is fully human and is so as a woman.[18]

Despite the traditions that emerge about God sparing his mother from pain and about an intact postpartum hymen, it is not shameful or impure for Mary to have given birth like a normal human woman (yet with divine conception).[19] The pious discourse that Jesus loved his mother enough to spare her pain and miraculously was born without breaking her hymen—thus reinforcing an androcentric testament to her virginity—also has the potential to diminish Mary's humanity and the free, consensual, synergistic labor of that humanity in bringing Christ into the world.[20] It may be that the birth of Christ was painful and bloody—not because Christ could not spare Mary, but because this testifies to her humanity. Of course, Christ's birth was beyond nature, but it was also *in* it. If one assumes a different interpretation, the pain could be an offering of love itself, a divine act that many women know, the messiness of birth a glorious witness to God's condescension and Mary's humanity. This is not to prescriptively valorize pain in childbirth but to recognize that labor pains are not divine retribution for some perceived impurity from which only Mary is exempt.[21] But this, of course, would be privileging women's own perspectives about their bodies and experiences that have rarely been given full voice in tradition.[22]

Reflecting on Mary's bodily experience and Christological contribution brings to the fore the ambivalence surrounding the body in the sources of Orthodox tradition. Due to the influence of ascetic and monastic teachings within Orthodoxy as representing a type of ideal, embodiment is often treated as a form of limitation that needs to be overcome in spiritual life. Surpassing the physical needs of sleep, food, companionship, medical care, and drink through prayer and austerity is viewed hagiographically as a sign of holiness that can lead to miraculous superhuman feats that defy physical limitations, such as levitation, walking on water, clairvoyance, no longer having to fulfill physical needs, and divine visions. Indeed, hymns, desert sayings, spiritual instructions, and patristic texts negatively associate the body with worldly "flesh" or unruly "passions," while surpassing the needs of the body is a sign of the "angelic life." Although some women are commemorated for ascetic feats, they are traditionally more negatively associated with the body, in terms of weakness, blood, emotions, maternity, and sexuality. Yet to affirm the fullness of the incarnation the body as perhaps the most obvious aspect of humanity should be honored. This is not to say that every bodily impulse should be given free rein but that the normalized punitive attitude Orthodox might have to their own physical conditions should be rethought to align with the Orthodox confession of the incarnation. Cyril of Alexandria, in particular, emphasizes the need to affirm that Jesus was subject to even unseemly bodily experiences in the incarnation as part of his assumption of the fullness of human nature.[23] That is, there is no part of the human body that was not assumed in the incarnation. If we continue to perpetuate taboos surrounding women's bodies or overemphasize control and suffering of the flesh as virtuous, we miss the ways these views are disproportionately damaging to many women (e.g., eating disorders, diminishment of women's health, bodily shame) and undermine theological claims. God took on humanity in its fullness, which includes the human body and the female body because it was by this that he became incarnate.

## DEIFICATION AND REDEMPTION

Orthodox theology drawing on Athanasius, Irenaeus, and others sees the incarnation and deification as two sides of the same coin. Athanasius reminds that in the incarnation "everything is filled with the knowledge of God" and that "he was incarnate that we might be made god."[24] Since I have argued that the full humanity of a woman needs to be acknowledged to affirm the incarnation, this means that full humanity in the saving work of Jesus Christ must be acknowledged. More directly, however, I focus on what Orthodox believe Jesus's incarnation, passion, death, resurrection, and ascension accomplish and make possible for those who are baptized into Christ within the Orthodox Church: theosis.[25] Deification, divinization, becoming god by grace, regaining the divine likeness through participation and divine communion: however one might configure or translate what this term means, theosis is the activity of divine love for and from within humanity. For Orthodox, it signifies in participative terms a transfiguring communion with God. John of Damascus describes the unitive action between deification and incarnation, saying, "For from the time when God the Word became flesh, and was made like us in every respect save sin, and was united without confusion with what is ours, and unchangingly deified the flesh through the unconfused co-inherence of his divinity and his flesh one with another, we have been truly sanctified."[26] In uniting his divinity to humanity, particularly humanity taken from a woman, there is no part of humanity that is not divinely restored and capable of participating in divinity. Women too can hope with Gregory of Nazianzus, "I might be made God to the same extent that he was made man."[27] More significantly, because in the words of Maximus the Confessor, man "has become God to the degree that God has become man," if God takes on full humanity from a woman, then women too are fully divinized.[28] Again, this should be an obvious theological point, but it is nevertheless worth drawing attention to its gendered dependence and implications for affirming the full humanity of women, their redeemed nature, and their invited divine participation like all humans. I would not make this point if the tradition of the church and those with ecclesial authority within it did not undermine the affirmation of women's capacity for equal deification through rites and teachings that continue to privilege androcentrism.

Of course, related to incarnation and deification is the Orthodox veneration of Mary, the Theotokos. If one first affirms that Mary is fully human as a woman and then considers her as God-bearer, the affirmation that women as women can receive and bear God in the world, and can be deified, resonates more clearly. The Orthodox dogmatic references to Mary as Theotokos hinges on the full unity of divinity and humanity in her womb at the moment of conception.[29] Calling Mary Theotokos requires an affirmation of her full humanity and the possibility of full deification of the human nature assumed from her. John of Damascus observes:

> Hence, the holy Virgin is understood to be Mother of God, and is so called not only because of the nature of the Word but also because of the deification of the humanity simultaneously with which the conception and the coming into being of the flesh were wondrously brought about—the conception of the Word, that is, and the existence of the flesh in the Word himself. In this the Mother of God, in a manner surpassing the course of nature, made it possible for the Fashioner to be fashioned and for the God and Creator of the universe to become man and deify the human nature which He had assumed, while the union preserved the things united, just as they had been united that is to say, not only the divinity of Christ but His humanity also.[30]

What Mary offers is not some sort of abstract sanitized humanity but her womanly (and here I reclaim the term used pejoratively in historical hagiographies and hymns) humanity and her female flesh, and she serves God as a mother—and is thus deified as a woman. God united himself to human nature from and within a woman.

Although Orthodox tradition has no difficulty lauding women as sanctifiable, this appears in androcentric and masculine terms. Christology and the confession of deification and redemption require instead an affirmation that it is Mary as a woman (and also a mystical virgin mother) who bears God in her body from her human nature and physically and spiritually bears God to the world. Maximus the Confessor reminds us that God "generously provided our nature with the gift of deification, which he could not possibly have failed to bestow since he was himself God incarnate, indwelling the flesh in the same matter that the soul indwells the body, that is thoroughly interpenetrating it in a union without confusion."[31] Christ did not take on humanity and first disconnect it from the female flesh that was offered to him or masculinize that flesh in perfecting it. The redemptive work of Christ is already inaugurated in the incarnation, and women's nature is not left somehow less holy or undeified. To treat women as if it were is unorthodox.

Orthodox patristic writers and contemporary theologians certainly affirm that women are redeemed in Christ. And as I have claimed about the hagiographic tropes in previous chapters, women are afforded equal opportunities for spiritual progress and sanctification in Christ. Passive claims of equality are not enough, especially in cultural and religious contexts that continue to otherwise render women marginalized. The reversal of the fall of Eve by the Theotokos is celebrated in Orthodox hymns and commemorations. In practice, however, many Orthodox women still find the shadow of the fallen Eve contouring their religious experience and understanding of what it means to be an Orthodox woman.[32] Living as if one is not fully offered redemption in Christ is in conflict with theological assertions. Athanasius explains that in the divine incarnation, "the Lord touched all parts of creation, and freed and undeceived them all from every deceit;"[33] and Cyril of Alexandria likewise observes, "The Only Begotten did not become man only to remain in the limits of the emptying. The point was that he who was God by nature should, in the act of self-emptying, assume everything that went along with it. This was how he would be revealed as ennobling the nature of man in himself by making it participate in his own sacred and divine honors."[34] Women are not naturally sinful or less redeemed than men based on sex, body, or gender. Theologically, this is a significant claim—because it affirms the fullness of the divinizing power of the incarnation.[35]

Any diminishment of women's fully redeemed humanity and potential for equal deification is a problem not only in confessing the incarnation but also in affirming God's love and grace toward humanity. If there is something in the commemoration or Orthodox engagement of women that diminishes their humanity, then the whole notion of deification and redemption for anyone is jeopardized. If women cannot be unequivocally affirmed as fully human, then there is a part of humanity left unassumed.[36] Maximus affirms that "God will also completely fulfill the goal of his mystical work of deifying humanity in every respect, of course, short of an identity with the essence of God; and he will assimilate humanity to himself and elevate us to a position above the heavens. It is to this exalted position that the natural magnitude of God's grace summons lowly humanity, out of a goodness that is infinite."[37] If women and human nature overall are fully assumed by God and therefore united to his divinity and released in his death and resurrection from the bondage of death, then to treat women or commemorate them in ways that render them less redeemed or still prone to a natural weakness, shame, impurity, or fallenness is to negate the resurrection and deification realized through the coming of Christ.[38] John of Damascus observes rightly that it is meet to "reverence the rest of matter and hold in respect that through which my salvation came, because it is filled with divine energy and grace" and that "the only thing that is dishonorable is something that does not have its origin from God."[39] Women's bodies should be included in this reverence especially to combat centuries of misogyny and social messages that tell them otherwise. The sex and gender of Christ may not matter for the salvation of women, but affirming women does matter for affirming the salvation offered in Christ.

## ICON VENERATION

In addition to the theological necessity of affirming full humanity for women for soteriological and Christological reasons, consistently confessing the full humanity and diverse realizations of women is important for the Orthodox theology of icons. Modern theologians, art historians, and iconographers have contributed much to the Orthodox understandings of what icons are and how they function in the tradition.[40] Most Orthodox churches and many homes are filled with icons, including many of holy women. However, as I indicated in previous chapters, often the presentation and commemoration of these sainted women is constrained or at least shaped in response to androcentric and patriarchal cultural expectations and determinations of holy womanhood. Indeed, icons in that they should be legible need to refer to images and symbols familiar to those who view them, and in that they refer to a divine archetype and timeless reality, they need to have certain stylized depictions that shape their expression.[41] This means that icons are limited in how they reflect the particularity of individuals, but they serve as an entry to and reminder of a transcendent relationship through which the one venerating and the one venerated might know each other more fully. The two most famous iconodule theological defenders, John of Damascus and Theodore the Studite, remind us that icons not only attest to the incarnation that renders the divine manifest and circumscribable, but also the saints and their image that allow us to see the divine archetype. There is a union of the divine and the human that is communicated through iconography, and when one addresses oneself to an icon through prayer and veneration that devotion passes to the saint, who in turn has revealed the divine likeness in their holiness. Icons point beyond themselves to reveal the divine image, and those viewing them should strive to know the divine referent that is communicated through a particular image. Icons of women (and men, for that matter) are in this way means of knowing, witnessing, and venerating the communion of divinity and humanity in a particular person. Women have the capacity to bear and reveal the divine image, and Orthodox believers should encounter both living and painted icons in ways that move them beyond a stylized or stereotyped representation.

In venerating the holy person, the holy female saint, for example, is venerated in material form, in a body, in the flesh—even if iconographically stylized to reflect spiritual continuity with Christ. Symbols of martyrdom, ministry, or miracles are often included in icons to indicate to the viewers who the saint is and what attributes are highlighted in their hagiographies and commemorations. These symbols and attributes display a variety of ways women and women's bodies are holy. The saint is not disembodied but represented as holy in the flesh—even if that flesh is transfigured in the resurrection. Indeed, it is regarded as a pious practice and embodied Orthodox confession for men and women to venerate female saints' icons, "for the honor which is paid to the image passes on to that which the image represents, and he who reveres the image reveres in it the subject represented."[42] While recognizing that icons are spiritually stylized and intended to facilitate spiritual participation, it is not theologically consistent to venerate a saint in only their spiritual likeness in a way that undermines their humanity. To do so would negate the theological justifications for veneration of icons as material, circumscribed, and human images of the divine.

The commemoration of men in the tradition is perhaps also limited. However, women's categories are arguably more limited and controlled by a history of patriarchal androcentrism. If women saints are commemorated only in certain established tropes and types, then there is an issue of selective veneration. The goal of iconography and icon veneration is not to bow before human values concerning who is holy but instead to praise the revelation of holiness in the material form by God. John of Damascus reminds us, "I do not venerate the creation instead of the creator, but I venerate the Creator, created for my sake, who came down to his creation without being lowered or weakened, that he might glorify my nature and bring about communion with the divine nature."[43] No flesh, nature, or body is somehow unfitting for divine presence aside from sin. The unique differentiated person and their material form matter in revealing holiness and God at work in the lives of others. Theodore the Studite likewise explains, "If the particular individuals did not exist, man in general would be eliminated. Therefore, humanity is not in Christ, if it does not subsist in Him as in an individual." And later he writes, "Although He assumed human nature in general yet He assumed it as contemplated in an individual manner; for this reason the possibility of circumscription exists."[44] The particular saint matters, and the particular human and their attributes matter as a divine revelation even if they diverge from established patterns. Theodore further reasons, "When anyone is portrayed, it is not the nature but the hypostasis which is portrayed. For how could a nature be portrayed unless it were contemplated in a hypostasis?"[45] The particularity of women as they are sanctified and perfected by God in their individual uniqueness matters. Therefore, any categorical objectification of women or privileging of some androcentric ideal over women's realities is theologically problematic. Venerating holiness as it has been revealed in the world and lives of individual holy women makes for authentic and theologically consistent iconography and icon veneration.

Venerating ideals is not the same as venerating a person, and it is the person who is venerated in the icon, not ideals like "asceticism" or "manliness" or "humility." To be as the hymn for St. Nicholas sings, an "icon of humility," does not mean Nicholas is a witness to some abstract ideal of humility; it means that the person Nicholas is an icon of the one who perfectly embodied humility, Christ.[46] Icons represent particular unique persons who reveal the divine archetype, not human ideals about some fictitiously constructed person who has idealized values. Certainly, there are historical hagiographic constructions that piously and fictitiously do appear in iconography, but if Christians are reverencing an icon of a saint, it is more theologically consistent to depict a real person in whom holiness was manifest than an abstract unembodied ideal—because to do so venerates the saving deifying actions of Christ uniting himself personally to humanity.[47] Consequently, Christians should affirm the whole united and unconfused person in the likeness of Christ in manifold and diverse forms. Theodore the Studite explains this:

> For Christ did not become a mere man, nor is it orthodox to say that He assumed a particular man, but rather that He assumed man in general, or the whole human nature. It must be said, however, that this whole human nature was contemplated in an individual manner (for otherwise how could he be seen?), so that He is seen and described, touched and circumscribed, eats and drinks, matures and grows, works and rests, sleeps and wakes, hungers and thirsts, weeps and sweats, and whatever else one does or suffers who is in all respects a man.[48]

God did not unite himself to and fill an ideal but creation itself through humanity as a divine person. Consequently, images, scriptural scenes, persons, the cross, of course, are venerated. I am not saying that only historical persons should be icons but that inasmuch as Orthodox commemorate female saints and recognize and venerate holy persons, they should do so faithfully in ways that foremost recognize God working in diverse humanity in diverse ways rather than collapse differentiation to promote a uniformity of holiness.

One cannot affirm the Orthodox theology and veneration of icons and negate the full humanity of those they depict. Even the practice of making and venerating icons is dependent on the full humanity of Christ in the incarnation, assumed from the Virgin. As Theodore the Studite explains, "The Word of the Father, conceived in the womb of the Theotokos, was present there and at the same time was above all things. For this reason, He is uncircumscribable and boundless as God, although as man, because He was born from the Virgin, He is circumscribed."[49] If one negates the true union of God with created matter, or deprecates the human, the flesh, or the physical to the spiritual and intellectual, then the theological rationale for icons and their veneration is diminished. Veneration of icons is precisely an honoring of the incarnation, that God became human and voluntarily lowered himself to enter into the material world to sanctify it by his divinizing presence. To venerate an icon implies a confession of divine-human unity in Christ, such that the possibility of humans to reveal a true divine likeness is restored—a likeness that requires full humanity and is manifest in it.

If women are fully equal and human but their commemorative representation as such has been artificial, restricted, or absent, then Orthodox have established a system of poor iconography—and veneration of artificially embodied ideals instead of a divinely created human person. John of Damascus explains that veneration of icons is necessary because "one who does not honor the saints does not honor the Lord himself."[50] I argue that this extends to living icons, by which I mean humans created in the image and likeness of God.[51] If God is made manifest in women in ways that the tradition, church leaders, and commemorations ignore, then there is a privileging of human expectations of women's piety rather than divine revelations of it. This is not to call for an improvement in iconographic skill but rather attention to better expressing the diversity that gives rise to our appreciation for embodied divine-likeness. Theodore the Studite explains about depictions:

> Even if we grant that the image does not have the same form as the prototype because of insufficient artistic skill, still our argument would not be invalid. For veneration is given to the image not insofar as it falls short of similarity, but insofar as it resembles its prototype. In this degree the image has the same form as the prototype; and the objects of veneration are not two, but one and the same, the prototype in the image.[52]

Here of course Theodore the Studite is referring to the physical icons written on walls, but again his optimistic logic can be extended to living holiness and recognition of female saints. Such teaching does not require a rejection of saints' lives or iconic depictions that are overly feminized or unrealistic based on conforming to androcentric preferences; rather they may be reverenced with acknowledgment of *more*. Instead of looking for or ignoring the ways that individuals are holy and looking for the ways they are not as holy as men, women's holiness should be considered as it refers to its archetype, Christ. Orthodox Christians assert women also are in the image of God, and to claim so while also maintaining an androcentric privilege—as if men are perhaps more directly so based on sex or gender—is to misname the divine archetype of their iconicity, both in painted images and in recognizing the working of God in human lives.

If Orthodox have a truncated image of women in commemorations and saintly venerations (both of women saints and of male saints whose holiness is dependent on interactions with women who appear as subhuman tropes of temptation, worldliness, or obstacles to the spiritual life), then their veneration of the incarnation is truncated. Sanitizing the lives of women through androcentric preferences and patriarchally controlled ideals limits the types of living icons that might be revealed and teach others about God incarnate. Consequently, the injunction against iconoclasts is appropriate here.

> Let everyone know, therefore, that anyone who attempts to destroy an image brought into being out of divine longing and zeal for the glory and memorial of Christ, or of his Mother the holy Theotokos, or of one of the saints, or for the disgrace of the devil and the defeat of him and his demons, and will not venerate or honor or greet it as a precious image and not as god, is an enemy of Christ and the holy Mother of God and the saints and a vindicator of the devil and his demons.[53]

When Orthodox sources and practices continue to limit and misconstrue the lives of women through the filter of androcentric patriarchalism, this is a type of iconoclasm. To denigrate the image of God by denying the full and equal humanity of women (and therefore God's image as created in them) is iconoclastic behavior. The image of holiness revealed in a particular person is destroyed—even perhaps out of zeal to conform to tradition. What Orthodox should be doing is venerating the manifold expression of God's presence in the world and acknowledging openly that human understandings of it fall short. To be consistent with the theology of icon depiction and veneration, the intent in recognizing and depicting women's holiness must be to inspire virtue, educate, and communicate the divine-human unity, not restrict the revelation of the divine image to patriarchal androcentric expectations.[54] Any belief or sentiment about gender that restricts, diminishes, or destroys the possibility of God being known and venerated in human women needs to be unsaid and rejected as theologically problematic.

## TRADITION AND WITNESS OF THE HOLY SPIRIT

Theologically, the Orthodox Church relies on continuity with tradition, continuity with the beliefs, practices, and teachings of what has been handed down from the apostles through the ecumenical councils and patristic teachings, among other sources. However, even as Orthodox traditions change and adapt to various cultures and times, there is a profundity with which Orthodoxy claim, "This is the faith of the apostles, this is the faith of the fathers, this is the faith of the Orthodox, this faith hath established the whole world."[55] More fundamentally, the church affirms tradition as the revelation, work, and witness of the Holy Spirit in time. The tradition is living, it is composed of people as the living body of Christ that is the church, but it is also known through sources and teachings passed down generationally that record Christians reflecting on their faith and communicating it to others by means of hagiography, homilies, icons, prayers, liturgical rites, canons, scripture, sacraments, patristic and desert teachings, acts of the ecumenical councils, and theological teachings and interpretations. If the church affirms tradition as the witness of the Holy Spirit in time but includes misogyny, or at the very least patriarchal androcentrism, then the doctrinal issues related to the humanity of women are not overcome. Affirming patriarchal androcentrism over the concerns and lives of women is also inconsistent with overt ethical claims of modern Orthodox theologians, hierarchs, and historical hagiographies on the fundamental equality of dignity that should be shown to all people reflective of being created in the image of God.[56]

To claim to have the fullness of the faith can never be an intellectual assertion, because the faith and its tradition are revealed in and through persons. It can only be relational and faith-based in knowing and loving God, in a way that does not assert with dominance what individuals think God is and how God should be but is open to meeting God in ongoing revelation of the Holy Spirit in the diversely unique lives of others.[57] John Zizioulas notes:

> We cannot give a *positive qualitative content* to a hypostasis or person, for this would result in the loss of his or her absolute uniqueness and turn a person into a classifiable entity. Just as the Father, the Son and the Spirit are not identifiable except simply through being who

they are, in the same way a true ontology of personhood requires that the uniqueness of a person escape and transcend any qualitative *kataphasis*.[58]

Thus, the fullness of faith is the fullness and truth of God united to and revealed in humanity (in Christ and in the indwelling of the Spirit), and therefore the particular human uniqueness is significant for tradition even as it disrupts assertive conceptions of how those within tradition should be. The naming of tradition by human perspectives in a way that excludes or confines according to culturally constructed expectations and seconding or ignoring what it is—an acknowledgment of God wherever God is revealed, even if it pushes or breaks open human expectations of divine action—is an intentional misnaming of tradition. Privileging human will and history above divine revelation has the potential to deny the full activity of the Holy Spirit. The inadvertent ignoring or intentional misrecognition of certain types of holiness and callings because they do not fit within particular gender expectations poses ecclesiological limitations for the development of tradition as *living*. Just as the commemoration of women in androcentric ways is problematic in terms of affirming the incarnation and the veneration and theology of icons, so a limited and humanity-diminishing representation of women poses questions for the reliance of theology on tradition overall because it misses half the church. If Orthodox can see only a partial view of tradition and so triumphantly represent it as the whole, then believers might consider what else of the tradition they are missing or have received as a misrepresentation.

We do not need to fault sainted fathers of the church for the ways they adopted and responded to gender norms of their times or even contemporary hierarchs in a way that cancels their other theological contributions, but there must be space to apophatically say that this is not the fullness of tradition, that this is not the full revelation of the faith, because it does not account for the full equal humanity of women within it. If Christians continue to privilege patriarchal androcentrism in readings of the past and their relevance for the present, then the affirmation and effects of the union between divinity and humanity in Christ are partially undone. Orthodox can certainly marvel in the faith they have received while acknowledging the infiltration of discriminatory and dehumanizing attitudes in theological decisions, discourse, and values. The fact that tradition can still communicate divinity (in belief and practice) to humanity despite human shortcomings should move believers to appreciate the power of God at work in the world and not be limited by human sinfulness but work within humanity cooperatively with divinity to overcome it. This latter incarnational calling is present in tradition and should not be overlooked. Tradition, as it is composed of human reflections on and revelations of divinity, needs to always be reassessed for its confession and production of divine-human unity in time. For the purposes of this book, that means including full humanity participating in divinity as known in the lives of diverse women.

This chapter points to several interrelated areas of theological troubling that emerge if Orthodox acknowledge that the presentation of women in many of the authoritative sources and practices of their tradition are androcentrically denied, limited, devalued, dehumanized, and patriarchally controlled. These are not the only areas of theological tension that emerge when starting from the basic feminist premise that women should be regarded as fully and equally human but just three areas that exemplify how foundational beliefs of Orthodox Christianity are undermined by implicit misogyny within the tradition. There are certainly more directly ethical issues and arguments to be explored, along with pastoral considerations, but this chapter focuses on three theological areas that are complicated by any equivocation on the full equality and goodness of women's human nature. The incarnation requires an unequivocal affirmation of women's full humanity that is equal to men. Deification necessitates Christ's full humanity that is given by a woman, a woman who for the sake of the deification of other women should be recognized as fully human in every way. Veneration of female saints and male saints for engaging with tropes of women is only authentic and theologically consistent if those women are presented and celebrated as full human persons—in as many diverse and messy ways as God has created them to be, no matter how these may affront or confound androcentric and patriarchal ideals. Icons are of human persons who by participative divine grace can reveal and communicate the divine image; they are not first ideals or abstract values. Orthodox venerate the image of God, the divinity united to humanity, and for this reason they can affirm it is meet and right to depict the circumscribable Logos. If Orthodox accept diminished humanity in women, then they diminish the theological justification for iconographic veneration and depiction and restrict imaging God in the world by privileging androcentric expectations. The misrepresentation of the divine image within human persons is closely tied to the final area of theological consideration—determining and relying on tradition for theological consistency. Tradition is a source of reflecting on the faith. If it presents women in these artificial and problematic ways without unsaying the limitations of these constructions, then it undermines its own authority because it privileges communicating patriarchal androcentric concerns over the incarnational realities experienced in the lives of real women.

For the sake of theological consistency, therefore, despite the spiritual ideals highlighted in the previous chapter, what one might call an Orthodox feminist commitment is warranted in the religious conceptual and commemorative tradition to disrupt and reject any line of thinking that does not affirm the full personhood and full and equal humanity of women. This must acknowledge the violence that has been done to women in the history of the church and present-day communities and strive to articulate and express itself beyond mere empty claims for equality amid a culture and discursive tradition that betrays ongoing patriarchal privilege. Grappling with such theological challenges related to the representation and misrepresentation of women in the Orthodox tradition lead me now to my final two chapters, in which I offer constructive approaches from within Orthodox spirituality that have the potential to foster greater theological consistency.[59]

**FIVE**

# Approaches for Unsaying Patriarchal Androcentrism

In a theological tradition that privileges the witness of the past as informing the theological articulation of the present and future, how might Orthodox theologians proceed with the acknowledgment of tradition's patriarchal androcentrism? How does one articulate the paradoxical logic of divine-human communion when half of that humanity is held in tension through a type of simultaneous veneration and subsumed denigration?[1] What do Orthodox do with a tradition that has produced profound spiritual understandings if they acknowledge that it is also a mechanism of potential oppression and ongoing piously rendered dehumanization?[2] Such questions need to be addressed if there is to be any relationship between what Orthodox Christians pray, what they believe, and the integrity of the historical witness of the church.[3] Tradition within Orthodoxy is variously conceived, but any conception that hardens around an idealized past instead of continually overcoming its temporal constraints in greater realization of the life in Christ offered "Today" is problematic for the equality of women.[4]

Unless the tradition is understood more as David Bentley Hart conceives it, apocalyptically, and the patriarchal androcentrism of its sources is intentionally unsaid, it can lead one to think that women are relegated to gender-specific roles or excluded from them as a confession of Orthodoxy.[5] Hart's explanation with reference to tradition that "faith is the will to let the past be reborn in the present as more than what until now had been known and the will to let the present be shaped by a future yet to be revealed. Hope is the conviction that revelation will not only fulfill but far exceed the promise that the tradition preserves within itself. And, in the end, faith and hope will both pass away, or rather pass over into perfect love," orients tradition as being known only with its revelation in Christ, who is perfect love.[6] Tradition in this light has resources for the present to help foster divine-human communion because it includes records of and reflections on human experiences of divine encounter (in the sacraments, in interactions with others, in mystical vision, etc.) and is itself reinterpreted in light of the transfiguring knowledge of God that comes through divine-human communion. The "mind of the fathers" and its modern articulations need not be jettisoned just because they limit the humanity of women by misrepresenting them, speaking for them, overidealizing, ignoring, or caricaturing them—especially when doing so was not motivated by malice but, often, to instill values of piety through appeal to widely accepted gender expectations of their times.[7] Rather, tradition needs to always be refocused through a communicative knowledge of God's love for humanity, women included. I suggest, then, that Orthodox Christians need to begin to intentionally unsay as a spiritual practice the patriarchal determination of women (and others) that is entangled with much of tradition.

Such unsaying is deeply consistent with the theological belief that we as finite creatures can never exhaustively name the infinite and as such are continually in a process of knowing through negation, that is, acknowledging limitations in theological assertions and then affirming that God is more so those assertions must be unsaid. This is apophasis. Such a negative approach to saying what God is not can be applied to an understanding of tradition if we take it to be the revelation of God in time. God is not oppressive, so if we have a tradition or teaching that is, then tradition or that teaching must be unsaid. Apophasis is often tied to cataphasis, the assertion of what can be claimed (even if then unsaid), such as God is love. This is indeed true, but to the extent that human conception of love is so far from God as perfect love, even this statement can be unsaid ("God is not love") to indicate the distance between what is claimed and understood through our very limited human knowledge and what is ineffably true in God's own being. Christian tradition, which is reflective of the humans that comprise it, should not be reduced to its shortcomings and definitively identified but reframed in light of its divinely reflective and participative potential through a type of apophasis of presumed limits. Apophasis is a way of acknowledging limits or boundaries and undoing their power to appear to control, opening instead a space to contemplate God and God's activity in the world in ways that remain beyond conception and definitive knowledge.

The Catholic theologian Catherine LaCugna observes that Christian feminism "exposes the profoundly harmful effects of patriarchy on the humanity of both women and men and rejects the part played by Christian piety and theology in sustaining patriarchy's hold upon society and church."[8] Having demonstrated Orthodox tradition's problematic entanglement with patriarchy in the previous chapters and in light of LaCugna's statement, I now turn to show that traditional teachings of piety and theology can be used to break patriarchy's hold on the church. I model a feminist and Orthodox reclamation of tradition and show that central aspects of Orthodoxy can be disentangled from patriarchal control to better reflect its doctrinal affirmations, particularly regarding women. Confessing the incarnation, resurrection, and possibility of theosis requires affirmation of women's voices, bodies, wills, and minds. As I have shown in the preceding chapters, within the commemorative genres of Orthodox tradition, women are affirmed as having equal spiritual potential to men, as being equally in the divine image, but in ways that often subvert and undermine claims to their full and equal humanity. I leave aside here the theological ideal that no one is fully human except Christ, raised in the third chapter, and instead observe that Orthodox tradition has difficulty affirming women's humanity to the same extent or from the same starting point it does men. Women are somehow not sufficiently redeemed in their bodies, are in many instances idealized only beyond their gender or "nature," and are associated with weakness and a pejorative "womanliness" that has seeped into liturgical practice even though it is in theological conflict with the doctrine of the incarnation.[9] This confluence of unintentional or intentional misogynistic views of women as being other, second, and so on, with the communication of religious values that diminish humanity presents several theological challenges for the whole church. As I indicated in the previous chapter, the dehumanization of women, even if through sanctification, calls into question Christological and soteriological dogmatic claims, restricts the authenticity of saint and icon veneration, and jeopardizes the authoritative reliability of the theological tradition. Therefore patriarchal androcentrism needs to be intentionally unsaid in the Orthodox use and conception of tradition.

## RECLAIMING TRADITION FROM ITS PATRIARCHAL LIMITATIONS

While there is no singular remedy for making the androcentric traditions of the past and inequalities of the present suddenly more inclusive and affirming, Orthodox can learn from the feminist and queer theological insights of other Christian denominations and begin to form their response to the gender inequalities entangled with their religious values in ways that are consistent with Orthodox theology and its expression in the current age. This does not necessarily mean that the patriarchal leadership of the church must be suddenly overthrown or that engagements from other traditions will fit neatly within Orthodoxy.[10] But, as the patristic authors drew on the non-Christian philosophy of their time to find a vocabulary for and an understanding of Christian doctrine, non-Orthodox thinking is still helpful for articulating the faith in a new and ultimately more authentic light. For example, Orthodox might take to heart bell hooks's suggestion, "We need to highlight the role women play in perpetuating and sustaining patriarchal culture so that we will recognize patriarchy as a system women and men support equally, even if men receive more rewards from that system. Dismantling and changing patriarchal culture is work that men and women must do together." This suggestion has the potential to better confess Orthodox faith and is consistent with the unitive ecclesiology of the church as the mutually uplifting Body of Christ.[11] The challenges that a patriarchal androcentric tradition pose for Orthodoxy are not an issue posed by men against women or problems for women to resolve. Rather, women have certainly been involved in upholding patriarchalism and androcentrism, men have been negatively affected by it, and it will take an effort that transcends gender divisions to overcome. It is important to acknowledge for both men and women that in the words of Sarah Ahmed, "an attempt to open up a space to others can be threatening to those who occupy that space," and that patriarchy as "a system is reproduced by rewarding those who are willing to reproduce the system."[12] To put it succinctly and in Orthodox terms, change that might undo the grasp of patriarchy on the church requires a divesting of the self to be reconfigured in greater divine similitude. As I argue in what follows, participating in such work is justified by and aligned with significant Orthodox ascetic and theological commitments to develop each person in divine likeness.

In addition, if one thinks about patriarchy as structural, systemic, and learned in the way that Kate Manne directs readers to think about misogyny (not just as an intentional feeling or habits of behavior), then as Ibrahim Kendi and others have urged an intentional commitment to undoing racism, I would suggest that something similar applies to patriarchal androcentrism within Orthodoxy.[13] Orthodox need to intentionally become "anti-misogynist"—by which I mean at the very least recognize and espouse a commitment to overcome the intentional and unintentional marginalization and dehumanization of women in all its forms in any way that is supported by Orthodox theology. Giving up the attachments one might have to the tradition (and church) one is comfortable with or privileged within might also be conceived as a type of kenosis, or self-emptying, and perhaps also repentance. Presuming a place of privilege within the Orthodox ascetic tradition is almost always aligned with the sin of pride, and it is only in shirking honor in lieu of service to others that one's holiness is cultivated. The religious value of humility might encourage those with privilege to put it to service on behalf of others rather than defend their privilege based on gender or clerical rank.

Patriarchal androcentrism that disadvantages women is structural, systemic, and often seemingly sacralized in Orthodox beliefs, traditions, and practice.[14] A commitment to anti-patriarchal androcentrism resonates with the Orthodox belief in salvation as deification and the universality of Christ's incarnation and resurrection. All are included in the love and work of Christ, so to perpetuate teachings and practices of tradition that exclude or oppress would be inconsistent with the revelation of Christ in scripture as being with and on behalf of the socially marginalized, as well as how Christ is worshipped in Orthodox liturgy as the life-giver and lover of all.[15] In the Orthodox spiritual life, one needs to continually "put on Christ" (Galatians 3:27–28) as an ongoing baptismal confession and in penitential striving for theosis. Intentionally unsaying the dominance of patriarchal androcentrism in order to better express and live the faith is deeply consistent with such active commitments. Orthodox spirituality evidences a rich tradition of the interior life as an ongoing penitential process, one wherein one never just stops being sinful but becomes increasingly filled with divine light and love and then more acutely aware of the imperfections of one's own love compared to God.[16] The view of development as gradual and unending transformation to become increasingly iconic and united to God through ongoing divine participation is consistent with a process of recognizing and increasingly unsaying behaviors, habits, practices, and thoughts that perpetuate the presumption of women as inherently less-than. Such a model could be extended and adapted to other forms of exclusion that exist within Orthodox tradition, but the need to nuance such application must be saved for another space.

Despite the complications and critique highlighted in previous chapters, I still maintain that when it centers a confession of divine-human unity as revealed and made possible in Christ, Orthodox spirituality and theological tradition have within it the resources for rejecting exclusion and patriarchal androcentrism and any behavior or thought that dehumanizes others in a similarly sustained penitential process. Audre Lorde's oft-cited quote, "the master's tools will never dismantle the master's house," if applied to the church, is only true if one mistakes who the master of the church is—for indeed, one cannot merely draw on the productions of patriarchy or turn to the patriarchs for patriarchy's own undoing. Alternately, if Christians recognize and reorient themselves with the understanding that the "master" is God, then his tools will not dismantle the church as it exists ultimately in him, but they can certainly undo oppressive patriarchy. The incarnation demonstrates that God works alongside and from within humanity to offer them tools to dwell with him as "joint heirs with Christ" (Romans 8:17).God offers a model of "master" (or of Father) that is not oppressive but liberative and divinizing.[17] These tools of reading tradition, with God as the self-emptying of power, to elevate the lowly and unite humanity to himself prioritized can undo the structures that might otherwise subjugate. Thus, deeply ingrained and widespread

Orthodox patriarchy and androcentrism need to be transformed over time and from within, as personal and communal spiritual transformations. Orthodoxy has the theological resources and justifications to support this.

In the discussion that follows, I draw attention to three areas within Orthodox spirituality and tradition that demonstrate how resources from within an ostensibly patriarchal tradition might be leveraged to develop a more inclusive and affirming theology. These approaches that might serve to initiate a type of corrective to Orthodox traditions that dehumanize or devalue women are rethinking kenotic (voluntarily self-emptying/giving) power, embracing an apophatic (negating assertive claims about boundaries and seeking what is beyond or missed by assertive claims) approach to tradition, and fostering a hesychastic (humble, quiet, penitential, and welcoming) encounter of others.[18] Admittedly, these are all androcentrically emphasized in Orthodox theology and consequently many of the sources I draw on to explain them are, as with most of this book, authored by men. However, the theological issues raised in the previous chapter prompt an intentional unsaying of patriarchal androcentrism and the possibilities of more inclusively appreciating what tradition has to offer in light of its Christocentric understanding. Instead, as with other chapters, I draw on this male-dominated tradition to see in it the spaces and fullness where the unvoiced (women) might be, reclaim it with a new interpretation that affirms women in their fullness, and penitentially unsay the spaces where women have been limited.[19]

Reclamation, in addition to being a feminist method, is an inherently Orthodox expression of tradition as living and the Orthodox method adopted in patristic interpretations of drawing on sacred sources anew in each age and diverse contexts to better articulate the faith. For example, John of Damascus urges "the people of God, the holy nation, to cling to the traditions of the Church" in his first defense of icons after he draws from scripture, hagiographies, and earlier patristic writings to affirm the Orthodoxy of icons. The examples he uses in previous contexts, however, would not necessarily have defended the point he is making with them (e.g., various scriptural citations, or veneration of the cross, or even that the "people of God" are the Orthodox rather than the Jews), yet he draws from the vast tradition to make the case that icons should be made and venerated in a way that is received by later Orthodoxy as compelling.[20]

The patristic tradition offers numerous examples of creatively drawing on the sources of the past to demonstrate a new possibility for articulating Orthodoxy in the present. They, like many feminists, engage in a type of reclamation of tradition. Thus, I offer a model of reclaiming theological teachings prevalent within Orthodox tradition that have been in some ways used to reinforce androcentric concerns to the detriment of women.

Patriarchal order has excluded and controlled women, and kenosis as a Christological imitation has been used to spiritually valorize women's sometimes obligatory self-giving. Apophasis has highlighted intellectual approaches to theological understanding and diminished the embodied incarnational realities of women. Hesychasm, like apophasis, has been primarily written about by men, often in privileged male monastic solitude that further associates women with worldliness and does not privilege them as narrators of their own divine encounters.[21] In what follows, I offer an Orthodox feminist theological interpretation of these androcentric theological approaches from within tradition. That is, I draw on theological themes and spiritual teachings that have largely excluded the voices of women and give them back to tradition with an interpretation that could begin to liberate them from their own androcentric limitations. Last, as I hope the previous chapters demonstrate, women's erasure, misrepresentation, and restriction in tradition through a patriarchal lens is among other things a *theological* problem. So what I offer are three distinctly Orthodox theological approaches that model how tradition has the resources nevertheless to communicate God who is "in all and for all" and thus intentionally undo its own patriarchal androcentrism.[22]

## A KENOSIS OF PATRIARCHY

The first approach I suggest is a self-emptying of patriarchy through a kenotic commitment.[23] As I have discussed elsewhere, Orthodox historical theology manifests multiple examples of spiritual authority being acknowledged or removed based on the iconicity of those in power—precisely in terms of kenotic imitation on behalf of others. Power inasmuch as it is from the only one who has or is powerful—God—is in fact power on behalf of, in service of, and self-giving through love. This *thearchical* power (i.e., divinely sourced power), this voluntary condescension to empower others, works to offer elevation to the unempowered others through love and self-effacement.[24] Although I hope someday for an Orthodox future that is not organized administratively in a gender-exclusionary way, for the present patriarchal reality, adopting a perspective of kenosis (here, self-emptying on behalf of others as Christ did in his incarnation) can begin to undo the pattern of perpetuating a sense of androcentric entitlement to lead and have authority over others. Indeed, Orthodox might come to understand ecclesial orders and leadership in a gender-inclusive way, a way that is contingent not on gender or sex difference but on one's ability to spiritually communicate God. Patriarchy emptied of its worldly constructs might return to a more theological center of communicating God's rule and principle as Father to the world. This is not a call for a paternalistic type of regendering of God as a male "father" but rather an expansion of how Christians understand who divine power includes and why.[25] Such a rule as revealed in Jesus Christ is not based in maintaining some sort of gender hierarchy but of offering kenotic love to elevate and offer divine life to even the most lowly.[26] Those who are called to lead should in their actions, not just their beards or bodies, be recognizable as the divine archetype that does not need to privilege a certain type of masculinity. This may certainly include women, and kenotic leadership should empty itself of the notion that a singular category of gender or sex has more suitability for leadership, ordination, or other vocations. Spiritual leadership and authority should not be dependent on one's sexual morphology or gender expression, apart from one's spiritual manifestation of divine likeness.[27]

If Orthodox want to maintain that patriarchy as an iconic and non-gender-specific type of spiritual hierarchy that is not associated with the oppressive control of women, as the term is used in secular feminist discourse, then the hierarchical structure of the church should function kenotically—selflessly on behalf of the other.[28] Indeed, ultimately the term "patriarchy" itself will need to be emptied from the tradition because of its association with power disparity along gendered lines. However, in the present, it is helpful to remind the church of the gendered power imbalance that needs to be intentionally undone. Dismissing the term altogether too early might result in erasing important work on gendered inequalities that still warrants action. For this reason, in the present I find the term "kenotic patriarchy" helpful to indicate that I am calling for those in gendered positions of power to offer of their privilege to empower others—that I am urging those with patriarchal privilege to embrace kenosis as a mode of leadership rather than further impose a kenotic calling on the already oppressed. Ruether offered decades ago that Jesus on the cross manifests in a kenosis of patriarchy—that is, an emptying of the structures of power that oppress in favor of equal humanity divinely ordained. Ruether explains, "Jesus as the Christ, the representative of liberated humanity and the liberating Word of God manifests the kenosis of patriarchy, the announcement of the new humanity through a lifestyle that discards hierarchical caste privilege and speaks on behalf of the lowly."[29] For gender and feminist theorists and theologians, this kenotic approach models a process and transformation that unyokes the normative aligning of gender with the signification of power. Instead, this interpretation of the kenosis of patriarchy reflects a type of paradoxical empowerment from voluntarily embracing vulnerability for the sake of the other (as Orthodox confess Christ does for the sake of human salvation in the incarnation).[30] A kenotic patriarchy works to elevate and include women's voices without concern for preserving one's gendered privilege and does so with love and longing to beautify the body of Christ. A kenotic patriarchy recognizes the cultural limitations related to misogyny and gender roles that would and do undermine women's spiritual authority and callings and works to show such attitudes are theologically incompatible with Orthodoxy. Ultimately, kenotic patriarchy, as I envision it, is unafraid to no longer exist as "patriarchy" in any sense other than communicating (either through iconicity of praxis or sacramental mediation) divinity to others.[31] That is, kenotic patriarchy might still remain as "patriarchy," only in the sense that it reveals the self-giving and life-bestowing love of God the Father, but this is certainly not correlative to gender or control of the tradition and those who participate in it.

If Orthodox believe in divine-human communion and strive to increase their divine likeness, then such a kenotic move from those in positions of privilege and authority to work on behalf of others is theologically imitative.[32] Even though Orthodox theology has yet to have a sustained engagement with liberation theology or address systems of structural oppression, it has within it already an assumed preferential option for those at the ecclesial, social, and cultural margins in a way that celebrates God's self-giving and voluntary condescension.[33] Christ reveals in the incarnation, his own passion, death, and resurrection, the power of God in the world on behalf of the world. After all, the goal of divine-human communion necessitates God filling the uttermost depths and a radically new understanding of power realized through voluntary service.[34] The modern theologian and saint, Maria Skobtsova of Paris, emphasizes the collapsing of hierarchical difference in the incarnation, saying, "The truth of the Lord abolishes the difference between the immense and the insignificant."[35] The self-emptying on behalf of another is not some patronizing self-congratulatory move that uses the lowly and depends on a separation of lowliness for its own piety; rather it should be in genuine recognition and yearning for the Other as an icon of God that has the potential to change oneself and elevate those it encounters through divine communion.[36]

Practically speaking, those who hold positions of privilege and influence (whether as a jurisdictional patriarch, a tenured theologian, or an influential layperson) could manifest a commitment to this type of kenosis of patriarchy in their engagement with others and the discourse they produce.[37] God's power is revealed in God's self-giving, in divine humility, and ultimately as love.[38] This power is not used to coerce, control, or limit those hierarchically below but to empower them to freely become increasingly more like God and realize their uniqueness as God has created them to be in his image. As Zizioulas notes, "The Christian ethos of otherness does not allow for the acceptance of the rejection of the Other on the basis of his or her qualities, natural or moral. Everyone's otherness and uniqueness is to be respected on the simple basis of each person's ontological particularity and integrity."[39]

Divine power, then, as connected to and the model of Christian administration of power and structures of ecclesial authority, should not be considered something wielded over others. Rather, it is power given up on behalf of empowering others to be realized in divine iconicity. It is the free gift of God's superabundant love, in which humans are invited to participate and share with others in his likeness. Human authority, particularly within the ecclesiastical hierarchy, should be dependent on a divinely imitative kenotic relationship with others.[40]

In terms of present-day Orthodox leadership, church leaders and those in the lineage of patriarchy should manifest this type of kenotic patriarchy to undo its dominating effects. In this way, a kenotic approach to patriarchal androcentrism might involve and begin to internally move the people whose religious lives and sense of identity are entangled with certain gendered expectations within Orthodox praxis that are normative in many Orthodox cultures to actively value gender equality. This is not an embrace of a gender-exclusive patriarchy as theologically acceptable but rather an admission of the incarnational realities of the Orthodox Church now and how it is called to be. This kenotic approach to patriarchal leadership does not call for sudden radical change, but as with all Orthodox practices of spirituality, it is a process of personal and communal ascetic transformation.

Scholarship of theology can include this kenotic commitment, as can constructive theology itself. It can empty itself of its inclination to valorize historical figures and contributions without acknowledging the ways they have been used to marginalize certain others. It can empty itself of its method, intellectual elitism, and androcentric engagements and make space for thinking differently and different thinkers.[41] This also means, as a practice, that those with more privilege, a certain type of academic, cleric, or hierarch, have to offer up their privilege to create space and authority for those who have traditionally been othered.[42] Such is the example offered by divine condescension in Christ's incarnation that results in human deification.[43] Those in positions of privilege need to make themselves voluntarily vulnerable to invite the communion of those in some ways unlike themselves. This is consistent with the Orthodox theology of Christ's kenotic and unitive incarnation. While I agree with Zizioulas that "the priority of the Other over against the Self reaches its climax on the Cross," I qualify that his conclusion that "the Other must always have priority, even if this means going against one's own conscience," might be taken to refer to preserving the freedom of the Other, and, as I argue in the next chapter, this involves a consideration of who is privileged in power. Exceptions should be made for those who are positioned at a disadvantage, because self-giving that is imposed is not iconic.[44] Kenotic praxis is predicated on Christ's freedom, his starting position of divine power, and is offered in love on behalf of the other.

Orthodox tradition may be marked by patriarchy to the detriment of women, but it can be carried forward with a kenotic impetus to empty itself of androcentrism and give itself up on behalf of the other. This is not to just swap out Orthodox theology for some new gender-liberal relativism, or keep the same patriarchal focus with an apology about the androcentrism of tradition. It might be instead a never fully realized self-emptying and self-giving of those in positions of privilege that manifests in elevating the voices and lived humanity of others. Kenotic patriarchy provides a mode to make space for diverse others and a way to retrieve a "usable past" by a willingness to empty oneself of uncritical attachments to tradition that might prioritize preserving "tradition" over communicating Christ-likeness.[45] Keeping the theological ideal of kenosis for those in positions of privilege is not naive idealism, but rather a witness to the reality of divine participation and likeness to which Orthodox Christians believe themselves to be called. This process of kenosis could be a start, certainly not the end, as a logical extension of its self-emptying eventual negation of its patriarchalness based on gender—demonstrated, expected, and acknowledged by Orthodox practitioners over time.

## MEETING GOD IN THE OTHER

For the next two approaches, I draw on the assumption that Orthodox theology requires a meeting of the neighbor and the other in a way that is not different from meeting God mystically. I take to heart the feminist philosopher Grace Jantzen's reminder that "a feminist aim of becoming divine . . . is an aim of increasing sensitivity to the face of the Other: the Other of this world, not of some other world beyond embodiment or beyond death," and find it deeply embedded in Orthodox theology and realized in practice with a sense of urgency by numerous, particularly female, saints.[46] It is in the other, as Zizioulas has explicated so robustly, that one meets and interacts with God.[47] Christians must first affirm the "other" created in the divine image, even before doctrinal affirmations, as a Christological encounter.[48] While I hope this simple ethical commitment is commonly accepted without significant elaboration, examples from scripture, liturgy, ecclesial documents, lives of saints, and spiritual instructions could be provided to affirm that the encounter and reverence for neighbor and God are not distinct or separate within Orthodox theology.[49] However, perhaps the most prominent recent example of this ethical alignment between God and humanity is found in the twentieth-century essay of Maria Skobtsova, "The Mysticism of Human

Communion."[50] In these short yet profound pages, Skobtsova emphatically notes that after the incarnation, "who ... can differentiate the worldly from the heavenly in the human soul, who can tell where the image of God ends and the heaviness of human flesh begins? In communing with the world in the person of each human being, we know that we are communing with the image of God, and, contemplating that image, we touch the Archetype—we commune with God."[51] Skobtsova provides a foundation for Orthodox theology of embracing the other as God, what she calls "an authentic, and truly Orthodox, mysticism, not only of communion with God but also of communion with man. And communion with man in this sense is simply another form of communion with God."[52] The encounter with all should be, according to Skobtsova, "an authentic and profound veneration," and it is a divine commandment to see in others "the image of God and in the world God's creation."[53] Skobtsova's martyric witness and social charity attest to her attempts to embody and live out the mystical communion with the people she encountered.[54] I suggest that this type of commitment to see and interact with others in their full humanness as a form of divine veneration and communion is essential to the two other approaches I describe below.

## APOPHASIS, HUMILITY, AND TRADITION

In addition to applying a kenotic commitment to how Orthodox think of and act in positions of authority and privilege, apophasis is a useful theological concept for finding ways to approach tradition while acknowledging its shortcomings for women. As I hope the previous chapter demonstrates, the power structure that patriarchy maintains via commemoration, and that tradition upholds based on gender privilege, is not theologically consistent. Trying to uphold and defend tradition in ways that categorically diminish the freedom, humanity, and spiritual potential of women privileges patriarchal control over a confession of divine-human unity. If ecclesial models of leadership are oppressive and diminish affirmations of full humanity and capacity for divinity, they are not iconic; that is, they do not reveal divine likeness. Welcoming diversity and honoring the humanity and gifts of women (and all others) are important theologically, as I have argued in chapter 4, to authentically acknowledge the work of the Holy Spirit in the church. Sarah Ahmed reminds us that "to hear with a feminist ear is to hear who is not heard, how we are not heard," with the latter phrase being particularly important for addressing the patriarchal androcentrism of tradition that speaks over or silences the autonomous voices of women. In the textual tradition women may be heard, and they may have a liturgical and commemorative presence, but the aspects of their lives that are obscured by gendered assumptions and how "woman" as a religious construct is used to authorize or restrict the lives of present-day women still are not heard.

There needs to be an unsaying of the aspects of tradition that impinge on women's Christologically gifted freedom and potential for divinized humanity. For example, where tropes exist in commemoration, they need to be amended or unequivocally explicated in ways that negate the possibilities of continuing to apply them in misogynistic or dehumanizing ways to now-living women. The privilege Orthodox give to tradition should not outweigh a theological obligation to affirm the full humanity of women. And yet, as I have argued elsewhere, the use of gender in hagiography and hymns often carries with it significant spiritual content that is dependent on certain gendered assumptions for being conveyed historically.[55] Other modes of religious expression and new ways of expressing spiritual values can be fostered while acknowledging the ever present finite limits of contexts that need to be unsaid as they are recognized in communicating religious values. Apophasis toward tradition thus may be useful for promoting a more inclusive and affirming Orthodoxy and Orthodox theology.[56]

In previous writing, I observed a type of apophasis toward the commemoration of female saints in terms of gender: they were negated as women in a way that indicated divine power and presence because the category "woman" was conceptually limited to express the holiness found in the saint. This both presumed "woman" as a limited category (somewhat problematically) and provided a theological rhetorical means of overcoming its limits and specific "roles" for women based on gender (somewhat theologically resourcefully).[57] Here, however, I suggest apophasis is a theological resource in a related but different way: to unsay the boundaries of tradition and foster a humbler approach to conceiving the breadth of tradition, as I indicated in the opening of this chapter. For the historical theological tradition to continue to hold authority, it needs to be approached through a mode of apophatic humility—recognizing that what has previously been named as tradition is only partial and any claims to universality need to be unsaid. Tradition may be missing its witness to the Holy Spirit at work in the lives of women in a plethora of ways because these women's lives may not have conformed to androcentric and patriarchal expectations. Several scholars of feminist and queer theology have noted the ways apophasis is useful for rejecting the seeming ultimacy of gender binary and rethinking desire in human conceptions of God.[58] In Orthodox hagiography and hymns historically, there are examples of negating the limits of gender in describing women's holiness—that is, an apophasis of human constructions to gesture to the infinite divine image manifest in individuals.[59] I suggest that a similar broadening of the apophatic approach is useful as a practice in approaching tradition as a whole. Apophatic theology has a rich heritage in Orthodoxy for speaking about God, but it also might serve as an unsaying reminder about what has been missed in tradition and theology. As Hart observes, "No one has the ability to discern from the vantage of this present moment within the life of the tradition just how much more that end may encompass, and how many local truths it may summon into existence and embrace within itself."[60]

As I discuss further in the next section on hesychast spirituality, what Orthodox know with any truth is God, but as the apophatic tradition reminds us, knowledge is relational and communicative, not a summative and assertive knowing that determines a subject. In Orthodox liturgy it is only after having received communion that the congregation sings in thanksgiving, "We have seen the true light; we have received the heavenly Spirit; we have found the true faith." The "true faith" is known through a communicative mystical encounter with Christ that further bestows the indwelling of the Holy Spirit and is reflected in "worshipping the undivided Trinity."[61] The understanding of what is true is based in divine communion with the one who is Truth (John 14:6). Relational knowledge in communion is necessarily always knowledge personally known and unknown to new understanding of the self and the other. It is a posture of nondominance and openness to revelation, an "unsaying" of claims that otherwise might result in exclusion, erasure, or artificial construction.

Apophasis might unsay the certitude and boundaries applied to recognizing God in time (tradition) and God in humanity (in women). This type of "ethical apophaticism" might be helpful in denying limiting constructions and expectations in encountering individuals rather than cataphatically laying a claim to who they are or how they should be aside from knowing them as already loved by God.[62]

Apophasis is also a mode by which believers might unsay the seeming triumphalist attitude present in some Orthodox sources and liturgical rites.[63] The Synodikon (synodal decree) of the "Triumph of Orthodoxy," proclaimed in various forms on the first Sunday of Great Lent, might be rearticulated or at least reinterpreted to celebrate the Orthodox faith not as a triumph over or against heresy but rather as an affirmation of the universality of the incarnation that is hopeful for the salvation even of the unorthodox.[64] This approach allows for the contingencies of culture, the semiotics by which saints are recognized as holy and liturgy feels familiar, and also the unsaying recognition that there is more that has been missed and that has not been seen. Such an approach might temper Orthodox claims to "tradition" and even to the "mind of the fathers" while acknowledging partiality. An apophatic approach to tradition and its sources would allow for Orthodox to retain that which is spiritually useful while also unsaying the aspects where a source or practice is now recognized to be theologically inconsistent.

For instance, historical normalized misogyny ingrained in the writings of beloved patristic theologians can be negated while retaining the contributions to doctrine.[65] Orthodox could choose to not limit historical authors to their disappointing mistakes or imbue them with a totalizing authority. Apophasis provides a method for unsaying the aspects of tradition that are entangled with assertions of patriarchal androcentrism and even blatant misogyny and seeing these limits overcome in God. For sainted authors who perhaps are problematic in their actions or views on others, one might negate the ways they are limited and instead marvel at how nevertheless God was able to work through them. Orthodox could ponder compassionately how these saints or "fathers" struggled to articulate their faith in their particular contexts and how they might now see things in a more capacious way dwelling in the glory of God—that their views in light of the experience of God more fully might have changed in ways that they would now unsay the problematic views of their past.

Such an approach asks that Christians humbly and compassionately see each other with spiritual eyes for what they could be in Christ rather than fixate on the aspects of perceived divine unlikeness that remain in themselves and others. Where unlikeness may be found, the faithful can name it plainly and unsay it as a limit. As Hart states, "The first often become last, and the last first. Reflective believers should always feel licensed to return to what went before and to reclaim certain things formerly rejected or forced to the margins, while perhaps at the same time demoting other things from the eminence formerly conferred upon them."[66] Orthodox theology should seek out God and marvel at God communicated in time through limited humanity. The apophatic approach does not ignore limitations but recognizes them as unlimiting for God and praises God as the one who helps believers see the more perfect possibilities that are in union with him.

Unsaying in humility allows space for maintaining the spiritual fruit of Orthodox tradition while rejecting the aspects of human failing and marginalization that are entangled in its articulation and ongoing expressions. Such an approach provides an example of how a gender-troubled past of a religious tradition might be reframed through a theological lens to be "usable" for fostering a more affirming future. If it might be hymnic phrasing that needs revision, Orthodox scholars and practitioners should be able to unsay it as some fixed aspect of tradition and instead explore the possibility opened to the church in communicating the faith in other words. The tropes about women in hagiography and hymns can be acknowledged as in need of unsaying, while their spiritual content may still be theologically fruitful.[67] I am aware of the controversy that arises when liturgical texts are revised or a new interpretation is offered that appears inconsistent with the sanctifying past. Yet the theological issues at stake necessitate that whole groups of people are not sung against or presented as holy in a way that caricatures or dehumanizes when alternatives are possible. Thinking within a tradition of apophasis might help Orthodox move forward and, in the meantime, see the limiting aspects of their tradition as something they can unsay with theological consistency that then leads them to critical contemplation of tradition and how God cannot be exhaustively expressed through it.

In such an apophatic approach there might be not only an unsaying of what Orthodox regard as complete and bounded but also an intentional welcoming of the witness of the Holy Spirit in times past and present and in places that have previously been ignored. It is an unsaying of assumptions and limitations and an openness to the reality of God with a radical affirmation. In this way, one might begin to liberate Orthodox discourse and tradition to make space for other voices. The humble apophatic approach to liturgy, saints, and clergy allows for change and ongoing witness because it denies tradition as a contained and bounded thing. Much like the open Royal Doors of the iconostasis in Bright Week, the apophatic approach can be adopted to burst open conceptual and contextually bound limits to marvel at a spiritual reality that is beyond comprehension.[68] Apophasis opens a space in which to constructively engage and draw on the richness of tradition while also acknowledging and unsaying its flaws and absences. All these male-authored sources may be tradition, but they are also not tradition, because tradition is *more*. It includes women, it includes all the historically marginalized, and it includes all the presently othered because it is the witness of God at work in time, God at work in humanity whether it is yet recognized or not.

## LESSONS FROM HESYCHASM FOR ENCOUNTERING OTHERS

The third approach I suggest is to have humility in approaching tradition, not only an apophatic unsaying of assertions, but also a penitential solicitation of the fullness of tradition and God at work in the church and human life to be revealed. In moving from rethinking engaging tradition to engaging each other, I suggest a similar attitude of humble apophasis in assertions of knowing the other.[69] This approach is one drawn from the Orthodox tradition of hesychasm, or quietude, and repeated prayer in response to and in order to prepare oneself for a direct encounter with God, often described as a vision of divine light.[70] Admittedly, the hesychast tradition has been primarily fostered in monastic contexts and therefore is associated with a particular totalizing obedience and ascetic submission that can be problematic when broadly idealized (see chap. 3). Moreover, the expressions of the hesychast heritage in contemporary Orthodoxy particularly outside of the monastic contexts often are associated with rigorous traditionalism and a type of self-righteous individual piety. Both these associations of hesychasm are problematic for improving the status of women in Orthodoxy: the first, because it can unequally restrict expressions of agency based on gender; and the second, because it limits women's future possibilities by idealizing a patriarchal past as the conditions for and expressions of holiness. However, in a refusal of having the boundaries and usefulness of Orthodox tradition dictated by its androcentric associations based on the unsaying emphasized in the previous section, I find some aspects of hesychasm useful in teaching individuals and Christian communities to encounter, honor, and be changed by others. What I offer is not the psychosomatic practices of controlled breathing along with the repetition of the Jesus prayer, or particular physical postures often associated with the hesychast tradition; rather the spiritual states that these indicate may be useful for thinking about how those who have been privileged within the Orthodox tradition might move toward greater inclusivity of women, as well as those who are marginalized more generally. I suggest hesychasm has much insight about divine encounter and therefore also about encountering the divine in the human. This hesychastic approach involves faith in seeing God in God's energies, and I would suggest this helps see the divine light as it is at work in others.

Hesychast spirituality includes practices and teachings of preparing oneself for, soliciting, receiving, and then responding to the experience of God. For example, the fourteenth-century defender of hesychasm, Gregory Palamas, teaches, "Spiritual light is thus not only the object of vision, but it is also the power by which we see.... [It] is a spiritual power ... made present by grace in rational natures which have been purified." He explains that the divine light encountered is not only an external encounter but also an internal divine cooperation to see God.[71] Nicholas Cabasilas's liturgical theology of the fourteenth century demonstrates that the same divine light and communion experienced by the praying mystic is encountered communally in the liturgical eucharistic celebration.[72] Skobtsova similarly extends the mystical encounter with God to the internal personal icons that are as worthy of veneration as those on the church walls.[73] And Zizioulas reconceives otherness as a prerequisite for communion and part of the divinely gifted divine image.[74] In bringing these teachings together, it is possible to apply approaches that are connected with appropriately encountering divinity to the encounter of God *within* others. Consequently, I propose that consistent with the teachings of encountering the other epitomized in Skobtsova, the practice of meeting and awaiting others is not different from the hesychastic awaiting and encounter of God. Embracing a hesychastic approach to encountering the other shifts the power dynamics from one of entitled privilege to know the other deterministically to one of humble and contemplative invitation to encounter the other relationally.

The Orthodox tradition of hesychasm prepares the practitioner through penitential self-emptying and humility, invites God's self-revelation, and awaits the presence of God.[75] This provides a spiritual practice that can be extended to encountering and communing with others. For instance, those with patriarchal privilege in Orthodox tradition could strive to intentionally empty themselves of preconceptions and gendered ideals and instead patiently await the self-disclosure of the ecclesially marginalized other, as they might the revelation of God.[76] Symeon the New Theologian, for example, explains that to "enjoy the ineffable blessings of the divine light," we must first "acquire a contrite heart, a soul humbled in mind, and a heart that by means of tears and repentance is pure from every stain and defilement of sin."[77] Indeed, it is in encountering the other that one meets God, just as Christians do in the sacraments and just as the hesychast mystics might in visions of divine light.[78] The same can occur interpersonally and, for the purposes of this book, let me emphasize, can occur with encountering women. This is not to overidealize women according to some sort of "feminine mystique" but to acknowledge their potential for bearing the divine image equal to that of men.[79] The idea is not to make women God and men penitents but to recognize that within the other *is* God and therefore mystery, diversity, and iconicity. There is in this model not the notion that individuals should imitate a divine experience, but that they should reverently and penitentially recognize that encounters with others *are already* meetings of the divine in humanity.[80] Such an acknowledgment should generate more respect for the other and appreciation for their self-disclosure of individuality as a gift to be received.

The teachings of hesychast spirituality that foster and respond to divine encounter offer a glimpse into an ascetic tradition that is useful for thinking about how those in positions of privilege might orient themselves to soliciting the participation of women and the self-disclosure of women in the church, that is, to offer a turning inward in penitence that prayerfully awaits and invites a divine disclosure, so that the encounter results in greater humility and self-knowledge. Hesychasm offers a penitential awareness of the ways ego and sinfulness have obscured vision of the divine light. For interpersonal application, this awareness can help Orthodox recognize and repent for the individual and structural ways that have prevented them from seeking and seeing others as being in the divine image and called to divine likeness. Drawing on the Orthodox spiritual practices of encountering God through quietude such as are evidenced in the mystical and hesychast traditions, I suggest a practice of emptying oneself of preconceptions and gendered ideals and instead patiently await the self-disclosure of the ecclesially marginalized others. This is not something distinct from the kenotic practice and apophatic approach but enmeshed in encountering the divine and the human response to iconicity. The humbling of the self in anticipation of the self-disclosure of another involves awaiting and joyfully hoping but not forcing to see the other through the practice of penitence. It should be noted that this could be a productive attitude for both men and women. In hesychasm, this is a type of mourning for one's sinfulness, unworthiness to behold God, and yet longing to be filled with vision of divine light.[81] Interpersonally, this could translate to repenting for the ways one fails to see the other with the love God has for them. This practice involves prayerfully and humbly working to change oneself (perhaps from androcentrism to more openness), rejecting a sense of entitlement to others' self-disclosure, and longing to encounter them in their unique particularity as God has created them to be.

Hesychast spirituality includes a dynamic of divine encounter that necessitates self-undoing for self-realization. After the divine light withdraws from the hesychast, there is a sense of internal prayer that recognizes one's own unworthiness and change of the self in greater repentance to be filled again with divine presence.[82] Much like kenosis mentioned above, this penitential practice of divine encounter is an ongoing transformation of the self in greater divine similitude. Encounter with God then leaves the hesychast with greater awareness of how unlike God they are and results in greater love and penitence.[83] This similar process might be useful for thinking about encountering God in the other. For instance, on meeting another, one should become increasingly aware of the ways one's perception of God in the other is limited by one's own constructs and repent of them and seek to encounter them more even though one is not entitled to know them. By adopting what we might call a hesychastic interpersonal practice, one might refrain from generalizing others or essentializing women. One might attend to the differences of others as they are significant to them rather than interpreting them for them, and there might be an openness to gender to function in a range of ways that cannot be fully communicated. Individual variations and experiences might be welcomed, and such a hesychastic approach would avoid the idolatry of social constructions and preconceived expectations. The goal is not to worship the other in place of God but to learn to see them with eyes of love as God does and to honor God at work in them.[84] Theologically, it could attend to the relationship with others in a way that is self-penitential rather than judgmental. It could foster accepting difference, welcoming the disclosure of others, seeking God in others, and rejoicing where divine love is encountered.

The knowledge of the other as God is relational and particular. It is not knowing about a category but meeting a unique divinely created hypostasis. Divine knowledge is not about an unhypostasized abstraction but is found in a personal seeking, meeting, and seeing God revealed in the other.[85] The hesychastic approach allows for spaces of self-definition and disclosure that are unique and anticipate continual change as one increases in the divine likeness. It does not pigeonhole individuals; rather in knowing the other, one longs to know more and understand the person encountered as a mystery in the process of attaining increasing personhood.[86] The emphasis on trinitarian personalism and the value of personhood found in some modern Orthodox theology, also grounded in a Christological emphasis on divine-human unity, has significant value for shaping such social and ecclesial interactions.[87] The people one might encounter are valued in their divinely given personhood, but it is the Orthodox obligation to also attend to their incarnational reality. To be in continuity with the Christological beliefs they claim to confess, Christians cannot love their personhood as some abstraction and ignore the conditions of their material and situational human existence, because to do so devalues the reality of the incarnation. Personhood in God as Trinity is foremost known through the embodied and human life of Christ. LaCugna rightly asserts that "the doctrine of the Trinity is ultimately therefore a teaching not about the abstract nature of God, nor about God in isolation from everything other than God, but a teaching about God's life with us and our life with each other" and that "the communion of divine life is God's communion *with us* in Christ and as Spirit."[88] Christ is incarnate in time and unites divinity to humanity, just as the Spirit is given in time to unite our humanity to divinity.

The activity of God in humanity and in time means one should look to encounter God at work in the differentiated and contextual circumstances of individual lives and identities. In Christ's divine "Godmanhood," we find the liberating impetus of Christ in the world.[89] This is not to elevate Christology over and against trinitarian theology as the justification for understanding how diverse persons should be in communion but rather to hold these two aspects of theology in unity. By doing so, a better understanding emerges of how to be in the world in a way that recognizes, venerates, and communicates God in increasing participation (and subsequent self-realization in divine likeness and personal uniqueness) and requires Orthodox more holistically to value the uniqueness of others. The hesychastic practice of inviting the disclosure of the other thus creates a practice that overcomes the challenges of difference and affirms universally the human person in the divine image and as a divine encounter. Differences in experience, identity, body, or expressions are not necessarily challenges to be overcome but could be encountered as revelations of the ways God is working in and through them. Differences can be affirmed and embraced, and the person can be affirmed as worthy of perfect and infinite love because they are already divinely created and divinely loved.

Knowledge of the other through encounter is nondominating and always held in an apophatic tension. One can know the other, just as the hesychast does in fact see God, but one also does not fully know the other, just as the hesychast is left with the sense that they cannot *fully* see God.[90] Such an approach fosters a meeting of the other in penitential patience and seeks to know them through a relationship of communion, which requires a change of the self, rather than assertive intellectual or social predetermination of the other.[91] The other, the divinely created person in the image of God, is ultimately mysterious and cannot be known in a dominating conception or perception but through ongoing encounters and relationships based on accepting love and participation.[92] This posture of humble invitation of others presents opportunities for honoring differences as divinely instrumental and particular in revealing a person as uniquely in God's image instead of erasing diversity to artificially assert equality. Such a hesychastic approach might address issues within Orthodox tradition and practice by rejecting gender constructions as determinative. It allows for more variety, diversity, and self-determination. It seeks women's contributions and the unbounding of expectations of women in parish life, welcomes the diversity of gifts and voices women might offer the church, and does not pressure women who have been hurt or ignored to suddenly return or offer themselves again, so that men can feel good about their positions and spiritual selves.

There is not a need for men to save women or to inadvertently perpetuate patriarchalism by telling women how else they can be in the church and directing them to other positions of unrecognized domestic or spiritual labor. Instead, one could be humbly and penitentially mindful of oneself as sinful and promote an openness and receptivity to what might be revealed in an encounter with another—not as one entitled to another's self-disclosure, but as one patiently hoping to receive the divine light. As Skobtsova explains, "the mystery of union with man becomes the mystery of union with God" in giving oneself up in love on behalf of another, that is, giving love freely to others without first knowing how, or if, they will reciprocate.[93] Such a hesychastic approach helps invite women's theological contributions and participation but also humbly awaits knowing anew those whom Orthodox sources have traditionally "othered." This could be a way of inviting the ongoing self-disclosure of others in the present without an ongoing inadvertent patriarchal determination of how women or others should be.

A similar approach could be used for inviting women's theological reflection on the gender-based omissions of the past and how they see themselves in tradition in more inclusive, affirming, and liberatory ways. It does not seek only women's involvement to speak to some essentialized women's perspective but acknowledges human situatedness and invites revelations of uniqueness. In seeking to include women more in the church, the academy, theology, various ministries, and even, perhaps in the future, ordination, there cannot be a demand or sense that women owe men something based on male entitlement to do religion correctly (that is, to be Orthodox). Having pointed out problems with tradition's current expression, some may want to quickly invite, include, cite, bless, or mention a woman in various contexts as a symbol that they are exempt from the critiques presented in the first few chapters, but men are not entitled to women fixing tradition for them and women are not obligated to fix men. There is an honoring of divine freedom in the hesychast's encounter that needs to be applied to encountering women on their own terms. This mystical way of inviting, anticipating, and welcoming others, particularly those who have been marginalized or partially constructed, does not persist in determining or demanding how or what someone else should be—but instead offers a radical joyful greeting in love and veneration of God in them.

I offer the approaches outlined in this chapter as examples of how tradition can be reclaimed from a feminist theological perspective that privileges confession of the divine-human unity and its potential for all people and is consistent with Orthodox tradition and theology. These approaches are not comprehensive or necessarily universally applicable (to do so would negate the approaches put forth), but they indicate contours of the Orthodox tradition that can be used to address and avoid reinforcing the gendered inequalities of patriarchal androcentrism and begin to undo them. Apophasis of assumptions and an ongoing kenosis of patriarchy can help open a space where a hesychastic approach to penitentially and anticipatively awaiting surprising encounters of God in uniqueness and the encounter of the other is sought in humble love. This provides a beginning for how those who recognize the patriarchal and androcentric (not to mention, class- and race-based) specters of the past that have formidably shaped Orthodox tradition might be able to foster spiritual values to shape a more inclusive and divinely reflective theology of the future.

The reframing of patriarchal privilege as a call to kenosis reflects the underlying kenotic patriarchy inaugurated by Christ observed by Ruether that empties itself of gendered oppression and empowers the lowly in a spiritual priesthood. Kenosis, debated for its usefulness for promoting the well-being of women, nevertheless provides a theological justification for realizing the divinely participative and iconic power that comes through voluntarily adopting vulnerability and self-giving to benefit others. Kenosis of patriarchy provides one way Orthodox might begin to transform existing power structures from within to make them less exclusionary and to rethink the significance of spiritual obligations of positions of authority. However, it must be admitted that adopting the kenotic premise of legitimate power does not do much to undo the often-internalized disproportionate and harmful ways that kenosis has been used to subjugate minorities in the history of Christianity.

The apophatic approach to tradition likewise offers a theological justification for reframing Orthodox engagements with its patriarchal and androcentric heritage in a way that rejects claims of ultimacy and triumphalism. It provides an intentional way for Orthodox to critique the limits of their sources while being open to the ways its historical and gendered positionality has resulted in lacunae. Orthodoxy's traditional past can thus be usable in a way that retains its lineage in full acknowledgment of its messiness as a spiritual value. The apophatic approach to the other is likewise useful in rejecting cataphatic claims to finitely determining and artificially constructing a person to particular roles or expectations, in favor of privileging the encounter with the other as an opportunity for meeting God. One must proceed cautiously, however, when applying apophasis to issues related to gender, because the significance of the body and gender expression for the individual can perhaps be too easily unsaid in a type of dehumanization.

The hesychastic welcoming of the disruption of expected norms through encountering the other in divine similitude and honoring difference as intrinsic to iconic revelation reflects a similar impetus to queer theological categorical openness.[94] Drawing on the practices of hesychasm as an anticipative, penitential, humble, relational knowing and encounter that results in ongoing self-learning through the voluntary self-disclosure of the other models a way for personal encounter without perpetuating oppressive determinations of others. The historical association of hesychasm with exclusionary and rigorist piety, however, may influence the contexts in which it might be considered resourceful to think with.

While these approaches may prompt an openness or seeming relativism, they are also framed within an understanding of Orthodox spirituality that is affirming and liberating at a personal level, without a triumphalist mode of asserting inclusion in a still-patriarchal system.[95] These approaches prompt a penitential and Paschal development of faith—one that is not just radically open to everything, but specifically attuning oneself to the Holy Spirit and the "still small voice" of God in humanity.[96] These approaches allow for the retrieval of traditional Orthodox sources and theology (while acknowledging the ways they are shaped by patriarchy), and welcome women's theological engagement—even in forms that may disrupt the androcentric intellectual practice and discursive modes of theology. Orthodox theology of the past needs to recognize its partiality, and the ongoing present needs to be charged with fostering greater diversity as an imperative of theological authenticity even among limitations. This humble apophaticism and hesychastic awaiting involves an openness to unsaying expectations of persons based on sex or gender. It means listening to what women say they need spiritually, inviting them to be agents of change for themselves in ways that are empowered by church leaders as vitally important to the universality of the church, honoring women's bodies with a Christological imperative, and recognizing their autonomy as a soteriological affirmation of what has been granted in the resurrection and made possible in the incarnation. I suggest that these approaches provide evidence of how rereading tradition through a type of Orthodox feminist theological lens can identify, unsay, and help mediate otherwise theological inconsistencies grounded in the religious celebration of patriarchy and the commemoration of its construction of women. Yes, these are ideals, but if normalized, the patriarchal determinations, the problems of commemorating constructs instead of full people, and the androcentric dominance of tradition would begin to be undone and become more welcoming for women and marginalized others.

These approaches also begin to address issues raised by feminist and queer theologians about the usefulness of a patriarchal tradition and the challenges of difference.[97] Addressing the challenges of a patriarchal ecclesial leadership and heritage for gender equality within Orthodox theology also offers potential insights to the study of gender and theology beyond Orthodoxy and beyond any limiting definition of women. Such thinking could also provide a conversation partner for others considering how a historically patriarchal tradition might nevertheless be employed for liberation, how solidarity can be found in an otherness grounded in a common divinely created humanity, and how theological approaches might reshape debates about the ontology of gender, the definition of sex, and intersectional issues of difference.[98] I suggest that the approaches offered in this chapter are grounded in Orthodox theology and are ripe for intentionally unsaying the limiting, diminishing, and androcentrically controlled aspects of the traditionally constructed "patriarchal woman" and fostering greater openness, unequivocal affirmation, and humility among those privileged in the tradition.

**SIX**

# Resources for Advocating for Women in Tradition

The previous chapter used a praxis of reclamation to provide three examples of how the limiting effects of an androcentric and patriarchal tradition can be undone by refocusing the theological and spiritual resources of Orthodoxy from a Christocentric reframing of tradition. The commitments to a kenotic, apophatic, and hesychastic theological approach I explore and recommend may be helpful for those who are in ecclesial positions of privilege to engage their tradition in a way that begins to resolve the problems associated with patriarchal androcentrism. That is all well and good for those privileged by the tradition, but what of women or the otherwise marginalized people in the not-resolved present? Orthodox spirituality teaches that penitence is not just about stopping sinful actions but also about increasing in divine likeness through the cultivation of love, goodness, and compassion. Accordingly, the previous chapter focused on undoing the problems of patriarchal androcentrism in tradition. The present chapter focuses on how Orthodox tradition might be drawn on for actively advocating for, affirming, and including women.

## MODELING AN ORTHODOX FEMINIST THEOLOGICAL APPROACH TO TRADITION

In the pages that follow, I highlight a few areas within Orthodox tradition and theology that demonstrate how Orthodox Christians can draw from their own sources and theological ways of thinking to advocate for women. However, to approach tradition in a way that is liberating and affirming for women requires a feminist theological starting point. This starting point rejects the premise that based on their gender or sex women are somehow categorically subordinate, obligated, or diminished in any way compared to men. It includes the Orthodox theological assertions that God is on behalf of and loves all people, that God calls all to divine communion, and that women's humanity is not "less" so that what is accomplished in Christ's divine-human unity is not somehow diminished for them.

How might women and others who are marginalized in the Orthodox tradition reclaim tradition in ways that affirm rather than deny and that spiritually empower rather than subjugate? In the diverse cultural and particularly post-communist, "diasporic," and conversion experiences of many contemporary Orthodox women, perceptions of gender, feminism, and even equality vary greatly. Consequently, any feminist theological development within Orthodoxy needs to come from within its resources, acknowledge the diversity of women within it, and leave space to invite unique self-voiced experiences. As I mentioned in the introduction, feminist theologies that attend to particularities of the identities and cultural contexts of various women, such as Mujerista, Womanist, and decolonial approaches, might model for Orthodox Christian women possibilities for improving the lives of women and advocating spiritually on their behalf in a way that is unique to their own traditions and attentive to local cultural particularities. Certainly, there is not a singular Orthodoxy or experience of being an Orthodox woman in such an ancient and global tradition that is shaped by diverse ethnic, cultural, racial, and political circumstances in both Orthodox majority and Orthodox minority contexts. As Spyridoula Athanasopoulou-Kypriou rightly notes:

> In order not to have one voice—an authoritarian male voice speaking on behalf of everybody and thus silencing other voices by reducing otherness to sameness—we [the Orthodox] need to listen to a

range of different voices, respect everyone's spirituality (respecting thus the Holy Spirit), sympathize with the other, and not feel fear of diversity. . . . New questions need to be asked, old teachings need to be phrased differently in order to convey the message to everybody.[1]

There must be space for different voices and different perspectives. An Orthodox feminist theological approach should be open to learning from others and reject self-ultimacy while remaining committed to theological integrity that promotes the well-being and full humanity of women in all their diversity, varied expressions, and social realities. This is consistent with the Orthodox spiritual value of humility and an apophatic theological approach. Attention to the circumstances of diverse women should be an expression of honoring the incarnational reality, the full humanity, of each person as uniquely created in the divine image.

Accordingly, the theological areas I present in this chapter are those that have been useful for my understanding as a scholar of theology and an American Orthodox woman. They come from deep reflection on Orthodox tradition as being already experienced and known by many women, as life-bestowing and liberating. That is, the thematic foci I discuss in this chapter are not imposed from some external Western feminist critique but rather exemplify how Orthodox tradition already includes and celebrates patriarchal subversion. I present them as contributions to what I hope will someday be a multitude of diverse women's theological voices reflecting and reclaiming their tradition and positions within it. I want to be very clear at the onset: for some women, the tradition and experience of Orthodoxy may be beyond repair, and they may for their own preservation and affirmation choose to sever or reimagine their spiritual lives outside of the formally recognized boundaries of Orthodoxy. Thinking with tradition may "nurture" some women but lead to a rupture with tradition for others.[2] For those who are looking for ways to advocate for themselves and their affirmation within a patriarchal faith tradition and practice, I invite consideration of the following three commitments as examples of how tradition can be centered as a further confession of the divine-human unity in Christ.

The first commitment reflects on the mysticism of human communion articulated so beautifully by Maria Skobtsova and referred to in the previous chapter: it is an iconodule commitment to the icon of God within oneself and others. The second commitment is to explore the examples of female saints within the Orthodox commemorative tradition whose holiness is manifest in righteous subversions of expected social and gender hierarchies. In Orthodoxy, it is not always the well-behaved women who are holy; rather there is a rich heritage of women's holiness being revealed and praised in defiance of patriarchal expectations. Saints who exemplify a rejection of earthly conditions model a type of holy disruption wherein humanity in communion with divinity is free from the expected constraints in the pursuit of greater expressions of love. The liberating impetus of some of these sources is still limited in their traditional and commemorative invocations and for unexamined reasons not extended into present-day action as an ideal of holy disruption, resistance, or righteous disobedience. Yet, even amid such constraints, these examples reveal that tradition has space for reconsidering the ways it is patriarchal and the ways it could be told on behalf of the historically marginalized. The third and final commitment is to the Paschal proclamation, that is, a determination to proclaim joy, life, and liberation "even to those that hate us."[3] This commitment shows a confession of what is offered to and proclaimed by women in Christ.

Each commitment draws on examples already anchored in what women are acknowledged to have done in tradition. In part, this is due to androcentric assumptions about them, but in refusal to let that be all or to let that determine how women relate and find empowerment in their examples, I raise these areas again here. There are sainted women iconodules, women who defied male authorities and androcentric gender expectations for their love of God, and women who first beheld and proclaimed the resurrection. These types of commitments demonstrate that there are resources for women from within tradition that may help Orthodox become advocates for women's voices, diversity, equality, and humanity in others and in themselves as a confession and defense of their Orthodox faith.

## ICONODULE COMMITMENT

The first approach, an iconodule commitment, is a theological commitment to protecting and honoring the divine image—in oneself and others.[4] Orthodox theology has frequently focused its anthropology and spiritual practices on understanding the human person in the "image and likeness of God."[5] While some patristic theologians equivocate on the completeness of women in the divine image, this has not been the consensus that has dominated in the tradition and shaped modern Orthodox theology. All human persons are created in the divine image and are therefore living icons of God. Orthodox theology is well known for its tradition of icon veneration and particular schools of iconography with associated spiritual practices and guidelines for creating new icons, that is, sacred imagery.[6] The Seventh Ecumenical Council in 787 affirmed that "the honor paid to the image passes over to the prototype, and whoever venerates the image venerates in it the hypostasis of the one who is represented."[7] There are indeed nuances that distinguish icons as material aesthetic objects presented intentionally to convey spiritual meaning and participative likeness manifest in imperfect living people. Yet the purpose of icons, "to reveal the true relationships between God and man," as Leonid Ouspensky writes, is the same for living and painted (Orthodox prefer the term "written") icons.[8] Similarly, the distinction between venerating the archetype of God manifest through the material depiction of sainted holiness and venerating the archetype of God manifest in human life is not easily made. Rather, much of Orthodox theology emphasizes the human calling and capacity for increasing divine likeness—that is, to ever improve the manifestation of God through the material.

Liturgically, the reverence offered to icons, the censing, the bowing, the kissing, are participative acknowledgments of the divine being mediated and imaged through the material, including the paintings on the church walls and the people standing in prayer. Skobstova explains, "During a service, the priest does not only cense the icons of the Savior, the Mother of God, and the saints. He also censes the icon-people, the image of God in the people who are present. And as they leave the church precincts, these people remain as much the images of God, worthy of being censed and venerated."[9] Skobtsova emphasizes that icons are not just inanimate objects but are present in the living human persons we encounter and that "our relations with people should be an authentic and profound veneration."[10] Thus, there is a theological precedent for a Christian obligation to protect the divine image and honor the icon within.[11] I offer a theological tradition and spiritual practice wherein women and others treat themselves as icons—not in the stylized and perhaps atemporal depictions of the face of Christ, but as internally bearing the image of God as a living icon—and should expect others to respect them in love as iconodules.[12]

I note here that this veneration of and in the other is not another type of idealism that contributes to gender essentialist views but rather seeks and venerates the particularity that is the person in their imperfect humanity with their potential to be realized in participating in divinity. As Cornelia Tsakaridou notes, "Christ's *hypostasis* (*prosopon*) unites his two natures and thus an image of him must show him as existing in these two natures fully, rather than as merely physical, finite being. It is therefore not enough to capture his human existence. An icon must also convey his divinity."[13] The same might be said of human persons, but it is not enough to see the other as a "soul" created by God worthy of veneration but also as a human already divinely loved and therefore worthy of love.[14] Not all humans are saints and therefore iconic in the sense of revealing in their holy lives a clear likeness to the divine archetype, but all humans are iconic in bearing the image of God within them.[15]

In considering human living icons, it is helpful to note that a material icon is no less worthy of veneration if it is damaged or poorly rendered. The image of God within it makes it holy. This means that every person is worthy of veneration, not on their own merits, but due to the one whose image they bear. Relatedly, the ability to recognize an icon depends not only on the likeness of its depiction but also on the spiritual ability of the one viewing it to know and recognize its likeness.[16] This means that if one does not perceive another as an icon of God, then there is spiritual work to be done on the part of the viewer. To be iconodulistic means supporting any measures of further beautifying the divine icon within as God has created it uniquely in that person, not as some external expectation or construct has determined it should be. Orthodox tradition contains stories of numerous icons being revealed rather than imaginatively constructed. This distinction is helpful when considering the icons in others so that one can avoid deterministically judging another or trying to make them into an image of how they think the person should be.[17]

Defending the divine image in oneself and others means reverencing and respecting the particular human person, the human creation, and the unique particularity of their hypostasis. If we recall Skobtsova's teaching, having an iconodule commitment means venerating God in people and also trying to adopt and honor God's love for them and love them the way God does and, I would suggest, even if it is directed toward one's self. Ascetic tradition encourages stripping down of the self in humility; this is not nihilistic but instead is the stripping away of sin and selfishness to reveal the person as God has willed it and as God has called the person to be united to Christ.[18] The spiritual direction to strip away the ego is intended to reveal more accurately the divine image. A spiritual leader should not shape a person in the way they think the person should be but instead as God has created and called the person to be uniquely in God's image. In light of the iconodule commitment, one should not be given more than one can bear or be forced to endure abuse under the pretense of pious obligation. An iconodule approach, I offer, should not be used as justification for avoiding external or self-correction, because ultimately the divine image is most glorified in divine similitude—which is something all Christians work toward and never fully attain. Those who seek help through confession or spiritual direction, however, should keep an iconodule commitment to protect the self as God has called that person to be, something that no one has the right to destroy or denigrate.

The love of the person as icon—here I mean love of the icon within, as Skobtsova urges—can serve as a balancing corrective to traditions of prioritizing humility and self-deprecation. For those whom Orthodox theology has taught that humility, obedience, and self-giving are preeminent virtues even among the already disenfranchised, it is important to affirm the ultimate un-Orthodoxy of fostering conditions of dehumanization and of enabling others to destroy an icon. Martyric witnesses may have shown there is holiness in suffering, but iconodules have taught there is holiness in protecting the divine image wherever it may be. The nun Theodosia famously led a group of women in casting down an imperial guard who was going to remove and destroy the icon of Christ above the Chalke Gate in Constantinople during the first wave of iconoclasm in the eighth century, the Empresses Irene and Theodora oversaw the overturning of the first and second waves of iconoclasm, respectively, and numerous women under modern communist persecution hid and protected family icons in their homes.[19] Women have an iconodule spiritual heritage that is worth centering in thinking constructively about aspects of tradition that can be used to argue for women's affirmation, inclusion, and equality, particularly in their incarnational humanity.

The protection and defense of the self in the face of dehumanization or abuse or denigration and even discrimination is not a self-justification of the sort "I am worthy" or "I deserve to be respected" based on any human accomplishment or characteristic but intrinsic to each human person. Humans are worthy of love, respect, compassion, and honor because God has created them out of love in his own image.[20] God already loves them. God already loves us. Iconodules work to defend this divine image and reiterate the necessity of its veneration by others as fundamental to Orthodoxy. Gender-based relationship abuses, misogyny, and objectification of the iconicity of another: often Orthodox reject such things but then ignore them as spiritual obedience, spiritual wisdom, and advice. Any way the tradition devalues or dehumanizes women gives room for using Orthodoxy to justify abuse, forced subordination, and acceptance of a secondary class, all of which, as I have shown, are theologically problematic. Within the commemorative, pastoral, and theological tradition of Orthodoxy, Beth Allison Barr's caution regarding her own Baptist tradition should be heeded: "Ideas that depict women as less than men influence men to treat women as less than men."[21] Orthodox Christians should do more to actively combat and correct misogynistic views as un-Orthodox on the basis of an iconodule commitment and on the basis of the incarnation.

No woman should be told being abused is her wifely duty. She first has a duty to protect the icon of Christ within her, and pious agency and self-determination might be realized in whatever way she finds possible. Orthodox Christians, women, in particular, can encounter their tradition with an acceptance of that which has passed down a rich spirituality and theology or meaningful forms of practice and religious experience but also have the iconodule commitment to hold it accountable and reject the spaces that have misrepresented them and led to their dehumanization. There are within Orthodox tradition resources for self-care and the undoing of patriarchal power. The iconodule commitment in this way offers an alternative within tradition that is theologically consistent and spiritually valuable, that can cultivate an Orthodox subject in ways that prompt humility and penitence to God—not to human-made constructs—and that can help one see oneself as loved by God, as an icon of God in the world.

If women and men adopt the practice of being iconodules in reference to others and themselves, then as a lover of the divine image one historically also protects, venerates, and defends the rightness of its veneration. Iconodule theology works not just for the right of icons to exist due to the incarnation, but the rich heritage of protecting the icons themselves from destruction out of love for the one they depict.[22] This too can be an attitude and an ideal for Orthodox striving that comes from its tradition and can be prioritized to protect the marginalized and at risk. Being an iconodule means loving the icon within and not purposefully abasing it or allowing it to be abased. It means expecting and protecting the dignity of the human person in the image of God universally, especially in those in whom the full iconicity has been traditionally called into question. The diverse incarnational realities (by this phrase, I mean taking seriously the full human and embodied experience) that shape humanity in our unique abilities to image God temporally and relationally to others should also not be obscured. As Vladimir Lossky observes, "Personhood belongs to every human being by virtue of a singular and unique relation to God who created him 'in His image.'"[23] Even though in stylized iconography there is often a blurring of the particular into a more atemporal liturgical or eschatological present, the uniqueness of the interior icon written by God is manifest in diversity.[24]

For even non-Orthodox scholars of gender and feminist theology, the iconodule commitment offers a fundamental recognition of the human as inherently worthy of dignity and respect regardless of activity or identity, perhaps even in light of these things. It also encourages agency and self-preservation as spiritual virtues and is theologically consistent. In traditions that do not have a theology of icon veneration, perhaps there is room to explore parallels at least of internally venerating the divine image and regarding individuals as living temples of the Holy Spirit based on scripture.[25] Certainly, for those in iconic traditions, it is relevant to draw on the theology of icons more directly, but the consequence is the same: an honoring and veneration of the divine in the human and not despite the human but as fully united to the human. This might support marginalized others in their efforts to preserve themselves even if it means removing themselves from or redefining the boundaries in relationships and environments that may otherwise appear religiously supported or expected but are personally experienced as iconoclastic. The iconodule approach provides a theological justification for prioritizing the divine image in oneself and others in a way that counters the ultimacy of the spiritual values of self-abasement and martyric self-giving. The person as an icon and divine encounter must be set first as a driving ethic of welcoming the marginalized into ecclesial participation and the lives of others. One can and should protect oneself and request respect for unique individuality as God has called one to be with spiritual and theological integrity. This approach works on behalf of the marginalized, in a liberating posture that acknowledges diversity and rejects any abuse or destruction of the divine image as religiously justified.

## HOLY SUBVERSION

A second aspect of tradition that is useful for providing theological justification for greater affirmation of women's agency and freedom from within tradition is the paradoxical subversion of worldly powers, expectations, and limits in Christ.[26] Orthodox hymns include celebration of the incarnational paradox of divine condescension.[27] Such celebration of God uniting Godself to lowly humanity, filling death with life, taking humanity to heaven in the ascension, and making the lowly "fishermen as most wise" in Pentecost shows a recurrence of celebrating the overcoming of presumed limits through the presence of divine power.[28] Mary is celebrated in this paradox as the virgin mother, as the container of the uncontainable, and as one "more spacious than the heavens."[29] A woman is at the heart of subverting expectations and limits for conception, birth-giving, motherhood, and, if one includes the traditions of her life after the crucifixion, apostolic leadership.[30] The realization of the lowly as empowered in Christ (Matthew 20:16) is a crucial aspect of Orthodox theology that can be further explored to justify centering the socially, traditionally, and even ecclesially marginalized (in this case, women). I will discuss more about the importance of centering the marginalized as a Christological confession of what is made possible and celebrated in the incarnation and resurrection, but here I focus on threads running through the tradition that celebrate subversion of normative hierarchies and gendered expectations.

There is a long history of saints (both male and female), from holy fools to virgin martyrs, who reject the authority and ways of the world to confess and witness their love and life in Christ.[31] There exists within

Orthodox spiritual commemorative tradition sainted exemplars who subvert and disobey presumed authorities and hierarchical structures. Subversion of expectations and worldly constructs is a hagiographic mode of conveying holiness—that with God one can be truly empowered, free, and so on. Although there are limits to what hagiography can be said to intend with such subversions when contextualized literarily and historically, I suggest such pious subversions also hold unexplored potential for an Orthodox feminist theology of liberation. Even as they might be hagiographically presented as "manly," many female saints are celebrated for independently choosing what to do with their lives and bodies even as they go against social norms. This trope, self-advocacy, and subversion toward divine liberation show the latent potential for valuing women's agency within Orthodox sources but, more significantly, the tradition of sanctified subversion of social, ecclesiastical, and gender hierarchies.

In this section, I present several hagiographic accounts of women who are praised for rejecting conformance to expected power structures and show that even though these examples of pious disobedience function more to identify power with God above worldly leaders than to give women a more generalized spiritual license for self-advocacy, in so doing, they also reveal that women empowered by their faith may act contrary to social and cultural expectations. Examples of subversive saints are somewhat limited by their situation related to androcentric spiritual concerns and phrasings, but they nevertheless indicate inversion of expectations of power within a spiritual framework, such that empowerment comes through communion with God rather than gender, clerical status, or social position. Christian women might find in these examples and others sainted justifications for rejecting oppressive authorities and models for casting off gendered limitations in realizing their potential callings in Christ. Individual hagiographic texts and depictions might be limited historically in terms of the types of values they can be said to endorse, but they are useful points of feminist reflection to imagine more widely the aspects of women's lives and experiences not included in the commemorative record. As an ongoing righteous subversion of the androcentric determination of tradition, Orthodox scholars and practitioners might ponder the real lives and experiences behind these texts and sainted figures and all the sainted forms of resistance and boldness left untold.

For example, given the common idealization in Orthodox tradition of voluntary suffering, it is perhaps unsurprising in the life of Mary/Marinos (ca. sixth/seventh century), a female saint who lives hidden as a eunuch in a men's monastery, that subversion of gender and perception of truth are deployed to bring about greater hardship for the saint. After being accused of fathering a child, Marinos accepts raising a child that is not his biologically.[32] However, he says, "I have sinned as a man," and replies to those who ask why he sits outdoors, "because I fornicated and have been expelled from the monastery." Yet Marinos is not a sinner in this way and in the text is not a man (the audience already knows that before entering the monastery, Marinos lived as a woman), so what this statement shows instead is a type of falsity and self-claimed subversion to bring about holiness.[33] Holiness is evident in this viewing and speaking of the self in ways that adopt reference to a spiritual rather than worldly conception of truth. In this instance, Marinos is subordinate to the situation of accused fatherhood, humbly accepting seemingly unjust consequences, and reinterprets the situation with a claim beyond its context in a way that subverts the authority of responding to human terms (Marinos did not fornicate, is not a "man" in the sense of the text, and is not the child's father), in favor of independently adopting an opportunity for spiritual progress (patience, penitence, and humility). Marinos rejects the expectations of the reader to reveal he is a woman and therefore innocent, to instead live as he feels called. Importantly, for this chapter, Marinos displays agency in discerning a path forward in holiness by understanding oneself foremost in relation to God and engaging on those terms rather than the limiting terms of the world. Marinos undoubtedly has sinned and in knowing himself as a sinner accepts the situation as a just punishment, yet the reader knows that Marinos is innocent of the crime of which he is accused. Marinos reframes and owns the sinfulness of the situation to apply it to the self and increase humility. The problematic dynamics related to the values of suffering and humility analyzed in chapter 3 are at play in this example, but so also is a liberating subversive reframing of what is true and possible by divine orientation.

Feminism requires a disruption of the patriarchal power and gender hierarchy that has historically rendered women limited and in subordinate positions compared to men. There is within Orthodoxy already such a disruption in its traditions of subversion of gender hierarchy and earthly assumptions of power. Orthodoxy prompts feminists to see within its tradition the celebration of inverting power expectations to reveal divine power at work even in those the world might marginalize. There is a way of reframing the situation much as Marinos does to make sense of unjust circumstances and apply them to oneself in a sanctifying way, and there is also a way of reframing to whom one is under authority and what divine zeal and love permits as righteous exceptions to expected hierarchies. Yet, while a mode of spiritual freedom and autonomy, subversion or even deception rendered true in a spiritual sense is only lauded in the tradition because it is a form of voluntary self-deprecation. The Marinos episode reveals subversive agency displayed in ways that simultaneously diminish the full humanity of the actor and spiritually advance it. Such ascetically motivated subversion and disruption of gender norms are valued, but they are troubling in response to the feminist claim of women being fully and equally human because they only laud women who advocate for placing themselves as the least of others.

Hagiographic depictions of holy subversions or reconstructions of reality such as that of the holy lie of Marinos do not lay out clear paths for women or call for an overthrowing of gender hierarchy categorically, yet they are worth serious interrogation for how they might serve to improve or restrict the lives of women and understandings of what is valued for women in the Orthodox tradition. One has to wonder, for example, in the case of the seventh-century life of Mary of Egypt and her numerous hagiographic variations if her retelling of her harlot-to-holiness life is accurate or an interpretation colored so much by penitence that it exaggerates sinfulness and then is sanctified by the church.[34] Is this an open trope known to the audience, which is used to holy people speaking about themselves in excessively disparaging ways as a model of holy self-reflection? Are we supposed to assume that any historical Mary's sinfulness was not as bad as she describes?[35] Why do we take her at her word? The hagiographer wants her depicted in this way, but is he also perhaps modeling a type of prescriptive holy self-reproach? After all, a desert saying states, "blessed is the monk who considers himself the 'offscouring of all things,'" which seems valued to the point of speaking in a way about God that exaggerates and names the self as the worst in humility, even when there are clear markers of holiness.[36] The desert father Abba Matoes notes this saying: "When I was young, I would say to myself: perhaps one day I shall do something good; but now that I am old, I see that there is nothing good about me." This is rendered meaningful in the Abba's knowledge of God as perfectly good, such that the term cannot be applied to himself in any sense.[37] Such attitudes are problematic, however, for those who are already involuntarily humbled by their station in life. I suggest that what subversive sainted stories evidence most consistently is that prioritizing communion with God in life reorients all other understandings so that they are open to new possibilities and greater expressions of truth in relation to God, who is Truth.[38] Speaking in a way that otherwise appears exaggerated or false by worldly standards in fact communicates something true about oneself in relation to God. Consequently, subversive stories help reinforce a shifted relation away from worldly expectations, understandings, power structures, and rules to a new self-identification foremost as a human communicant in divinity. This can be liberating and empowering.

Aside from tropes of subverting ostensible truth, there are more overt subversions of gender. There is a recurrence of female martyr saints who are unexpectedly smart and divinely emboldened to put down the "clever among the godless" through a rebuke of sinfulness and pointed defense of the faith in a way that inverts expected gender performance and subverts an expected gender hierarchy.[39] Numerous sainted late antique examples such as Perpetua, Thecla, and Catherine's hagiographies and hymns recall women martyrs giving speeches to put down an impious male authority and confound the opposing male intellectual arguments.[40] As explained in chapter 2, such women are celebrated for transgressing androcentric gender expectations, but importantly for this chapter, they are celebrated for subverting gender hierarchical norms of obedience and submission on behalf of defending their faith. Gender limits, like all limiting constructs, are overturned in communicating divine power. As participants in divinity, these women saints overcome the expectations of their humanity. Consequently, it seems logical that as a confession of divine-human unity, subversion of oppressive power structures might be normalized as a theological witness to the structure's or person's ultimate impotence if not participating in divinity and God's ultimate power.

The most well-known female hymnographer, Kassia, for example, famously theologically rebuffs the emperor Theophilos during the bride show organized by his mother. Theophilos taunts, "Through a woman [came forth] the baser [things]," blaming Eve for the fall, and Kassia wittily replies, "And through a woman [came forth] the better [things]," referring to the Theotokos.[41] Given that Theophilos was an iconoclast emperor, such a rebuke could be read as a gendered insult to the emperor (as if to say, Theophilos was upbraided by a woman), but Kassia's legacy suggests that she was an impressive poetic theologian in her own right. Nevertheless, the narrative celebrates a laywoman correcting the gendered taunt of an emperor with a theological claim. Kassia was not selected as the emperor's bride and instead founded a monastery and wrote poetry and hymns that persist even in present usage (with endorsement from the highly influential and iconophile Studite Monastery). Kassia exercises surprising authority over the emperor and is praised in holiness for censuring the cleverness of this man, rejecting marriage, and fulfilling a role dominated by men, as a hymnographer.[42] Kassia and her legacy do not subordinate themselves unquestionably to some sort of gender hierarchy, nor does she conform to a type of quiet monasticism. Instead, Kassia is a celebrated example of a woman piously displaying authority of faith and leaving a legacy of developing a voice for ecclesial participation and perspective. However, in this example, if the emperor were not an iconoclast, one could imagine Kassia being equally lauded for accepting the humbling remark of the emperor and remaining in modest silence. Her example nevertheless celebrates putting aside gendered expectations (silence, deference, marriage, etc.) to realize spiritual priorities.

There are other examples of hagiographers depicting female saints as having righteous zeal that leads them to disobedience or insubordination of male hierarchs, who—unlike the impious emperor—do not need rhetorical schooling to validate the faith and expression of the readers.[43] In identifying the true source of authority in divine reality, some female saints are lauded for successfully rejecting and exercising authority over the male clerics and leaders who would otherwise have authority over them. But, and there is a "but," such idealized pious subversions of male authority do not translate to liberation of women from patriarchy. Rather, Kassia and others are lauded for being exceptions due to their holiness. This is what licenses the humbling of the men around them; the female saints are divinely protected or divinely saved from male retribution because they are pious defenders of faith above earthly authority. Subversion of authority when it occurs in the home or the parish for anything less than purely pious martyric witness or divine zeal evident of saintliness is not more generally idealized. Equality of the sexes or subversion of oppressive or abusive situations is not lauded in hagiographies to show that God loves men and women and created them equally but rather appears as a rhetorical device to teach men that divine power can even exist in an otherwise foolish, worldly, or submissive woman in a way that might disrupt social expectations.[44] There may be other women's stories or other more meaningful truths to women's lives, but these are obscured, so what dominates instead is a narrative of independence and subversion written by and, perhaps more importantly, for men. Even where women's agency is highlighted or lauded according to an androcentric worldview, when motivated by their faith, it is celebrated nevertheless.

On behalf of righteousness, and divinely directed, these female saints serve to model that divine aims and presence allow women to break beyond patriarchal roles and oppression. Female saints' determination, boldness, agency, freedom, and choice to express their holiness in the face of adversity is ecclesially lauded, even if presented through an androcentric gaze. Orthodox hagiography and hymns honor female saints for freely making choices for themselves and their bodies, even if these commemorations are also patriarchally constrained. Women martyrs choose to suffer and have their bodies disfigured in disobedience to their husbands and fathers. Women ascetics choose to emaciate their flesh and live in celibacy. The tropes marking women's holiness are indeed reflective of patriarchal androcentric values, but the commemoration of women saints also includes a collective and public celebration of women's choices and freedom for witnessing to their faith. These women are holy, which is demonstrated in their actions, which are more like men's, or in a type of divinely relative gender reversal by which expectations of order, obedience, leadership, and so on, are inverted to reveal divine presence and power. This reversal has the potential to improve the status of women, as do the empowered ways women are presented, even if they are held in tension with the other tropes of valorized obedience and self-deprecation, a constant state of becoming fully human, virtuous suffering, and a theologically ingrained preference for ordered hierarchy over equality.

Present-day readers of Orthodox tradition, however, can reclaim interpreting tradition to both acknowledge the limits of what can be inferred historically and faithfully imagine the theological meaning of those examples more constructively. A long tradition of hymnic and poetic pious imagining within Orthodoxy supports subverting even historical knowledge and spiritually reflecting on women behind and left out of the texts.[45] Present-day Orthodox women already draw on female saints as models for their own lives in interpretive and imaginative ways that often go beyond what might be recorded and commemorated in the church.[46] If one reads and imagines sainted subversive exemplars through the paradoxical power of Christ, however, there is room to see how these subversive models of holiness might be understood more broadly to reflect a Christological similitude wherein greater freedom is realized precisely in the spaces where one expects its limits. One could certainly take these stories beyond their patriarchal and androcentric contextual limits and claim that such commemorative tropes theologically reinforce a present-day overcoming of limits imposed on the marginalized.

## PASCHAL PROCLAMATION

This brings me to the final thematic suggestion for refocusing theological reflection on supporting women from within an admittedly androcentric and patriarchal historical and present-day tradition: the Paschal proclamation. Pascha, the celebration of the resurrection in Orthodox Christianity, is the climax of the festal year. Celebrated annually, weekly, and by the saints daily, the resurrection of Christ is not just a remembrance, but a vocation to which "all peoples" are called to participate in and "rejoice."[47] Obviously, this is a calling for all Christians. However, intentionally recalling the joy, life, and freedom that have been offered in the resurrection can be useful for theologically advocating for those who are still categorically subjugated or systematically marginalized. The resurrection is not only the promise of a life to come but also the breaking in of liberation from all the *power* of everything that proclaims death (e.g., structures and systems of oppression) in the present. This, of course, does not mean that if we just believe enough in the resurrection of Christ all political and social oppressions will stop and that human death will no longer occur but rather that the power of those forces to control the interior meaning of human life (through fear, obligation, helplessness, social pressure, etc.)

is negated and recognized as false.[48] The ultimacy of anything other than radical freedom, love, and life in Christ is undone.

Such a perspective results in an affirmation of agency to act in a way that confesses this spiritual orientation and that should have real-world and political impacts. Athanasius remarks, "If one were to watch men and women and young children rushing and leaping towards death on account of their devotion to Christ, who is so silly . . . as to not understand and reason that it is Christ, to whom human beings are bearing witness, who provides and grants the victory over death to each, rendering it fully weakened in each of those having his faith and wearing the sign of the cross?"[49] I highlight this quotation not as a way of reinforcing a valorization of suffering and a martyric ideal that is already overly established in Orthodox tradition but to demonstrate the precedent of Christians being known for orienting themselves in a Paschal present to affirming life and rejection of the power of death as a confession of faith. This confession, for present-day Christian women, might take the form of self-preservation or care of the self as a testimony to Christ's life-bestowing gift to them. It could be a liberatory attitude of self-agency and reclaiming meaning in unavoidable suffering. It might be a persistent hope for change in a church that moves slowly toward its full proclamation of the Gospel. Not only is it as icons of Christ that women should defend their particularity, but also as those fully *living* in the possibilities offered in the resurrection and as a faithful confession of its universality.[50] What I suggest is not a naive false optimism in the face of systemic oppression or subjugation but rather a continual calling to mind and orientation to what is already accomplished for humanity in Christ and proclaimed in much of Orthodox worship.

Like the previous two areas of reflection, women are central to the tradition of the proclamation of Christ's resurrection. The myrrh bearers, for example, were "anticipating the dawn" to anoint the body of Christ and then instead go and proclaim the impossible and the unbelievable to the world (I might note, the androcentric world).[51] This is not to reinforce an essentialist role of proclamation just for women based on scriptural precedent but rather to reinforce their being already central to the tradition of proclaiming joy, life, and the victory of Christ to the whole universe when it was expecting death and mourning. The myrrh-bearing women in Orthodox commemoration effectively serve as apostles to the apostles, demonstrating the value of women's voices and contributions to the church and their ability to offer something central to the church that would otherwise be missing. The proclamation of the myrrh-bearing women who were other adds something to tradition that Orthodox now see as worth celebrating and valuable and that if the church only privileged the voices of men would be missing. Topping aptly remarks, "Jesus made a woman the 'first apostle' and the 'apostle to the apostles.' The male disciples, however, did not believe her (Mark 16:11), since traditionally women's witness was considered worthless.... And yet, two thousand years later, Christian faith and belief in the Resurrection depends solely on the testimony of women, from whose lips fell the first XRISTOS ANESTI (Christ is Risen)."[52]

I also note that such a determined commitment to proclaim (even if subversively) "Christ is Risen!" is not to deny the very real suffering that many in the church may experience. It may indeed be challenging to proclaim Pascha in a way that is spiritually meaningful for those who have experienced ecclesial marginalization. However, for others, it may be an anchor of spiritual hope, a way to generate commitment to realizing the life in the risen Christ; if there is some aspect of life that is not also proclaiming the life and freedom offered in Christ, then it needs to be overcome. This is not some sort of delayed expectation of joy that will come in the afterlife but a witness of divine power breaking into and offering life even in the present. Christ is risen, so the power of patriarchy is already undone.

Two aspects of the Paschal proclamation may be highlighted in the Orthodox tradition: universal joyful freedom offered in Christ and Christ descending into the uttermost depths to raise up those held there.[53] The Paschal proclamation unites the iconodule commitment to affirm the self as valued in Christ and is the epitome of subverting the expectations of the world by the presence of divine power. It sees Christ as descending to the lowest space of captivity and offering those there liberation through his own unifying and liberating presence.[54] The Paschal proclamation sees Christ as working alongside women and already offering women freedom from the bonds of patriarchal androcentrism and its vestiges.

The resurrection may be a celebrated reflection point of resistance to a world, a society, or a church that might proclaim death or limitation to another. Women and marginalized others could take up the resurrection as a sign of victory and urge that their participation in the Paschal celebration be affirmed. One of the Paschal hymns sings, "Though Thou didst descend into the grave, O immortal One, yet didst Thou destroy the power of Hades, and didst arise as victor, O Christ God, calling to the myrrh-bearing women, Rejoice, and giving peace unto Thine Apostles, O Thou Who dost grant resurrection to the fallen."[55] Pascha is universal. In this hymn, however, Christ tells the women to "rejoice" and gives "peace" to the apostles. A feminist theological reading of this difference might be one that sees it as if Christ is affirming women's joy and cause of rejoicing at being liberated from subjection and telling the male apostles to peacefully accept that this indeed undoes their patriarchal privilege. Consequently, women choosing to affirm themselves fully when they are faced with a proclamation of effacement is a confession of the universality of the resurrection. In terms of ascetic instructions to women, this resurrection proclamation is somewhat lacking if it does not consider lived realities. Subduing women who are already subdued does not proclaim the freedom from oppressive patriarchal structures of death in the resurrection. It is more consistent with proclaiming the resurrection to reject subordination to gendered systems of control and power, as an expression of being no longer under the power of death but life united to Christ.

Calling to mind the Paschal proclamation is also useful for rejecting the claiming of power that is sometimes negatively associated with feminism. A Paschal approach instead proclaims that women and all are called to an equal celebration of and participation in the resurrection of Christ.[56] For women who have been hurt by the church, this might be a mode of liberation from the power of resentment and active resistance to the seeds of anger that might have power over them. It is certainly right for women to feel anger and frustration and to meet this with action in a way that they find consistent with their spiritual situation, but they might also choose to refuse the shortcomings of those who seek to steal from them their Paschal joy. Instead, they might, as the myrrh-bearers, proclaim it all the more loudly "to the disciples"—that is, proclaim by their own lives the liberation affirmed in the resurrection of Christ to the rest of the church. This is not a misogynistic type of telling women to smile and be happy in a system of oppression but to resist that system from determining them and having them mistake the structures of the world for the freedom already offered in Christ. Women's joy should be affirmed.[57]

And their proclamation of their participation in Pascha as a proclamation of Christ on behalf of women's freedom, equality, and divine potential realized in the church should be heard.

To address in a practical manner the issue of patriarchal androcentric perspectives within Orthodox tradition, the Paschal proclamation reminds Orthodox believers to listen to women, for it is to them that Christ first appeared. Much of Orthodox theology is anchored in the authority of priests, hierarchs, and monastics, with male voices being significant and often entangled with an internalized patriarchy that results in a not-so-subtle exclusion, diminishment, or silencing of women. Men are privileged with being prospective ordinands in seminary education, and women are welcome but remain optional, floating in a man's world. When one considers who is at the margins of theology, one is referring to who is recognized and expected to have authority on theological issues rather than who is actually at the center of the church. One might think of the many women who attend church and have their own ways of knowing, which are unacknowledged in official church statements and representations. There is an exclusion based on gender, among other characteristics and categories, that renders women and women's insights less important. Remembering Christ's own example of appearing first in a woman and to women should make one attentive to the theological expressions of women. Theology as a discipline and a practice, at both the parish and synodal levels, cannot be a "boys club," for this has the theological implication that God is not able to be known by, born, proclaimed, or imaged in a woman—all of which are inconsistent with Christology. Yet there is little initiative to address the representative gender disparity in the thinking of the church as *a matter of theological importance*.

The social reasons for the dominance of a certain class of male theologians in many cultures are no longer valid. Imagine if Orthodox Christians were at the forefront of advocating for women's education, equality, and inclusion because of the incarnation, resurrection, and belief in their potential for deification. What a Paschal proclamation that would be! Even where women might not be professional theologians employed by a seminary or university, women's understandings of God and their own tradition are important to hear. Men speaking about or on behalf of women in the church to reinforce certain values of patriarchy is not the same as women speaking for themselves in a way that reflects their knowledge of being uniquely and equally valued, divinely liberated from oppression, and full communicants in divinity. In confessing the power of God to overcome, to manifest in impossibility, and to rise from the dead, Orthodox should seek God in the historically ignored and unexpected and be unafraid of change that reflects the commitment to honoring and acknowledging the image of God in all of humanity and proclaiming the resurrection.

This chapter explores three areas that feature women working within tradition to confess their faith against the norms of the times and resisting the limits of what men have told them they could be. These are centered in tradition. Reclaiming them through a feminist theological premise is not a break from tradition but a building on and contribution to it. By adopting an iconodule commitment to others and to oneself, it is possible to advocate for oneself theologically. In addition, prioritizing preserving and further beautifying the divine image within helps counter a tradition of ascetic spirituality that can be destructive if not carefully safeguarded. A hagiographic tradition that includes sainted examples of subverting social, ecclesial, and gendered expectations in pursuit of expressing divine love and self-identification provides precedent for women to exercise autonomy as a mode of being foremost oriented to God. By living in a way that negates the authority of worldly constructs and orders, women can reclaim their own lives and self-expression while prioritizing their identities as known through communion with God rather than social expectations. Last, the Paschal proclamation provides a reminder of the importance of women's voices and God being known through them. It includes rejecting the power of any system or structure that proclaims death and instead overcoming it with a proclamation of life in Christ. This might take the form of self-advocacy, affirmation of one's liberty, or the rejection of the power of patriarchy to control one's life in Christ. All three of these commitments exemplify the type of reclaiming that is possible when women are acknowledged to be full participants in divine-human unity and live their lives as a confession of that faith.

The points presented in this chapter are not exhaustive but demonstrate the theological resources latent within the Orthodox tradition to argue on behalf of including, listening to, and affirming women theologically. Although much of tradition, as I argued in the first two chapters of this book, is entangled in problematic patriarchal and androcentric domination, it does not need to be reduced to and by its limits. The patriarchal androcentrism of Orthodox tradition is not something that can just be undone and no longer perpetuate itself without intentional advocacy for women. Women already are engaging in their tradition in ways that demonstrate active (even if unacknowledged) reclamation, resistance, and reinterpretation of tradition. Although I certainly do not want to put the burden of undoing patriarchal androcentrism on women alone, there are resources within tradition for women to advocate for themselves with theological continuity. Even though the commitments I highlighted in this chapter come from androcentric contexts, the myrrh bearers and their Paschal proclamation, the defense of living and material icons amid historical and figurative iconoclasm, and hagiographic subversions of male authority and gender expectations in holiness are indicative of the rich resources possible within tradition for resisting the single story of the "patriarchal woman."[58]

# Conclusion

This book started with the critique of the religious construction of women within Orthodox Christian sources by taking seriously the systemic and structural effects of androcentrism and patriarchy on shaping gendered spiritual values. Certainly, people have used tradition and what they think will produce divinizing outcomes for others to subject women to patriarchy. This is the path to holiness, they might say, or this is how an Orthodox woman is supposed to be. Perpetuating visions of prescriptive gender categories truncate the reality of women as fully human unique persons called by God to participate in the divine-human unity of the Body of Christ. With Orthodox Christianity's identity and theological formulation so deeply tied to continuity with tradition and inseparable from broader cultural experiences, the radical excising of the patriarchal past would do nothing to resolve the tensions in the critique I offered in the first four chapters. The historical androcentrism of Orthodox tradition and even the present ecclesial structures as limiting its usefulness for women need to be acknowledged. With such acknowledgments in mind, Christians cannot uncritically turn to what the fathers say, what the church has always done, or what canons teach to affirm women without reflection and apophatic hope about where God was that was not recorded because it was in the life of women, or how God was speaking to the church but ignored because it was in the voice of a woman.

I acknowledge in the critique I offer that I disrupt not just approaches to tradition but also what could be conceived by some as a culture and heritage that are meaningful because they have been meaningful to loved ones who have come before. Tradition is also a source of memory, and it can be localized to how individuals have told, lived, or otherwise passed on tradition. I hope in this case readers will reflect again on the varieties of ways Orthodox tradition might be understood and how theology can be better articulated when we look to those often unacknowledged yet most meaningful sources of its preservation (perhaps in the lives of many women) with greater authority. Accordingly, I have argued that the Orthodox tradition has within it theological justifications and spiritual resources for unequivocally affirming the full and equal humanity of women in a way that is consistent with tradition and pushes beyond its presumed patriarchal limits. I have explored possible Orthodox approaches for beginning to overcome the challenges of constructing and commemorating a patriarchal "woman" and the privileging of androcentrism that continues even in contemporary tradition.

Acknowledging that the affirmation of the full humanity of women is essential for theological consistency but is something that has been traditionally eclipsed, I suggest kenotic, apophatic, hesychastic, iconodule, and Paschal commitments for an Orthodox theology on behalf of women, as well as other marginalized individuals and groups within the Orthodox tradition. These are just several theotic approaches that come from within Orthodox theology and spiritual practice; they do not fully or immediately resolve patriarchal tensions in Orthodoxy but have the potential to develop more inclusive and doctrinally consistent affirmations of those who have been othered in the sources and practices of tradition. Recognizing the pervasive hold patriarchal androcentrism has on the sources of Orthodox tradition, as well as its theological problems, necessitates its intentional rejection and the affirmation of its opposite. I am not rejecting tradition or the authority of the church overall but rather stressing the importance of recognizing the limits of what it has to say about women because it was primarily filtered through men or at least into an ecclesial system that prioritizes upholding the authority of men.

Nevertheless, I have claimed that if grounded both within feminist affirmation of women as full human beings and within Orthodox theology, commemorations, and spiritual practices, patriarchal androcentrism does not need to dominate Orthodoxy. Unless Orthodox Christians acknowledge and intentionally unsay the androcentrism of their tradition, the tradition itself is problematic for women because it asks them to participate in an identity-shaping religious system that disadvantages them structurally and reinforces their subordination. It denies to them the very Paschal message that it asserts to proclaim.

When there is recognition and repentance of the dominating influence of patriarchal androcentrism on tradition and on Orthodox communities, of tradition's resistance to being used to better support and advocate for women, of the church's subtle silencing, ignoring, devaluing and subjugating of women, of the Christian community for remaining a silent bystander to or an overt enforcer of cultural and social misogyny—when all that is recognized as being antithetical to the life in Christ, then change that renders the church and her heritage as more divinely communicative can take place. When Christian tradition is referred to by the faithful to center and intentionally privilege the marginal in Christological imitation, then the ecclesial community is doing the work of Christ. It is in this type of activity, of working to realize all others as participants in the divine-human unity of Christ and to confess the reality of the incarnation as deification for all classes, races, genders, and peoples, that an appreciation and application of tradition as living—because it is bestowing life—is possible.

Orthodox Christians need to recognize and treat women as fully redeemed, fully human, fully capable of deification to affirm the incarnation and its soteriological effects and affirm the universality of the resurrection. Women also need to be affirmed in this way to actively dismantle a type of patriarchal power that entitles itself based on gender rather than Christologically emptying itself on behalf of elevating those who are socially othered. Any way that the tradition devalues or dehumanizes women and gives room for using Orthodoxy to justify abuse, forced subordination, and acceptance of a secondary class within the church is theologically problematic because it subverts the universality of the incarnation and resurrection. Thinking along with these commitments provides ways that Orthodox theologians might acknowledge the patriarchal heritage and structures of their tradition, yet still find within it a usable past and liberating present. They suggest highlighting spiritual practices of empowerment through vulnerability that are balanced by theological justifications for honoring self-preservation and attending to the challenges of difference by promoting a love of diversity and fundamental humble openness to encountering and honoring the divine united to the humanity of the other.

With the critiques and suggestions offered in the previous pages, I am not looking for women to just be included more fully in the patriarchal social order as post-Enlightenment free rational subjects. I am also seeking to pull an initial thread to undo the tapestry of tradition that has given rise to multiple forms of accepted (and even sacred) marginalization within the church. Throughout this book, I have pointed to the problem that in much of Orthodox tradition women are not regarded as fully human in the same way men are. As a solution to this problem, I do not propose that women should be treated and thought of as the same as men, over men, as counterparts to men, or to reinforce gender binarism. That would ignore aspects of meaningful difference and further inscribe likely androcentric privileges and hierarchical competitions of power. In much of the tradition, men of various classes, races, and other statuses and identities are not fully recognized in their humanity and diversity either. Moreover, any Orthodox theology addressing gender must provide space to elevate the numerous individuals who do not fit in such artificial and essentialist binary expectations and boundaries, yet have been subject to the oppression of patriarchal androcentrism. Ultimately, the response to seeing the false and problematic constructions of women in the tradition cannot be one of seeking mere parity or redefining women. Instead, such recognition should prompt a reconsideration of how these and other absences, constructions, practices, and determinations within religious sources reflect spaces and ways in which human power and preferences elide rather than illumine the divine image in humanity, the full confession of the incarnation, and witness the unbounded work of the Holy Spirit in the church.

The analysis of the problematic patriarchal nature of Orthodox tradition, its theological effects, and its resources for subverting the seeming dominance of its androcentric heritage might appear to some people as a type of interpretive gymnastics. Indeed, I offer suggestions for ways

Orthodox might realign their praxis with theological understanding by drawing on varied aspects and features of the Orthodox theological, commemorative, and spiritual tradition. I emphasize that these are not the only approaches and model a type of feminist reclaiming of an otherwise patriarchally framed past. Beyond a mere feminist assertion that the androcentric ways of theology, spiritual texts and practices, and tradition need not be the official narrative of tradition, I show that tradition can be a resource for and on behalf of everyone if Christians privilege the communication and confession of God united to humanity. These approaches reflect a theological method of drawing on tradition by prioritizing confessing the divine-human unity of Christ and the potential for all, especially the marginalized, to participate in Christ. This confession should orient the Orthodox view of tradition.

If we reflect on Orthodox beliefs about God and God united to and on behalf of humanity and use that as the lens to see and use tradition, then it becomes more about conceiving tradition as that which produces humans in communion with God and confesses God in communion with humanity and what that starting point does for our understandings of ourselves, each other, and how we interact and less about preserving continuity with a past in order to construct identities as *we expect* them to be. This emphasis on divine-human unity suggests not only divinization, but that any imposed limitation on the humanity of women is also an imposed limitation on God. The communication of properties and Orthodox doctrinal affirmation that in Christ there is a true unity between divinity and humanity means that to say women should be subordinate to men would be to say that Christ united to some should be subordinate to Christ united to others based on gender—creating an inequitable hierarchy within humanity's capacity for divine communion. If, on the other hand, one privileges the confession and communion of divinity united to humanity and humanity united to divinity inclusive of the most marginalized, then every aspect of Orthodox tradition is salvifically oriented. Tradition becomes useful for those it has been used against, and the church becomes more Christ-like because it unequivocally affirms Christ's divine-human unity as universal. The paradox celebrated in the incarnation, the inversion of expectations, the inversion of power structures, the undoing of subjugation, and the overcoming of the power of death needs to be confessed in the Orthodox use of tradition. In the previous chapters, I have demonstrated what that confession might look like and how it might bear the fruit of fostering and proclaiming divine-human communion: it affirms women in their humanity and their participation in divinity. If women are fully human in the same way men are and are fully united to Christ, then they cannot be categorically subjugated to others—only voluntarily and freely choose to be on behalf of others in humility as Christ is. Being united to Christ and a voluntary participant in him offers a mutuality where God is also voluntarily active in the person, working in her to become increasingly united to him. A divine-human unity starting point allows one to see and engage with tradition in terms of its divinizing potential rather than its human shortcomings.

But why should the women stay in what remains a frustratingly slow-moving, male-led religious structure? My personal answer to the "why stay" question is based deeply in my own experience of God through the teachings, traditions, and practices of Orthodoxy as love that cannot possibly be limited and is always at work in undoing our limitations. I do not have a universal answer to the question, but I offer this book as one example of acknowledging the limits and resources of Orthodox tradition for women in a critical assessment and constructive reclaiming of a woman's right to critique, redefine, and draw on her religious tradition for herself. It is my hope that it will soon be one among many. Granted, within Orthodoxy, tradition is anchored in consensus of the church; it is not individual interpretation and meaning-making. Yet it is also anchored in the historical witness and acknowledgment of God at work in the church through individual human persons. Women may not be represented enough, or on their own terms, or through their own voices in tradition, but they are still a part of it. Bringing forward and reclaiming tradition in women's lives, imagining women (as fully human) beyond what is depicted in the historical record, and listening to women share how tradition is for them, for us, and for all—despite all its human limitations—is a feminist theological and deeply Orthodox approach. It is a seeking of God at work in the world and a greater understanding of divinity united to humanity, particularly in the lives of women.

While some feminist theologians have found Christianity irredeemably patriarchal, I find within Christianity the theological resources and justifications to begin to overcome and address the problems of its patriarchal heritage and work on behalf of women and others whom it has previously marginalized and rendered partial. Likewise, while some Orthodox might see the critical reassessment of tradition in these pages as problematically "innovating," I have tried to show that thinking about women in tradition through engagement with external contemporary premises can foster greater internal consistency. Orthodoxy gives a space to recognize the fallenness and ongoing sinfulness of humanity while simultaneously realizing that the ongoing perfection in Christ is already available. That is, Orthodoxy has within its spiritual heritage a central admission of penitence of human failings alongside faith in divine possibility, and this includes a recognition of the problems of the past that is not stagnant or triumphalistic but in constant penitential development toward greater divine similitude. Acknowledging that the affirmation of the full humanity of women is essential for theology but has been traditionally undermined in much of Orthodox tradition is not a contradiction; rather it points to an area in need of spiritual development. In continuity with the spiritual practices of Orthodoxy and its theological claims to ongoing theosis, this tradition has resources for honoring the other in the divine image, even amid a living construction of tradition that struggles consistently to do so. The systemic and structural change of Orthodox tradition is grounded in a theological center of affirming divine-human unity, of theosis, and that is personal. Such a unitive centering of affirming full humanity with transformative divine participation helps elucidate that undoing the limits of patriarchal androcentrism is first and foremost through the people of the church.

In the introduction to this book, I noted that while some branches of Christianity have developed robust feminist theological perspectives, Orthodox feminist theological discourse has yet to develop a response to its patriarchal heritage and present practices.[1] Existing Orthodox engagement with feminist theology and gender theory has proved insightful, but developing approaches to address uniquely Orthodox feminist concerns from within Orthodox theology has gained little traction and is often met with significant resistance or dismissal from those who lead and participate in the church.[2] Framing Orthodox theology as already being universal (and therefore already inclusive of women's or other marginalized individual's concerns), or transcendent of such embodied, temporal, secularly constructed, and gendered differences as being at all theologically significant, permits a continuation of a commemorative and theological tradition that in its presentation of women is problematic. Alternately, framing Orthodoxy as above or antithetical to feminism in any conception equally side-steps addressing Orthodox sources and practices that perpetuate a subtle, sometimes not subtle, sacralized misogyny. To critique the tradition as patriarchal in this way does not mean that is unusable but, as other feminist theologians have demonstrated, that it warrants different approaches by women that acknowledge and unsay its impetus to control them. The suggestions I have offered in the previous two chapters, however, are not just for women to make sense of a tradition that otherwise restricts them. The acknowledgment of the patriarchal androcentrism of tradition, the problems it poses, and the theological resources Orthodoxy offers to overcome them in becoming more communicative of who and how they confess God to be is for everyone. In reflecting on the limits of tradition for women, perhaps this book will raise other issues that need to be addressed and unsaid—not to undo tradition, but to find a more authentic theological expression of it for *all* the members of the Body of Christ.

Acknowledging the constructive suggestions of this book as a start does not diminish those who have come before or erase their contributions but rather invites reaction and construction in ways that produce new thinking. Thus, I invite the reader to wrestle with the critiques and approaches I have offered and use them as an interlocutor for developing further Orthodox theological engagements from traditionally marginalized perspectives and greater interdisciplinary and comparative insights into the limits of affirming equality while maintaining patriarchy in other religious contexts. For the scholarship and theology of women specifically, I note the importance of the robust scholarship on women's lived religious lives in the anthropological, ethnographic, and sociological disciplines that emphasize the partiality of conceiving tradition through a patriarchal or androcentric lens and suggest a more receptive, anticipative, and inclusive tradition is at play that calls for acknowledgment of theological consistency. Scholarship on women's religious lives in history, anthropology, ethnography, and sociology is important for developing Orthodox theology that honors and affirms women's full humanity, because these fields help give voice to the diversity of ways women participate in and enliven their tradition that have historically been ignored or diminished.[3] By attending to the fullness of women's humanity and welcoming its diverse forms and expressions, we can better appreciate the diverse and empowering ways women have participated in, subverted, and come to know Orthodox Christianity as their own. This too is an important theological source and aspect of undoing the patriarchal grasp on tradition.

In the study and practice of Orthodox Christianity, more needs to be done to explore the ways patriarchal androcentrism poses theological and practical problems for women and the whole church. This book has focused primarily on historical commemorative examples of women and spiritual values—hymns, hagiography, and spiritual instructions or sayings—and briefly engaged liturgical contexts, iconography, and doctrine. Attending to such sources brings to light dissonance between how an androcentric patriarchal leadership might conceive and communicate about gender and the multivalent impacts such constructions and expressions have on women. Other genres, periods, cultural particularities, and ways of framing tradition could be analyzed to find resonances with or challenges to the observations I have made and the responses I have offered. Perhaps the critiques of androcentrism offered in the previous chapters and the approaches for overcoming existing structures of patriarchalism might be adapted or applied to Orthodox theology as a discipline, not to mention reshaping conversations about androcentrism in liturgical/pastoral contexts and prompting explorations of the spiritual value of human equality. Theology needs to be broadened to include more than clerical, monastic, and academic voices. This is not to dilute a rigorous study of the religious intellectual tradition but to more capaciously and faithfully account for the diverse aspects of the incarnational reality in which theology might be reflected. Such a move might include more women's voices and different types of theological reflections that include more personal and lived connections. Similarly, religious studies scholars might highlight the alternative ways tradition is engaged by diverse women and elevate issues of equality among marginalized members of and beyond the Orthodox community. Scholarship on Orthodox women's religious lives and understandings can reveal a new understanding of tradition, one that more fully includes the actual rather than constructed lives of women.

The analysis and reflections in this book prompt a rethinking of religious constructions of gender and their theological entanglement beyond

Orthodox Christianity. For scholars and practitioners of religions with a patriarchal past, this book offers a model for taking seriously the androcentrism of still-influential traditional sources and its impact on belief and current practices. Rather than dismiss Orthodoxy as obviously patriarchal and therefore simplistic in terms of gender, the examples I have drawn on demonstrate the dynamic ways gender can function to communicate power and religious values historically and into the present—even if bearing limits for equality. The significance of gender for communicating and cultivating spiritual ideals should not be underestimated, and the significance of spiritual commitments for cultivating more affirming openness cannot be overstated. The notion that powerful and prominent women in religious traditions are not androcentric must be rejected, but at the same time such exemplars should not be reduced only to their androcentric constructions. The examples from Orthodox commemoration as well as a kenotic conception of patriarchy model a subversion of normative power and gender expectations to communicate spiritual values. The power the Orthodox feminists seek is not some sort of male or clerical power to control but the divine power to liberate, create, and realize iconicity through communion with its archetype. There is a salience and hierarchy of religious and gender identities that is inflected by prioritizing spiritual progress but that is nevertheless inflected by social and ecclesial realities of difference. Attending to the ways gender, power, and the realization of the self are shaped *religiously* is important for understanding and addressing seemingly sacred traditions of inequality.

I hope that the preceding chapters show the insights that can be gained about Orthodoxy from engaging with a feminist premise and one that is already theologically significant for Orthodoxy (that women are fully and equally human) but also that Orthodoxy has valuable resources for engaging in a broader feminist theological discourse with other Christian denominations and sister churches. For example, Orthodox theology's emphasis on the incarnation and divine-human communion provides doctrinal justifications for affirming the human body and mediating between the imperfect culturally specific conditions and the liberative and affirming divine ideal. Thinking alongside Orthodoxy's conception of salvation as theosis also validates a process of ongoing development toward greater divine likeness, which negates any justification of an oppressive religious status quo. The theology of humans as bearers of the divine image is shared across Christian traditions, but Orthodoxy shows the possibilities of recognizing that image and honoring it in embodied and transformative ways. Last, the diversity of sources and practices that inform Orthodox theology shows that theology is living and appreciates the multivocality of a tradition, not just its scriptures or official documents, and allows space for creative reclamation and response. Some feminist theologians already engage in this type of work. However, the unboundedness of the Orthodox apophatic approach to theology and tradition might also be useful for unsaying what otherwise appear as fixed or authoritative boundaries.

Although this book will likely prove unsatisfactory to some, I offer it as a sincere attempt to make sense of how gender, patriarchy, theology, and tradition within Orthodoxy can be productively informed by critically reflecting on the insights of gender and feminist studies. While Orthodox theology equivocates on its conception of gender, adopting the normative view of gender's performative and constructed nature allows recognition of its multivalence in Orthodox commemorations. Orthodox leaders may claim the inherent dignity of all, but the androcentric privilege and structural impact of patriarchy on the religious construction and practices of women reveal deeply embedded inequality and marginalization. Considering misogyny and patriarchy in terms of the effects women experience and sources evidence, rather than feelings men have, provides a method for acknowledging the problematic impact of androcentrism on the church even when perpetuated by sainted men and women. Overall, this book's analysis, critiques, connections, and suggestions prompt a conversation that is greatly needed in Orthodoxy to make sense of how gender, patriarchy, theology, and tradition can be engaged to promote more inclusive and affirming religious values.

I close with a personal and what I see as a particularly Orthodox feminist reflection. In bringing life into the world, as a woman, as a mother, I have, like many others, quite literally torn my body apart to allow something more vibrant and beautiful, full of potential, and in need of care to enter into a space that I, along with those who helped me, brought forth. In birth and caregiving, the body is sacrificed, the shape distorted in some ways forever, and the drain on the body to raise and foster life is perhaps just beginning. But the sacrifice is offered with joy, anticipation, and persistent hope. In some ways I present this book to Orthodox, feminist, gender, and theological studies with a similar sense of giving space to change. I know it will be torn apart, it needs to be torn apart, to make way for something more vibrant, for discussions with fuller potential, and for the next generation of scholarship that has been born out of pushing back against the disagreements, lacunae, and places where this book and what it offers fails to take into account. In offering it this way, I do not apologize for it but rather am hopeful of a future that takes seriously women's voices and the voices of others who are underrepresented, even where they question tradition itself. May this too be an iconic witness in its claims.

# NOTES

## INTRODUCTION

1. There are a few prominent saintly "mothers" in this tradition; however, the "patristic" voices certainly dominate. This volume focuses on Eastern Orthodox tradition, which has some significant overlap with Oriental Orthodox traditions but also significant variation. On problematizing the term "Eastern Orthodox," see Zachary Ugolnik, "Names Matter: How to Better Represent the Orthodox Churches in Textbooks and the Academy," *Journal of Religion* 96.4 (2016): 506–43.

2. "The Mission of the Orthodox Church in Today's World," Official Documents of the Holy and Great Council of the Orthodox Church, June 26, 2016, https://www.holycouncil.org/-/mission-orthodox-church-todays-world. See women's reflections on this hierarchical meeting in Carrie Frederick Frost, ed., *The Reception of the Holy and Great Council: Reflections of Orthodox Christian Women* (New York: Greek Orthodox Archdiocese of America, Department of Inter-Orthodox, Ecumenical, and Interfaith Relations, 2018).

3. The petition to include women in the Council received over one thousand signatures and was sent to the Ecumenical Patriarch. See Patricia Bouteneff, "Create a special delegation of women as consultants at the Pan-Orthodox Council," change.org, accessed January 27, 2023, https://www.change.org/p/centreorthodoxe-gmail-com-create-a-special-delegation-of-women-as-consultants-at-the-pan-orthodox-council.

4. "Theotokos," meaning "God-bearer," is a title used in Orthodox Christianity for the Virgin Mary as affirmed in the Third Ecumenical Council in Ephesus in 431.

5. Certainly, there are more robust and contested ways of understanding tradition, e.g., David Bentley Hart, *Tradition and Apocalypse: An Essay on the Future of Christian Belief* (Grand Rapids, MI: Baker Academic, 2022); these will be engaged in subsequent chapters. See also Cornelia Tsakiridou, *Icons in*

*Time, Persons in Eternity: Orthodox Theology and the Aesthetics of the Christian Image* (Burlington, VT: Ashgate, 2013). Tsakiridou explains tradition as "the ongoing creative synergy of divine and human activity in ecclesial life" and says that "despite some critical voices, the prevailing view of tradition equates it with the animating energy and presence of the Holy Spirit in the life of the Church" (22).

6. For a discussion of the "dynamism of tradition," see Vladimir Lossky, "Tradition and Traditions," in *In the Image and Likeness of God*, ed. John Erickson and Thomas Bird (Crestwood, NY: St Vladimir's Seminary Press, 1974), 140–68, 159.

7. Doxastikon of the Eighth Eothinon, "The 11 Resurrectional Matins (Eothina) Exapostilaria, Theotokia and Doxastica," Greek Orthodox Archdiocese of America, accessed March 20, 2024, https://www.goarch.org/-/the-11-resurrectional-matins-eothina-exapostilaria-theotokia-and-doxastica.

8. For the centrality of the relationship between what is believed and what is prayed in contemporary Orthodox theology, see Alexander Schmemann, *Introduction to Liturgical Theology* (Crestwood, NY: St Vladimir's Seminary Press, 1966).

9. I discuss this issue especially in chapter 2, as well as how patriarchal androcentrism shapes Marian devotion (especially in liturgical contexts) in chapters 3 and 4.

10. On liturgical subject formation in historically Orthodox Byzantine contexts, see Derek Kruger, *Liturgical Subjects: Christian Ritual, Biblical Narrative, and the Formation of the Self in Byzantium* (Philadelphia: University of Pennsylvania Press, 2014).

11. See the richly diverse ways women engage their religious identities with agency and autonomy in various parts of the Orthodox world in Ina Merdjanova, ed., *Women and Religiosity in Orthodox Christianity* (New York: Fordham University Press, 2021).

12. For an overview of Orthodox reflections on the female diaconate, see John Chryssavgis, Niki Papageorgiou, Marilyn Rouvelas, and Petros Vassiliadis, eds., *Deaconesses: A Tradition for Today and Tomorrow* (Brookline, MA: Holy Cross Orthodox Press, 2023); and for a brief summary of past and present developments, see Carrie Frederick Frost, *Church of Our Granddaughters* (Eugene, OR: Cascade Books, 2023), 82–97. The ordination in Harare, Zimbabwe, on May 2, 2024, of Angelic Molen to the diaconate with the support of the Alexandrian Synod, however, is hopeful for this office's renewal.

13. Judith Bennett, *History Matters: Patriarchy and the Challenge of Feminism* (Philadelphia: University of Pennsylvania Press, 2006), 54.

14. Nadiezda Kizenko, "Feminized Patriarchy? Orthodoxy and Gender in Post-Soviet Russia," *Signs* 38.3 (2013): 595–621; Anne Marie Adams, "Naming and Re(claiming) Feminism in Orthodoxy: Voicing the Gender and Religious Identities of Greek Orthodox Women" (PhD diss., DePaul University, 2021).

15. See the brief description of a woman negotiating this dynamic in a Baptist context in Beth Allison Barr, *The Making of Biblical Womanhood: How the Subjugation of Women Became Gospel Truth* (Grand Rapids, MI: Brazos Press, 2021), 69.

16. On the "patriarchal bargain," see Deniz Kandiyoti, "Bargaining with Patriarchy," *Gender and Society* 2.3 (1988): 274–90.

17. For an insightful rethinking of women's religious agency, see Saba Mahmood, *Politics of Piety: The Islamic Revival and the Feminist Subject* (Princeton, NJ: Princeton University Press, 2012).

18. For instance, in no Orthodox majority countries does a majority support women's ordination. See Pew Research Center, "Orthodox Christianity in the 21st Century," November 8, 2017, https://www.pewresearch.org/religion/2017/11/08/orthodox-christianity-in-the-21st-century/.

19. Ariana Salazar and Michael Lipka, "On Gender Issues, Many in Orthodox Christian Countries Have Conservative Views," Pew Research Center, May 16, 2017, https://www.pewresearch.org/short-reads/2017/05/16/on-gender-issues-many-in-orthodox-christian-countries-have-conservative-views/.

20. Despite numerous calls for revitalizing the female diaconate, the Orthodox Church remains without a normalized ordained position for women. See the recent developments, scholarship, canons, and appeals at the St. Phoebe Center for the Deaconess, accessed July, 5, 2024, https://orthodoxdeaconess.org.

21. Kyriaki Karidoyanes-FitzGerald, "Orthodox Women in Theological and Ecumenical Context: Assessing Concerns for Today and the Future (The More Things Seem to Change the More They Stay the Same?)," in *Many Women Were Also There . . . : The Participation of Orthodox Women in the Ecumenical Movement*, ed. Eleni Kasselouri-Hatzivassiliadi, Fulata Mbano Moyo, and Aikaterini Pekridou (Geneva: World Council of Churches Publications, 2010), 52.

22. Carrie Frederick Frost, "The Legacy of Rhodes—St Phoebe Center," YouTube video, 1:28:08, May 11, 2023, https://www.youtube.com/watch?v=1YTcAje5jC0.

23. Sarah Ahmed, *Complaint* (Durham, NC: Duke University Press, 2023), 2; original emphasis. See also Karidoyanes-FitzGerald, "Orthodox

Women in Theological and Ecumenical Context," 37. She notes that women's ministries are often perceived as "less important."

24. Ahmed, *Complaint*, 7; original emphasis.

25. For example, in 2013, Russian Patriarch Kyrill made several public statements condemning the dangers of feminism. See also the views described in Eleni Kasselouri-Hatzivassiliadi, "Orthodox Women and Theological Education," *Ecumenical Review* 4 (2014): 471–76; Nonna Harrison, "Orthodoxy and Feminism," *St. Nina Quarterly* 2.2 (1998): 5–7. Harrison observes, "Some Orthodox Christians describe feminism as a dangerous heresy, an enemy they fear is already 'within the gates' of the Church, threatening to destroy it" (5).

26. See the observations and reflections in Kasselouri-Hatzivassiliadi, Myo, and Pekridou, *Many Women Were Also There* . . . .

27. Cf. the Christian theological justifications from other traditions for some of these issues: Margaret Kamitsuka, *Abortion and the Christian Tradition: A Pro-Choice Theological Ethic* (London: Westminster Knox Press, 2019); Margaret Farley, *Just Love: A Framework for Christian Sexual Ethics* (New York: Continuum, 2008).

28. Kristina Stoeckl, "The Rise of the Russian Christian Right: The Case of the World Congress of Families, Religion," *State and Society* 48.4 (2020): 223–38.

29. For a case study on conservative Orthodoxy in the United States, see Sarah Riccardi-Swartz, *Political Apostasy: American Conversions to Russian Orthodoxy in the Trump-Putin Era* (New York: Fordham University Press, 2022); see also the attitudes toward gender in popular writings by the Orthodox convert Frederica Mathewes-Green, *Selected Writings*, vol. 1: *Gender: Men, Women, Sex, Feminism* (Ben Lomond, CA: Conciliar Press, 2002).

30. Pew Research Center, "Orthodox Christianity in the 21st Century," November 8, 2017, 59–61; Eleni Sotiriou, "Contested Masculine Spaces in Greek Orthodoxy," *Social Compass* 51.4 (2004): 499–510.

31. Nicholas Denysenko, "An Appeal to Mary: An Analysis of Pussy Riot's Punk Performance in Moscow," *Journal of the American Academy of Religion* 81.4 (2013): 1061–92; Vera Shevzov, "Women on the Fault Lines of Faith: Pussy Riot and the Insider/Outsider Challenge to Post-Soviet Orthodoxy," *Religion and Gender* 4.2 (2014): 121–44.

32. See, e.g., the relatively conservative Orthodox responses to feminism for a lay audience published by Orthodox presses in Deborah Belonick, *Feminism in Christianity: An Orthodox Christian Response* (Crestwood, NY: St Vladimir's Seminary Press, 2012); Lawrence Farley, *Feminism and Tradition: Quiet Reflections on Ordination and Communion* (Crestwood, NY:

St Vladimir's Seminary Press, 2012); Sarah Cowie, *More Spirited Than Lions: Orthodox Responses to Feminism and a Practical Guide to the Spiritual Life of Women* (Salisbury, MA: Regina Orthodox Press, 2007).

33. See, e.g., the strategic positioning of some women in Greece in Eleni Sotiriu, "'The Traditional Modern': Rethinking the Position of Contemporary Greek Women in Orthodoxy," in *Orthodox Christianity in 21st Century Greece: The Role of Religion in Culture, Ethnicity and Politics*, ed. Victor Roudometof and Vasilios N. Makrides (Farnham: Ashgate, 2010), 131–53. See also the important critique about needing to sufficiently attend to local understandings of gender before applying a "Western" feminist approach in Orthodox contexts in Romina Istratii, "A Decolonial Critique of Western Feminist Hermeneutics in Theology / Religious Studies in Relation to Orthodox Communities," Gender and Orthodoxy series, Orthodox Outlet for Dogmatic Enquiries, August 19, 2020, https://www.oodegr.com/english/koinwnia/koinwnika/Gender_and _Orthodoxy.htm.

34. Elina Vuola, "Religion, Intersectionality, and Epistemic Habits of Academic Feminism: Perspectives from Global Feminist Theology," *Feminist Encounters* 1.4 (2017): 1–15.

35. Within religious discourse, for example, Womanist, Mujerista, and Muslima theology distinguish themselves.

36. Most recently this has been because the term "feminist" is associated in some contexts with exclusion of transwomen; however, I use the term with inclusivity in mind.

37. See, e.g., the integration of feminist ideals with Russian Orthodoxy in the Soviet context in the reflections of Tatiana Goricheva, *Talking about God Is Dangerous: My Experiences in the East and in the West* (London: SCM Press, 1986).

38. See the influential contributions to learning and performing gender in Simone de Beauvoir, *The Second Sex*, trans. Constance Borde and Sheila Malovany-Chevallier (New York: Vintage Books, 2011); Judith Butler, *Gender Trouble: Feminism and the Subversion of Identity* (New York: Routledge, 2006).

39. E.g., Elizabeth Clark, "The Lady Vanishes: Dilemmas of a Feminist Historian after the 'Linguistic Turn,'" *Church History* 67.1 (1998): 1–31; Derek Krueger, *Liturgical Subjects: Christian Ritual, Biblical Narrative, and the Formation of the Self in Byzantium* (Philadelphia: University of Pennsylvania Press, 2014); Patricia Cox Miller, "Is There a Harlot in This Text? Hagiography and the Grotesque," *Journal of Medieval and Early Modern Studies* 33 (2003): 419–35; Joan Scott, "Gender: A Useful Category of Historical Analysis," *American Historical Review* 91.5 (1986): 1053–75; Blossom Stefaniw, "Feminist

Historiography and Uses of the Past," *Studies in Late Antiquity* 4.1 (2020): 260–83.

40. Audre Lorde, "An Open Letter to Mary Daly," in *Sister Outsider: Essays and Speeches* (New York: Random House, 1984); bell hooks, *Feminist Theory: From Margin to Center* (Cambridge, MA: South End Press, 2000); Kimberlé Crenshaw, "Mapping the Margins: Intersectionality, Identity Politics, and Violence against Women of Color," *Stanford Law Review* 43.6 (1991): 1241–99.

41. On intersectional theology, see Grace Ji-Sun Kim and Susan Shaw, *Intersectional Theology: An Introductory Guide* (Minneapolis: Fortress Press, 2018). On the importance of intersectional theology for Orthodoxy in particular, an excellent case is made by Rachel Contos, "Intersectionality and Orthodox Theology: Searching for Spandrels," *Journal of Moral Theology* 12.1 (2023): 132–56.

42. Luce Irigaray, *Speculum of the Other Woman*, trans. Gillian Gill (Ithaca, NY: Cornell University Press, 1985); Gayatri Chakravorty Spivak, "Can the Subaltern Speak?," *Die Philosophin* 14.27 (1988): 42–58.

43. Sarah Ahmed, *Living a Feminist Life* (Durham, NC: Duke University Press, 2017), 29, 36–42.

44. Sarah Ahmed, "Making Feminist Points," September 11, 2013, https://feministkilljoys.com/2013/09/11/making-feminist-points/.

45. I have in mind the Paschal image of the "Harrowing of Hell" and the hymnic celebration of Christ breaking open the gates of Hades/Hell and liberating those held in bondage.

46. For an explanation of gaslighting and its philosophical application, see Kate Manne, "Moral Gaslighting," *Aristotelian Society Supplementary Volume* 97.1 (2023): 122–45.

47. This is addressed in the next two chapters.

48. Kate Manne, *Down Girl: The Logic of Misogyny* (Oxford: Oxford University Press, 2018).

49. Kate Manne, *Entitled: How Male Privilege Hurts Women* (New York: Penguin Random House, 2020).

50. Carol Gilligan and Naomi Snider, *Why Does Patriarchy Persist* (Cambridge: Polity Press, 2018), 71.

51. Gilligan and Snider, *Why Does Patriarchy Persist*, 71.

52. Nancy Hirschmann, *The Subject of Liberty: Toward a Feminist Theory of Freedom* (Princeton, NJ: Princeton University Press, 2003), 205.

53. Manon Garcia, *We Are Not Born Submissive: How Patriarchy Shapes Women's Lives* (Princeton, NJ: Princeton University Press, 2021).

54. Belonick, *Feminism in Christianity*; Anca Manolache, *Problematica feminină în Biserica lui Hristos: Un capitol de antropologie creștină* (Timișoara:

Editura Mitropoliei Banatului, 1994). Valerie Karras identifies as a feminist theologian in "Eschatology," in *The Cambridge Companion to Feminist Theology*, ed. Susan Frank Parsons (Cambridge: Cambridge University Press, 2006), 244. See also Spyridoula Athanasopoulou-Kypriou, "The Essentials of Theology in Feminist—That Is to Say Ecclesial—Perspective," in Kasselouri-Hatzivassiliadi, Myo, and Pekridou, *Many Women Were Also There . . .* , 117–31.

55. Elisabeth Behr-Sigel, *The Ministry of Women in the Church*, trans. Steven Bigham (Crestwood, NY: St Vladimir's Seminary Press, 1999); Maria Skobtsova, *Mother Maria Skobtsova: Essential Writings*, trans. Richard Revear and Larissa Volokhonsky (New York: Orbis Books, 2003); Myrrha Lot-Borodine, *La déification de l'homme selon la doctrine des Pères grecs* (Paris: Éditions du Cerf, 2011). See the helpful discussion and overview in Pauline Kollontai, "Contemporary Thinking on the Role and Ministry of Women in the Orthodox Church," *Journal of Contemporary Religion* 15 (2000): 165–79.

56. Women's voices and concerns from different Orthodox perspectives as an initiative of the World Council of Churches are also represented in Kyriaki Karidoyanes-FitzGerald, ed., *Orthodox Women Speak: Discerning the "Signs of the Times"* (Geneva: World Council of Churches Publications, 1999).

57. Leonie Liveris, *Ancient Taboos and Gender Prejudice: Challenges for Orthodox Women and the Church* (Burlington, VT: Ashgate, 2005); Kasselouri-Hatzivassiliadi, Myo, and Pekridou, *Many Women Were Also There . . . .*

58. Liveris, *Ancient Taboos and Gender Prejudice*, 137.

59. Eleni Kasselouri-Hatzivassiliadi, "Feminist Hermeneutics: The 'Gender Factor,'" in *Modern Biblical Hermeneutics* (Thessaloniki: Pournaras, 2003); Aikaterini Tslampouni, "'Aner-Gyne': Feminist Approaches and Paul's Theology," in *Proceedings of the Symposium, "The Human Being According to Apostle Paul"* (Beroea: Metropolis of Beroea, 2002), 249–59; Nonna Verna Harrison, *God's Many Splendored Image: Theological Anthropology for Christian Formation* (Grand Rapids, MI: Baker Academic, 2010); Eva Catafygiotu Topping, *Holy Mothers of Orthodoxy: Women and the Church* (Minneapolis: Light and Life Publishing, 1987); Valerie Karras, "Orthodox Theologies of Women and Ordained Ministry," in *Thinking through Faith: New Perspectives from Orthodox Christian Scholars*, ed. Aristotle Papanikolaou and Elizabeth Prodromou (Crestwood, NY: St Vladimir's Seminary Press, 2008), 113–60.

60. Carrie Frederick Frost, *Maternal Body: A Theology of Incarnation from the Christian East* (New York: Paulist Press, 2019); Frost, *Church of Our Granddaughters*.

61. Kateřina Bauerová, "Motherhood as a Space for the Other: A Dialogue between Mother Maria Skobtsova and Hélène Cixous," *Feminist Theology* 26 (2018): 133–46.

62. Gabrielle Thomas and Elena Narinskaya, eds., *Women and Ordination in the Orthodox Church* (Eugene, OR: Cascade Books, 2020); Ashley Purpura, Thomas Arentzen, and Susan Ashbrook Harvey, eds., *Rethinking Gender in Orthodox Christianity* (Eugene, OR: Pickwick Publications, 2023); Ina Merdjanova, ed., *Women and Religiosity in Orthodox Christianity* (New York: Fordham University Press, 2021); Helena Kupari and Elina Vuola, eds., *Orthodox Christianity and Gender: Dynamics of Tradition, Culture and Lived Practice* (London: Routledge, 2019).

63. Paul Evdokimov, *Woman and the Salvation of the World: A Christian Anthropology on the Charisms of Women*, trans. Anthony Gythiel (Crestwood, NY: St Vladimir's Seminary Press, 1994); Thomas Hopko, *Women and the Priesthood* (Crestwood, NY: St Vladimir's Seminary Press, 1983); John Behr, "A Note on the Ontology of Gender," *St Vladimir's Theological Quarterly* 42.3–4 (1998): 363–72; Luis Josué Salés, "To Kill a Matriarchy: Makədda, Queen of Ethiopia and the Specter of Pauline Androprimacy in the Kəbrä Nägäśt," *African Journal of Gender and Religion* 26.1 (2020): 1–28.

64. Susan Ashbrook Harvey, *Song and Memory: Biblical Women in Syriac Tradition* (Milwaukee, WI: Marquette University Press, 2010); Stavroula Constantinou, "Male Constructions of Female Identities: Authority and Power in the Byzantine Greek Lives of Monastic Foundresses," *Wiener Jahrbuch für Kunstgeschichte* 60 (2012): 43–62; Amy Singleton Adams and Vera Shevzov, eds., *Framing Mary: The Mother of God in Modern, Revolutionary, and Post-Soviet Russian Culture* (Dekalb: Northern Illinois University Press, 2018); Ina Merdjanova, ed., *Women and Religiosity in Orthodox Christian Contexts* (New York: Fordham University Press, 2021); Kupari and Vuola, *Orthodox Christianity and Gender*.

65. For examples of engagement with Orthodoxy, see Heleen Zorgdrager, "Is *theosis* a Gendered Concept? Theological Pitfalls and Perspectives for an Inclusive Affirmation of Human Dignity," *Journal of Eastern Christian Studies* 71.3–4 (2019): 343–68; Michele Watkins, "Differentiation as Disfigurement: A Womanist Polemic against the Co-Option of the Divine Essence," in *Faith, Reason, and Theosis*, ed. Aristotle Papanikolaou and George Demacopoulos (New York: Fordham University Press, 2023).

66. See, e.g., Butler, *Gender Trouble*; Manon Garcia, *We Are Not Born Submissive*.

67. Rosemary Radford Ruether, *Sexism and God-Talk: Toward a Feminist Theology* (Boston, Beacon Press, 1993), 18–19.

68. Mary Catherine Hilkert, "Experience and Tradition: Can the Center Hold?," in *Freeing Theology: The Essentials of Theology in Feminist Perspective*, ed. Catherine Mowry LaCugna (San Francisco: HarperCollins, 1993), 59–82, 72.

69. Elisabeth Schüssler Fiorenza, *Bread Not Stone: The Challenge of Feminist Biblical Interpretation* (Boston: Beacon Press, 1984), xvi.

70. Janet Martin Soskice, *The Kindness of God: Metaphor, Gender and Religious Language* (Oxford: Oxford University Press, 2011), 23–25.

71. Serene Jones, *Feminist Theory and Christian Theology: Cartographies of Grace* (Minneapolis: Fortress Press, 2000),18.

72. Elena Procario-Foley and Susan Abraham, Preface to *Frontiers in Catholic Feminist Theology: Shoulder to Shoulder* (Minneapolis: Fortress Press, 2009), 2.

73. Sarah Coakley, *Powers and Submissions: Spirituality, Gender and Philosophy* (Oxford: Blackwell, 2002); Shawn Copeland, *Enfleshing Freedom: Body, Race, and Being* (Fortress Press, 2010); Elizabeth Johnson, *She Who Is: The Mystery of God in Feminist Theological Discourse* (New York: Crossroad, 1997); Catherine Mowry LaCugna, *God for Us: The Trinity and Christian Life* (New York: HarperCollins, 1993).

74. See, e.g., Catherine Keller, "The Apophasis of Gender: A Fourfold Unsaying of Feminist Theology," *Journal of the American Academy of Religion* 76.4 (2008): 905–33; Mary Daly, *The Church and the Second Sex* (Boston: Beacon Press, 1986); Grace Jantzen, *Becoming Divine: Towards a Feminist Philosophy of Religion* (Bloomington: Indiana University Press, 1999); Ruether, *Sexism and God-Talk*; Elisabeth Schüssler Fiorenza, *Changing Horizons: Explorations in Feminist Interpretation* (Minneapolis: Fortress Press, 2013); Tina Beattie, *New Catholic Feminism: Theology and Theory* (London: Routledge, 2005).

75. Rosemary Radford Ruether, "The Future of Feminism and Theology," *Journal of American Academy of Religion* 53.4 (1985): 703–13.

76. While there are numerous introductory volumes to Orthodox Christianity, none has been more prominent in the anglophone world than Kallistos Ware, *The Orthodox Way* (Crestwood, NY: St Vladimir's Seminary Press, 1995); and *The Orthodox Church: An Introduction to Eastern Christianity* (New York: Penguin Books, 2015).

77. For example, icon veneration and the theology behind it that I highlight in chapters 3 and 6.

78. For a concise and helpful overview of patriarchy, androcentrism, and the various trajectories of Christian feminist theological responses to them, see the introductory discussion in Rebecca Moore, *Women in Christian Traditions* (New York: New York University Press, 2015), 1–19.

79. Tertullian, *The Prescription against Heretics*, Early Latin Theology, Library of Christian Classics V, trans. S. L. Greenslade (London: SCM Press, 1956), 36.

80. See a related discussion of methodological reflections about gender and religious sources in Shelly Matthews, "Thinking of Thecla: Issues in Feminist Historiography," *Journal of Feminist Studies in Religion* 17.2 (2001): 39–55.

81. For accounts of women's lived religiosity, see Merdjanova, *Women and Religiosity in Orthodox Christianity*.

82. Orthodox Christianity has within its tradition a rejection of a strict cisgender binary. See my article, "Beyond the Binary: Hymnographic Constructions of Eastern Orthodox Gender Identities," *Journal of Religion* 97.4 (2017): 524–46.

83. See the related critique of inclusion in Linn Tonstad, "The Limits of Inclusion: Queer Theology and Its Others," *Theology and Sexuality* 21.1 (2015): 1–19.

84. On problematizing an essentialist gender binary, see Bryce Rich, *Gender Essentialism and Orthodoxy: Beyond Male and Female* (New York: Fordham University Press, 2023).

85. See, e.g., the very useful theological reflection on tradition by Hart, *Tradition and Apocalypse*.

## CHAPTER ONE

1. Eva Catafygiotu Topping, *Holy Mothers of Orthodoxy: Women and the Church* (Minneapolis: Light and Life Publishing, 1987), 4.

2. Cf. the "narrative" and "system" of patriarchal Christianity described in Serene Jones, *Feminist Theory and Christian Theology: Cartographies of Grace* (Philadelphia: Fortress Press, 2000),18.

3. Contrast, for example, the various definitions given in Sergius Bulgakov, *The Orthodox Church*, trans. Lydia Kesich (Crestwood, NY: St Vladimir's Seminary Press, 1988); Vladimir Lossky, *The Mystical Theology of the Eastern Church*, trans. Fellowship of St. Alban and St Sergius (Cambridge: James Clarke & Co., 1957); and the categories that might express it in Eugen Pentiuc, *The Old Testament in Eastern Orthodox Tradition* (Oxford: Oxford University Press, 2014), 136–66. For a different approach to conceiving Orthodox tradition, see David Bentley Hart, *Tradition and Apocalypse: An Essay on the Future of Christian Belief* (Grand Rapids, MI: Baker Academic, 2022).

4. Oliver Herbel, "Resolving the Tension between Tradition and Restorationism in American Orthodoxy," in *Fundamentalism or Tradition: Christianity after Secularism*, ed. Aristotle Papanikolaou and George Demacopoulos (New York: Fordham University Press, 2020), 152.

5. Sergius Bulgakov, *The Orthodox Church*, trans. Lydia Kesich (Crestwood, NY: St Vladimir's Seminary Press, 1988),10; see also 32–33.

6. Eugen Pentiuc, *The Old Testament in Eastern Orthodox Tradition* (Oxford: Oxford University Press, 2014), 156 for additional components.

7. 1 Corinthians 6:19–20.

8. Deification in Orthodox theology is a common term to describe *theosis*, or becoming increasingly like God through participation in divine grace, although variations of understandings and emphases are present across various interpreters.

9. Valerie Karras, "Eschatology," in *The Cambridge Companion to Feminist Theology*, ed. Susan Frank Parsons (Cambridge: Cambridge University Press, 2006), 257.

10. This reflects an adoption even in theological knowledge of a type of feminist standpoint theory. For an overview of this approach in other disciplines, see Sandra Harding, ed., *The Feminist Standpoint Theory Reader* (New York: Routledge, 2004).

11. Feminist theological critique is expansive, but here I mention just a few formative examples: Mary Daly, *The Church and the Second Sex* (Boston: Beacon Press, 1985); Grace Jantzen, *Becoming Divine: Towards a Feminist Philosophy of Religion* (Bloomington: Indiana University Press, 1999); Rosemary Radford Ruether, *Sexism and God-Talk: Toward a Feminist Theology* (Boston: Beacon Press, 1983); Janet Martin Soskice, *The Kindness of God: Metaphor, Gender, and Religious Language* (Oxford: Oxford University Press, 2007); Aysha Hidayatullah, *Feminist Edges of the Qur'an* (Oxford: Oxford University Press, 2014); Judith Plaskow, *Standing Again at Sinai: Judaism from a Feminist Perspective* (San Francisco: HarperCollins, 1991).

12. Daly, *The Church and the Second Sex*.

13. Eva Catafygiotu Topping, "In Defense of the Men of a Certain Parish," in *Holy Mothers of Orthodoxy*, 81–82.

14. See, e.g., the rubrics for reading the hagiography and the related hymns in the Matins service of Thursday of the fifth week of Lent in *The Lenten Triodion*, trans. Mother Mary and Kallistos Ware (South Canaan, PA: St. Tikhon's Seminary Press, 2002), 377–416.

15. A lay-oriented guide for understanding and developing this "mind" can be found in Eugenia Scarvelis Constantinou, *Thinking Orthodox: Understanding and Acquiring the Orthodox Mind* (Chesterton, IN: Ancient Faith Publishing, 2020).

16. Kimberlé Crenshaw, "Mapping the Margins: Intersectionality, Identity Politics, and Violence against Women of Color," *Stanford Law Review* 43.6

(1991): 1241–99; Blossom Stefaniw, "Masculinity, Historiography, and Uses of the Past: An Introduction," *Journal of Early Christian History* 11.1 (2021): 1–14.

17. Notably, there are many feminine and maternal images of God used in patristic reflections and poetry, but liturgically these have yet to be incorporated in any official way. For a discussion of the gendered language for God in Orthodoxy and an example of Orthodox feminist engagement about it, see Nonna Verna Harrison, "The Trinity and Feminism," in *The Oxford Handbook of the Trinity*, ed. Gilles Emery and Matthew Levering (Oxford: Oxford University Press, 2011), 519–30.

18. Kate Manne, *Entitled: How Male Privilege Hurts Women* (New York: Crown, 2020), 8–12.

19. Kate Manne, "Brett Kavanaugh and America's 'Himpathy' Reckoning," *New York Times*, Sept. 27, 2018.

20. Leonie Liveris, *Ancient Taboos and Gender Prejudice: Challenges for Orthodox Women and the Church* (Burlington, VT: Ashgate, 2005), 109. Liveris observes that Orthodox women have gained equality in professions and many social contexts but remain conservative regarding gender equality in the church.

21. Kyriaki Karidoyanes-FitzGerald, "Orthodox Women in Theological and Ecumenical Context: Assessing Concerns for Today and the Future (The More Things Seem to Change the More They Stay the Same?)," in *Many Women Were Also There . . . : The Participation of Orthodox Women in the Ecumenical Movement*, ed. Eleni Kasselouri-Hatzivassiliadi, Fulata Mbano Moyo, and Aikaterini Pekridou (Geneva: World Council of Churches Publications, 2010), 52.

22. See the discussion about the inaction of hierarchs on allowing women and girls to serve in the altar as acolytes or deaconesses in St. Phoebe Center for the Deaconess, "What Is the Legacy of Rhodes," YouTube, 1:28, May 11, 2023, https://www.youtube.com/watch?v=1YTcAje5jC0&t=2s.

23. Nancy Hirschmann, *The Subject of Liberty: Toward a Feminist Theory of Freedom* (Princeton, NJ: Princeton University Press, 2003), 204.

24. See the broader discussion and definition of patriarchy in bell hooks, *Understanding Patriarchy* (New York: Washington Square Press, 2004).

25. Nadia Zasanska, "New Producers of Patriarchal Ideology: Matushki in Digital Media of Russian Orthodox Church," *ESSACHESS* 12.24 (2019): 99–128.

26. Lavinia Tanculescu, "'Old Church Women': An Insight into the Less Understood and Their Contribution to the Life of the Orthodox Church," *Societies* 9.63 (2019): DOI:10.3390/soc9030063.

27. Blossom Stefaniw, "Feminist Historiography and Uses of the Past," *Studies in Late Antiquity* 4.3 (2020): 265.

28. Stefaniw, "Feminist Historiography and Uses of the Past," 271–72; original emphasis.

29. On Orthodox theology and antinomic traditions, see Pawel Rojek, "Pavel Florensky's Theory of Religious Antinomies," *Logica Universalis* 13 (2019): 515–40.

30. On the centrality of divine and personal communion for realizing personhood, see John Zizioulas, *Being as Communion* (Crestwood, NY: St Vladimir's Seminary Press, 1985), 15.

31. See my earlier work on the need for iconicity to legitimize authority: *God, Hierarchy, and Power: Orthodox Theologies of Authority from Byzantium* (New York: Fordham University Press, 2018).

32. Manon Garcia, *We Are Not Born Submissive: How Patriarchy Shapes Women's Lives* (Princeton, NJ: Princeton University Press, 2021), 13; my emphasis.

33. Judith Bennett, *History Matters: Patriarchy and the Challenge of Feminism* (Philadelphia: University of Pennsylvania Press, 2006), 10.

34. Manne, *Entitled*, 9; original emphasis.

35. Manne, *Entitled*, 8–9.

36. Kathleen McVey, "Syriac Christian Tradition and Gender in Trinitarian Theology," in *The Holy Trinity in the Life of the Church*, ed. Khaled Anatolios (Grand Rapids, MI: Baker Academic, 2014), 199–216.

37. Susan Ashbrook Harvey, "Feminine Imagery for the Divine: The Holy Spirit, the Odes of Solomon, and Early Syriac Tradition," *St Vladimir's Theological Quarterly* 37 (1993): 111–39.

38. Symeon the New Theologian's Hymn 50, in *Divine Eros: Hymns of Saint Symeon the New Theologian*, trans. Daniel Griggs (Crestwood, NY: St Vladimir's Seminary Press, 2010), 353; and Symeon's Ethical Discourse IV, in *On the Mystical Life: The Ethical Discourses*, vol. 2: *On Virtue and Christian Life*, trans. Alexander Golitzin (Crestwood, NY: St Vladimir's Seminary Press, 1996), 20.

39. E.g., reflecting on Matthew 23:37; Luke 13:34. John Penniman discusses the maternal and nursing imagery used by Gregory of Nyssa's scriptural reflections in *Raised on Christian Milk: Food and the Formation of the Soul in Early Christianity* (New Haven, CT: Yale University Press, 2017), 138–64.

40. Daly, *The Church and the Second Sex*, 38; for an Orthodox rejection of gender essentialization, see Bryce Rich, *Gender Essentialism and Orthodoxy: Beyond Male and Female* (New York: Fordham University Press, 2023).

41. Nicolae Mosoiu, "God Language: An Orthodox Perspective on Feminist Theology," *International Journal of Orthodox Theology* 7.2 (2016): 57–80.

42. Soskice, *Kindness of God*, 4.

43. Linn Marie Tonstad, *God and Difference: The Trinity, Sexuality, and the Transformation of Finitude* (London: Routledge, 2016), 205.

44. Contrast this with the type of muscular Christianity that is popular in U.S. Protestantism but also linked to some associations of representing Orthodoxy as "hard core" or "manly," especially linked with nationalism. See Kristen Kobes Du Mez, *Jesus and John Wayne: How White Evangelicals Corrupted a Faith and Fractured a Nation* (New York: Liveright, 2020); Nicholas Denysenko, "Orthodox Ideology and Masculinity in Putin's Russia," *Concilium* 2 (2020): 74–84.

45. Elisabeth Schussler Fiorenza, *Jesus, Miriam's Child, Sophia's Prophet: Critical Issues in Feminist Christology* (New York: Continuum, 1994); Elizabeth Johnson, *She Who Is: The Mystery of God in Feminist Theological Discourse* (New York: Crossroad, 1993); Carol Christ, "Sophia, Goddess, and Feminist Spirituality: Imagining the Future," *Journal of Feminist Studies in Religion* 38.1 (2022): 93–110.

46. See, in particular, Sergei Bulgakov, *Sophia the Wisdom of God: An Outline of Sophiology*, trans. Patrick Thompson, (Stockbridge, MA: Lindisfarne Press, 1993); and the relation between the Holy Spirit and Sophia in Sergius Bulgakov, *The Comforter*, trans. Boris Jakim (Grand Rapids, MI: Eerdmans, 2004).

47. For situating sophiology across several theologians and its controversy, see Marcus Plested, "Modern Russian Sophiology and Its Discontents," in *Wisdom in Christian Tradition* (Oxford: Oxford University Press, 2022), 13–69.

48. See the helpful situation of this comparison between feminism and sophiology in Brenda Meehan, "Wisdom/Sophia, Russian Identity, and Western Feminist Theology," *CrossCurrents* 46 (1996): 149–68. See also Sarah Livick-Moses, "The Kenotic Iconicity of Sergii Bulgakov's Divine-Humanity: A Feminist Retrieval" (paper presented at Building the House of Wisdom: Sergii Bulgakov—150 Years after His Birth International Conference, Fribourg, Sept. 3, 2021); Walter Nunzio Sisto, *The Mother of God in the Theology of Sergius Bulgakov* (New York: Routledge, 2017).

49. *Protoevangelium of James*, trans. Lily Vuong (Eugene, OR: Cascade, 2019); Thomas Arentzen and Mary Cunningham, eds., *The Reception of the Virgin in Byzantium* (Cambridge: Cambridge University Press, 2019).

50. Leslie Brubaker and Mary Cunningham, eds., *The Cult of the Mother of God in Byzantium: Texts and Images* (Burlington, VT: Ashgate, 2011).

51. See her various depictions as militant protector of Constantinople, ascetic disciple, and virgin mother in Mary Cunningham, *The Virgin Mary in*

*Byzantium, c. 400–1000: Hymns, Homilies and Hagiography* (Cambridge: Cambridge University Press, 2021).

52. Athanasius, *On the Incarnation*, trans. John Behr (Crestwood, NY: St Vladimir's Seminary Press, 2011), 166–67; Mary Daly, *Beyond God the Father: Toward a Philosophy of Women's Liberation* (Boston: Beacon Press, 1985), 3.

53. On Orthodox reading of scripture as Christocentric, see John Behr, *The Mystery of Christ: Life in Death* (Crestwood, NY: St Vladimir's Seminary Press, 2006). See, e.g., Ephesians 5:22–24; 1 Timothy 2:11–15; 1 Corinthians 11:3–16.

54. The discussion of feminist approaches to the Bible are too numerous to detail in a note, but most influential are the critiques of Ruether, *Sexism and God-Talk*; and Elisabeth Schussler Fiorenza, *In Memory of Her: A Feminist Theological Reconstruction of Christian Origins* (New York: Crossroad, 1983).

55. E.g., Aikaterini Tsalampouni, "'Aner-Gyne': Feminist Approaches and Paul's Theology," In *Proceedings of the Symposium, "The Human Being According to Apostle Paul"* (Beroea: Metropolis of Beroea, 2002), 249–59 (in Greek). Ambivalence to the feminist critiques of other Christian sources, traditions, and practices is evident in Kasselouri-Hatzivassiliadi, Moyo, and Pekridou, *Many Women Were Also There . . .*, where there is a clear preference for developing a uniquely Orthodox response to the status of women and the issues they face.

56. Eleni Kasselouri-Hatzivassiliadi, *Feminist Hermeneutics: The "Gender Factor" in Modern Biblical Hermeneutics* (Pournaras: Thessaloniki, 2003) (in Greek).

57. Orthodox Divine Liturgies of John Chrysostom and Basil. See examples of related reflection on the actions of the liturgy in Nicholas Cabasilas, *A Commentary on the Divine Liturgy*, trans. J. M. Hussey and P. A. McNulty (Crestwood, NY: St Vladimir's Seminary Press, 2002); Germanus, *On the Divine Liturgy*, trans. Paul Meyendorff (Crestwood, NY: St Vladimir's Seminary Press, 1984).

58. Anthony Kaldellis, "The Study of Women and Children: Methodological Challenges and New Directions," in *The Byzantine World*, ed. Paul Stephenson (New York: Routledge, 2010), 61–71.

59. For an exploration of the New Testament's tension between hierarchy and egalitarianism and an example of its modern relevance, see Jennifer Slater, "Inclusiveness—An Authentic Biblical Truth That Negates Distinctions: A Hermeneutic of Gender Incorporation and Ontological Equality in Ancient Christian Thought," *Journal of Early Christian History* 5.1 (2015): 116–31. For consideration of women's equality in scripture in particular, see Rosemary

Radford Reuther's *Religion and Sexism: Images of Women in the Jewish and Christian Traditions* (New York: Simon and Schuster, 1998) and *Women and Redemption—A Theological History* (Minneapolis: Fortress, 1998).

60. Kate Cooper, "Approaching the Holy Household," *Journal of Early Christian Studies* 15.2 (2007): 131–42; Kate Cooper, "Closely Watched Households: Visibility, Exposure and Private Power in the Roman 'Domus,'" *Past & Present*, no. 197 (2007): 3–33, 7; Angeliki Laiou, "Family Structure and the Transmission of Property," in *The Social History of Byzantium*, ed. John Haldon (Malden, MA: Wiley-Blackwell, 2009), 57. Laiou contests the designations patrilineal and patriarchal for Byzantine family and household structures because there were limits to father's rights in the family and inheritance was not only through sons.

61. See the classic yet still compelling critique by Elaine Pagels, "What Became of God the Mother? Conflicting Images of God in Early Christianity," *Signs* 2.2 (1976): 293–303.

62. 1 Corinthians 5; John Chrysostom, "Homily 19," in *St. John Chrysostom, On Marriage and Family Life*, trans. Catherine Roth and David Anderson (Crestwood, NY: St Vladimir's Seminary Press, 1986), 28.

63. Numerous hymns begin with the word *Today* in a way that is a liturgical mystical time rather than a historical moment, making present events and characters liturgically recalled and commemorated in a spiritual present without any explanation. See, e.g., the fourteenth antiphon from the service of the Twelve Gospels, "Today He who hung the earth upon the waters is hung upon the Cross," in *Lenten Triodion*, trans. Mother Mary and Kallistos Ware (South Canaan, PA: St. Tikhon's Seminary Press, 2002), 587; Bogdan Bucur, "Exegesis of Biblical Theophanies in Byzantine Hymnography: Rewritten Bible?," *Theological Studies* 68 (2007): 92–112.

64. See, e.g., the number of sayings attributed to Ammas compared to the Abbas in the *Apopthegmata Patrum*. For an accessible English translation, see *Give Me a Word: The Alphabetical Sayings of the Desert Fathers*, trans. John Wortley (Crestwood, NY: St Vladimir's Seminary Press, 2014). Liturgically, I have observed one priest close services with "through the prayers of our holy fathers and mothers . . . ," but this is far from widespread and questions who this closing liturgical phrase does or should refer to (all the people present, the saints, male clerics actually serving in the altar, or the hierarch?).

65. From my research, it seems to be the case that there is not a significant difference between the historical texts authored by women and those authored by men that have been preserved in the tradition due to the dominance of androcentric patriarchalism in society, which determines what gets preserved and transmitted in the church. It is my hope that this impression will be proved

wrong over time, with either new ways of reading texts or new discovery of texts themselves.

66. Kurt Sherry, *Kassia the Nun in Context: The Religious Thought of a Ninth-Century Byzantine Monastic* (Piscataway, NJ: Gorgias Press, 2011).

67. John Thomas and Angela Constantinides Hero, eds., *Byzantine Monastic Foundation Documents: A Complete Translation of the Surviving Founders' Typika and Testaments* (Washington, DC: Dumbarton Oaks, 2000).

68. "Dismissal Hymn of the Fathers," in *The Pentecostarion*, trans. Holy Transfiguration Monastery (Boston: Holy Transfiguration Monastery, 2014), 219.

69. See the "Decree of the Seventh Ecumenical Council" or the "Synodikon," in *The Seven Ecumenical Councils of the Undivided Church*, trans H. R. Percival, Nicene and Post-Nicene Fathers, 2nd series, ed. P. Schaff and H. Wace (repr. Grand Rapids MI: Eerdmans, 1955), XIV, 549–51.

70. For an influential compilation of Orthodox canons, see Nicodemus and Agapius, *The Rudder of the Orthodox Catholic Church: The Compilation of the Holy Canons*, trans. D. Cummings (Brookfield, MA: Orthodox Christian Educational Society, 1957). For discussion of the canons with regard to gender, see Vassa Larin, "What Is Ritual Im/Purity and Why?," *St Vladimir's Theological Quarterly* 52.3-4 (2008): 275–92; Patrick Viscuso, "Theodore Balsamon's Canonical Images of Women," *Greek, Roman and Byzantine Studies* 45 (2005): 317–26.

71. See, e.g., the study by Patrick Viscuso, *Sexuality, Marriage, and Celibacy in Byzantine Law: The Alphabetical Collection of Matthew Blastares* (Brookline, MA: Holy Cross Orthodox Press, 2008).

72. There are spiritual mothers (often nuns) who provide spiritual counsel, but sacramental absolution still requires an ordained (male) priest.

73. Nonna Verna Harrison, "Women, Human Identity, and the Image of God: Antiochene Interpretations," *Journal of Early Christian Studies* 9.2 (2001): 205–49; Nonna Verna Harrison, *God's Many-Splendored Image: Theological Anthropology for Christian Formation* (Grand Rapids, MI: Baker Academic, 2010), 92–96; Constantine Yokarinis, "A Patristic Basis for a Theological Anthropology of Women in Their Distinctive Humanity," *Anglican Theological Review* 84 (2002): 585–608. See also the discussion of various early Christian perceptions of women in Susanna Elm, *Virgins of God: The Making of Asceticism in Late Antiquity* (Oxford: Oxford University Press, 1996).

74. See the discussion of patristic womanhood relating to biblical figures, social norms, Marian devotion, and various exemplary women of early Christian writers in Nonna Verna Harrison, "Eve, the Mother of God, and Other Women," *Ecumenical Review* 60 (2008): 71–81.

75. Johannes Zachhuber, *The Rise of Christian Theology and the End of Ancient Metaphysics: Patristic Philosophy from the Cappadocian Fathers to John of Damascus* (Oxford: Oxford University Press, 2020); Ilinca Tanaseanu-Döbler and Marvin Döbler, *Religious Education in Pre-Modern Europe* (Leiden: Brill, 2012); Guy Stroumsa, "Scripture and Paideia in Late Antiquity," in *Homer and the Bible in the Eyes of Ancient Interpreters*, ed. Maren Niehoff (Leiden: Brill, 2012), 29–41.

76. Aristotle, *History of Animals*, 608b1–14, *Generation of Animals*, 728a, *Politics* I, 1259a–b, 1277; Plato, *Republic*, 455d, 469d, 605e; Jean-Baptiste Bonnard, "Male and Female Bodies according to Ancient Greek Physicians," trans. Lillian Doherty and Violaine Sebillotte Cuchet, *Clio: Women, Gender, History* 37 (Apr. 2014), http://journals.openedition.org/cliowgh/339. David E. Fredrickson, "Hellenistic Philosophy and Literature," in *The Oxford Handbook of New Testament, Gender, and Sexuality*, ed. Benjamin Dunning (Oxford: Oxford University Press, 2019), 239–56; Nicholas Smith, "Plato and Aristotle on the Nature of Women," *Journal of the History of Philosophy* 21 (1983): 467–78; Rebecca Flemming, *Medicine and the Making of Roman Women: Gender, Nature, and Authority from Celsus to Galen* (Oxford: Oxford University Press, 2000).

77. Elisabeth Behr-Sigel, *The Ministry of Women in the Church*, trans. Steven Bigham (Crestwood, NY: St Vladimir's Seminary Press, 1999), 156.

78. Maximus Confessor's discussion of male and female in *Ambiguum 41*. See Maximos the Confessor, *On Difficulties in the Church Fathers: The Ambigua*, vol. 2, trans. Nicholas Constas (Cambridge, MA: Harvard University Press, 2014), 102–21. For a discussion of Maximus and androprimacy, see Luis Josué Salés, *Maximos the Confessor: Androprimacy and Sexual Difference* (Cambridge: Cambridge University Press, 2025).

79. Of course, it is useful for Orthodox to learn about how those sainted within their tradition thought about these things, but there also needs to be an acknowledgment that these views leave a great deal out. A short excellent compilation of Orthodox thought on marriage and sexuality across various time periods that nevertheless remains primarily androcentric is John Chryssavgis, *Love, Sexuality, and the Sacrament of Marriage* (Brookline, MA: Holy Cross Press, 1998).

80. There are some exceptions, notably, Amma Sarah, Amma Theodora, and Amma Syncletica, as well as nuns writing about the lives of those sainted in their community. See Claudia Rapp, "Figures of Female Sanctity: Byzantine Edifying Manuscripts and Their Audience," *Dumbarton Oaks Papers* 50 (1996): 313–44.

81. *Life of Macrina*, trans. Joan Petersen, in *Handmaids of the Lord* (Kalamazoo, MI: Cistercian Publications, 1996), 51.

82. Susan Ashbrook Harvey, "Women in Byzantine Hagiography," in *That Gentle Strength*, ed. L. Coon (Charlottesville: University of Virginia Press, 1990), chap. 3.

83. See, e.g., the discussion of gender and holiness in Stephanie Cobb, *Dying to Be Men: Gender and Language in Early Christian Martyr Texts* (New York: Columbia University Press, 2008), 60–128.

84. Rapp, "Figures of Female Sanctity"; Ecaterina Lung, "Depictions of Women in the Works of Early Byzantine Historians and Chroniclers," *Historical Reflections / Réflexions Historiques* 43.1 (2017): 4–18.

85. See Derek Krueger, "Hagiography as an Ascetic Practice in the Early Christian East," *Journal of Religion* 79 (1999): 216–32; Stephos Efthymiadis, Vincent Deroche, Andre Binggeli, and Zissis Ainalis, eds., *The Ashgate Research Companion to Byzantine Hagiography* (Abingdon: Routledge, 2011).

86. Alexander Kazhdan, "Byzantine Hagiography and Sex in the Fifth to Twelfth Centuries," *Dumbarton Oaks Papers* 44 (1990): 143; Christa Gray and James Corke-Webster, eds., *The Hagiographical Experiment: Developing Discourses of Sainthood* (Leiden: Brill, 2020).

87. See the foundational observations of Gillian Cloke, *"This Female Man of God": Women and Spiritual Power in the Patristic Age, 350–450* (London: Routledge, 1995).

88. Gregory of Nazianzus, *PG* 37.1542–50; John Chrysostom's Letter 8, in *Saint John Chrysostom: Letters to Saint Olympia*, trans. David Ford (Yonkers, NY: St Vladimir's Seminary Press, 2016), 73–75, esp. 74.

89. Behr-Sigel, *The Ministry of Women in the Church*, 153. See also discussion of gender division in patristic texts in Harrison, *God's Many-Splendored Image*, 128–37.

90. For a discussion of Mary's veneration in historical Orthodox contexts, see Cunningham, *The Virgin Mary in Byzantium*; and for a contemporary example of Orthodox women relating to Mary in both these authoritative and more personal ways, see Carrie Frederick Frost, *Maternal Body: A Theology of Incarnation from the Christian East* (New York: Paulist Press, 2019).

91. *Wider Than Heaven: Eighth-Century Homilies on the Mother of God*, trans. Mary Cunningham (Crestwood, NY: St Vladimir's Seminary Press, 2008), 67.

92. Examples of these hymns are found especially in the services for Holy Friday and Saturday; see, e.g., *The Lenten Triodion*, 612, 617–21, 651.

93. *The Lenten Triodion*, 651; Ode 4 of the Canon for the Annunciation (Mar. 25), in *Greek Menaion*, vol. 7 (Boston: Holy Transfiguration Monastery, 2005), 109.

94. Elina Vuola, "Finnish Orthodox Women and the Virgin Mary," *Journal of the European Society of Women in Theological Research* 24 (2016): 63–80; Daly, *Beyond God the Father*, 81.

95. Nicholas Denysenko, "An Appeal to Mary: An Analysis of Pussy Riot's Punk Performance in Moscow," *Journal of the American Academy of Religion* 81.4 (2013): 1061–92; Graham McGeoch, "Pussies Rioting and Indecent Praying: Transforming Orthodoxy in the Company of Marcella Althaus-Reid," *Feminist Theology* 26 (2018): 279–307; Vera Shevzov, "Women on the Fault Lines of Faith: Pussy Riot and the Insider/Outsider Challenge to Post-Soviet Orthodoxy," *Religion and Gender* 4.2 (2014): 121–44.

96. Certainly, there are hagiographic and interpretive ways to view women such as Mary as serving as priest or bishop of the early Christian community, but this is not something currently acknowledged, commemorated, or widely held among Orthodox communities. See the historical evidence in Carolyn Osiek and Kevin Madigan, *Ordained Women in the Early Church: A Documentary History* (Baltimore: Johns Hopkins University Press, 2011); Mary Cunningham, "The Mother of God as 'Priest' in the Eastern Christian Tradition: A Response to Recent Scholarship," in *Women and Ordination in the Eastern Orthodox Church: Explorations in Theology and Practice*, ed. Gabrielle Thomas and Elena Narisnskaya (Eugene, OR: Cascade Books, 2020), 114–28.

97. Perhaps as a reaction to late antique religious sects that did have women leaders. A challenge to this view is argued by Ally Kateusz, *Mary and Early Christian Women: Hidden Leadership* (London: Palgrave Macmillan, 2019); see also discussion in Valerie Karras, "Priestesses or Priests' Wives: Presbytera in Early Christianity," *St Vladimir's Theological Quarterly* 51.2–3 (2007): 321–45.

98. Eva Catafygiotu Topping, "Orthodox Women and the Iconic Image of Christ," in *Holy Mothers of Orthodoxy*, 125.

99. The Synodikon of the Seventh Ecumenical Council is greatly abbreviated in some present-day usages; see, e.g., "Procession of the Holy Icons," Digital Chant Stand of the Greek Orthodox Archdiocese of America, https://dcs.goarch.org/goa/dcs/dcs.html. For the critical edition of the full text, see Jen Gouillard, "Le Synodikon de l'Orthodoxie: Edition et commentaire," *Travaux et memoires* 2 (1967): 1–313.

100. John 20:11–18. For a brief discussion of women as "equal to the apostles," see Paul Ladouceur, "The Ordination of Women to the Priesthood:

A Theological Issue or a Pastoral Matter?," in *Women and Ordination in the Orthodox Church: Explorations in Theology and Practice*, ed. Gabrielle Thomas and Elena Narinskaya (Eugene, OR: Wipf & Stock, 2020), 180.

101. One can even view the lineage of particular patriarchates maintained on their respective websites; see the list that goes back to the apostle Andrew on the website of the Ecumenical Patriarch, "List of Ecumenical Patriarchs," https://www.patriarchate.org/list-of-ecumenical-patriarchs.

102. Nadieszda Kizenko, "Feminized Patriarchy? Orthodoxy and Gender in Post-Soviet Russia," *Signs* 38.3 (2013): 595–621.

103. Paul Ladouceur, "The Ordination of Women to the Priesthood: A Theological Issue or a Pastoral Matter?" in Thomas and Narinskaya, *The Ordination of Women in the Orthodox Church*, 166–86.

104. Petros Vassiliadis, Niki Papageorgiou, and Eleni Kasselouri-Hatzivassiliadi, eds., *Deaconesses, the Ordination of Women and Orthodox Theology* (Newcastle: Cambridge Scholars Publishing, 2017). This is not to say that the educational efforts of those promoting its restoration are not without impact, only that there has yet to be widespread ordination of women to this office.

105. Behr-Sigel, *The Ministry of Women in the Church*, 104.

106. See, e.g., the role of the empress Pulcheria discussed in Vasiliki Limberis, *Divine Heiress: The Virgin Mary and the Creation of Christian Constantinople* (New York: Routledge, 2012). Other imperial women are notable in the spread and defense of Orthodox faith: Irene, Theodora, Olga, and Pulcheria held significant influence in the church and state in ways that did not necessarily translate to nonroyal women. Pulcheria's role, as well as women's involvement in the Marian controversy, has been the subject of some scholarly debate; see Richard Price, "Marian Piety and the Nestorian Controversy," in *The Church and Mary*, ed. R. N. Swanson, Studies in Church History 39 (Woodbridge: Boydell & Brewer, 2004), 31–38; Liz James, "The Empress and the Virgin in Early Byzantium: Piety, Authority, and Devotion," in *Images of the Mother of God: Perceptions of the Theotokos in Byzantium*, ed. Maria Vassilaki (Aldershot: Ashgate, 2004), 145–52. For discussion of royal women and their influence in various contexts, see Lynda Garland, *Byzantine Empresses: Women and Power in Byzantium AD 527–1204* (New York: Routledge), 1999.

107. "The Mission of the Orthodox Church in Today's World," Official Documents of the Holy and Great Council of the Orthodox Church, June 26, 2016, https://www.holycouncil.org/-/mission-orthodox-church-todays-world.

108. Sarah Ahmed, *Living a Feminist Life* (Durham, NC: Duke University Press, 2017), 40.

109. Many resources for current conversations on the diaconate can be found at St. Phoebe Center for the Deaconess, orthodoxdeaconess.org.

110. See my earlier discussion on this issue: "Constructing the Patriarchal Woman: Liturgical Challenges for Orthodox Christian Gender Equality," *Journal of Orthodox Christian Studies* 1.2 (2019): 167–88. See also Liveris, *Ancient Taboos and Gender Prejudice*; Gassin, "Eastern Orthodox Christianity and Men's Violence against Women."

111. On the Orthodox liturgical context, see Alexander Schmemann, *Introduction to Liturgical Theology* (Crestwood, NY: St Vladimir's Seminary Press, 1966); Christina Gschwandtner, *Welcoming Finitude: Toward a Phenomenology of Orthodox Liturgy* (New York: Fordham University Press, 2019). For an overview of the liturgy as perceived by the laity, see Nicholas Denysenko, *The People's Faith: The Liturgy of the Faithful in Orthodoxy* (Minneapolis: Fortress Academic Press, 2018).

112. Frost, *Maternal Body*, 59–67; Brian Butcher, "Gender and Orthodox Theology: Vistas and Vantage Points," in *Orthodox Christianity and Gender: Dynamics of Tradition, Culture and Lived Practice*, ed. Helena Kupari and Elina Vuola (New York: Routledge, 2020), 23–46.

113. Carrie Frederick Frost, *Church of Our Granddaughters* (Eugene, OR: Cascade Books, 2023), 45. Frost discusses the current and historical practices and offers a possibility for the future (46–54).

114. Frost, *Maternal Body*.

115. The visibility of women in the church as parish council leaders, readers, chanters, choir directors, acolytes/altar servers, procession participants, ushers, etc., often varies from parish to parish, geographically, or by jurisdiction without widespread hierarchical approval or even unofficial consensus.

116. See the discussion of Topping and Behr-Sigel's rejection of the "iconic" argument in Pauline Kollontai, "Contemporary Thinking on the Role and Ministry of Women in the Orthodox Church," *Journal of Contemporary Religion* 15.2 (2000): 165–79, 173.

117. In women's monasteries, the abbess has more authority than most other women, and certain nuns may serve as acolytes, read the gospel, cense, and perform other liturgical functions that typically exclude laywomen. In addition, in many parishes the priest's wife may have greater authority to take on more pastoral roles and have greater liturgical access than other laywomen and may be said to participate in the priesthood of her husband.

118. See my "Constructing the Patriarchal Woman: Liturgical Challenges for Orthodox Christian Gender Equality," *Journal of Orthodox Christian Studies* 1.2 (2019): 167–88.

119. See the relevant discussion in Behr, *The Mystery of Christ*, 119–34.

120. I thank Susan Ashbrook Harvey for raising this insight in conversation.

121. For discussion from Byzantine examples, see Judith Herrin, *Unrivalled Influence: Women and Empire in Byzantium* (Princeton, NJ: Princeton University Press, 2013); Vasiliki Limberis, *Divine Heiress: The Virgin Mary and the Making of Christian Constantinople* (New York: Routledge, 2012); Alice-Mary Talbot, ed., *Byzantine Defenders of Images: Eight Saints Lives in English Translation* (Washington, DC: Dumbarton Oaks, 1998); Francis Butler, "Ol'ga's Conversion and the Construction of Chronicle Narrative," *Russian Review* 67 (2008): 230–42.

122. Kurt Sherry, *Kassia the Nun in Context: The Religious Thought of a Ninth-Century Byzantine Monastic* (Piscataway, NJ: Gorgias Press, 2011). Donald Nicol, "Theodora Raoulaina, Nun and Scholar, c. 1240–1300," in *The Byzantine Lady: Ten Portraits, 1250–1500* (Cambridge: Cambridge University Press, 1994), 33–47.

123. Elisabeth Behr-Sigel, "Feminine Images and Orthodox Spirituality," *Ecumenical Review* 60 (2008): 15; Eva Catafgyiotu Topping, "Reflections of an Orthodox Christian Feminist," *Greek-American Review* (1991): 41–45, 44; Leonie Liveris, "Authority in the Church as the Body of Christ—The Orthodox Vision," *Ecumenical Review* 60 (2008): 108.

124. Frost, *Maternal Body*, 34.

125. Most significantly from scripture, see, e.g., Ephesians 5:22–23 and Genesis 3:16.

## CHAPTER TWO

1. Susan Ashbrook Harvey, "Women, Men, and Gender in Christianity: Historical Reflections on Past and Present," in *Rethinking Gender in Orthodox Christianity*, ed. Ashley Purpura, Thomas Arentzen, and Susan Ashbrook Harvey (Eugene, OR: Pickwick Publications, 2023), 46.

2. For instance, the short saints' lives retold on various jurisdictional websites such as Orthodox Church of America, "Lives of the Saints," https://www.oca.org/saints/lives (accessed December 7, 2020); Greek Orthodox Archdiocese of America, "Saints Search," https://www.goarch.org/chapel/search (accessed December 7, 2020); the liturgical reading of the synaxarion, and more popularized editions with daily saints' readings such as those included in Nikolai Velimirovic, *The Prologue of Ohrid: Lives of Saints, Hymns, Reflections and Homilies for Every Day of the Year*, 2 vols., trans. T. Timothy Tepsic (Alhambra, CA: St. Sebastian Orthodox Press, 2017).

3. On tropes of women in Orthodox texts, see the classic Catia Galatariotou, "Holy Women and Witches: Aspects of Byzantine Conceptions of Gender," *Byzantine and Modern Greek Studies* 9 (1985): 55–94.

4. On the ways liturgical and hagiographic texts construct desirable religious subjects, see Derek Krueger, *Liturgical Subjects: Christian Ritual, Biblical Narrative, and the Formation of the Self in Byzantium* (Philadelphia: University of Pennsylvania Press, 2014).

5. The challenge of women's scholarship and scholarship on women in Orthodox studies is an issue within both the church and the academy (especially globally). Resonances with issues across the scholarship of religion more broadly, especially the study of historically patriarchal religions, have yet to be explored. See, e.g., the issues raised in Kecia Ali, Alison Joseph, Sharon Jacob, Sarah Imhoff, Toni Bond, Natasha Heller, and Stephanie Buckhanon Crowder, "Living It Out: Manthologies," *Journal of Feminist Studies in Religion* 36.1 (2020): 145–58.

6. Blossom Stefaniw, "Feminist Historiography and Uses of the Past," *Studies in Late Antiquity* 4.3 (2020): 260–83, 281. Stefaniw highlights the importance of feminist perspectives in historical accuracy. For the negative way women are portrayed in hagiography, see Galatariotou, "Holy Women and Witches."

7. See Eva Catafygiotu Topping, "Reflections of an Orthodox Feminist," in *Holy Mothers of Orthodoxy: Women and the Church* (Minneapolis: Light and Life Publishing, 1987), 3–11. Topping notes also the limiting views of women presented in hymns and the patristic tradition, noting that "this sexist theology has determined the attitudes and praxis of the church" (4).

8. Judith Butler, *Gender Trouble: Feminism and the Subversion of Identity* (London: Routledge, 1990); Simone de Beauvoir, *The Second Sex*, trans. Constance Borde and Sheila Malovany Chevallier (New York: Knopf, 2010); See also Candace West and Don H. Zimmerman, "Doing Gender," *Gender and Society* 1.2 (1987): 125–51.

9. See, e.g., Bryce Rich, *Gender Essentialism and Orthodoxy: Beyond Male and Female* (New York: Fordham University Press, 2022); Valerie Karras, "Patristic Views on the Ontology of Gender," in *Personhood: Orthodox Christianity and the Connection between Body, Mind, and Soul*, ed. John Chirban (Westpoint, CT: Bergin & Garvey, 1996), 113–19; John Behr, "A Note on the 'Ontology of Gender,'" *St Vladimir's Theological Quarterly* 42 (1998): 363–72; Verna Harrison, "Male and Female in Cappadocian Theology," *Journal of Theological Studies* 41 (1990): 441–71; Timothy Patitsas, "The Marriage of Priests: Towards an Orthodox Christian Theology of Gender," *St Vladimir's Theological Quarterly* 51, no. 1 (2007): 71–105.

10. For some examples of this in Orthodox contexts, see Elina Vuola, "Finnish Orthodox Women and the Virgin Mary," *Journal of the European Society of Women in Theological Research* 24 (2016): 63–80; Carrie Frederick Frost, *Maternal Body: A Theology of Incarnation from the Christian East* (New York: Paulist Press, 2019); Ina Merdjanova, ed., *Women and Religiosity in Orthodox Christianity* (New York: Fordham University Press, 2021).

11. Monastic, clerical, and ascetic views dominate. In addition, while masculinity may transform significantly in moving toward holiness, it does not become associated with giving up its priority over femininity. See also Virginia Burrus, *"Begotten Not Made": Conceiving Manhood in Late Antiquity* (Stanford: Stanford University Press, 2000).

12. See the excellent study of overlapping structures of marginalization in historically Orthodox contexts in Roland Betancourt, *Byzantine Intersectionality: Sexuality, Gender, and Race in the Middle Ages* (Princeton, NJ: Princeton University Press, 2020).

13. Luis Josué Salés, "Androprimacy," *Religion and Gender* 12.2 (2022): 195–213.

14. The problems of male entitlement to tell women about their own stories and how they should be in their lives brings to mind Rebecca Solnit, *Men Explain Things to Me* (Chicago: Haymarket Books, 2014), 4; Kate Manne, *Entitled: How Male Privilege Hurts Women* (New York: Crown, 2020).

15. "The Service of Marriage—Liturgical Texts of the Orthodox Church," Greek Orthodox Archdiocese of America, March 1, 2018, https://www.goarch.org/-/the-service-of-the-crowning-the-service-of-marriage. For a brief overview of the development of the Orthodox marriage service and additional versions of the rites, see John Meyendorff, *Marriage: An Orthodox Perspective* (Crestwood, NY: St Vladimir's Seminary Press, 2000).

16. Kate Manne, *Down Girl: The Logic of Misogyny* (Oxford: Oxford University Press, 2018), 46–47, 192.

17. Manne, *Down Girl*, 47, 176.

18. Donna Rizk-Asdourian, "Women and Their Position within the Liturgical Life of the Coptic and Oriental Orthodox Churches," in Purpura, Arentzen, and Harvey, *Rethinking Gender in Orthodox Christianity*, 182–83; original emphasis.

19. See my "Constructing the Patriarchal Woman: Liturgical Challenges for Orthodox Christian Gender Equality," *Journal of Orthodox Christian Studies* 1.2 (2019): 167–88.

20. For example, the claim for equal dignity based on sex mentioned in "The Mission of the Orthodox Church in Today's World," Official Documents of the Holy and Great Council of the Orthodox Church, June 26, 2016,

https://www.holycouncil.org/-/mission-orthodox-church-todays-world; not to mention other hierarchically issued documents. Although the consensus on women being fully in the divine image is not consistent through all of the patristic tradition, see Nonna Verna Harrison, "The Image of God in the Antiochene Tradition," *Journal of Early Christian Studies* 7.4 (1999): 613–14.

21. One example, as notable as it was for its time in taking seriously questions of feminism and theology but nevertheless perpetuating a depersonalizing ideal feminine, is Paul Evdokimov's *Woman and the Salvation of the World*, trans. Anthony Gythiel (Crestwood, NY: St Vladimir's Seminary Press, 1994).

22. "Life of St. Mary the Younger," trans. Angeliki E. Laiou, in *Holy Women of Byzantium: Ten Saints' Lives in English Translation*, ed. Alice-Mary Talbot (Washington, DC: Dumbarton Oaks, 1996), 254.

23. Alexis Torrance and Symeon Paschalidis, eds., *Personhood in the Byzantine Christian Tradition: Early, Medieval, and Modern Perspectives* (London: Routledge, 2018); Aristotle Papanikolaou, "Personhood and Its Exponents in Twentieth-Century Orthodox Theology," in *The Cambridge Companion to Orthodox Christian Theology*, ed. Elizabeth Theokritoff and Mary B. Cunningham (Cambridge: Cambridge University Press, 2008), 232–45.

24. Anne Alwis, trans., *Narrating Martyrdom: Rewriting Late Antique Virgin Martyrs in Byzantium* (Liverpool: Liverpool University Press, 2010), 145–46, 167.

25. Amma Sarah, in *Give Me a Word: The Alphabetical Sayings of the Desert Fathers*, trans. John Wortley (Crestwood, NY: St Vladimir's Seminary Press, 2014), 301. See also Wortley's fuller explanation of "logismos" on p. 24.

26. This is expounded in chapter 4 in greater detail.

27. *The Life of Melania the Younger*, trans. Elizabeth Clark (New York: Edwin Mellen Press, 1984), 35.

28. See the rich discussions of Melania and gender amid historical considerations in Catherine Michael Chin and Caroline Schroeder, eds., *Melania: Early Christianity through the Life of One Family* (Berkeley: University of California Press, 2017).

29. Rosemary Radford Ruether, *Sexism and God-Talk: Toward a Feminist Theology* (Boston: Beacon Press, 1983), 18–19.

30. Elena Chernyak, "What Is a Woman Created For? The Image of Women in Russia through the Lens of the Russian Orthodox Church," *Feminist Theology* 24.3 (2016): 299–313.

31. Elisabeth Behr-Sigel, *The Ministry of Women in the Orthodox Church*, trans. Steven Bigham (Crestwood, NY: St Vladimir's Seminary Press, 1999), 36.

32. Rich, *Gender Essentialism and Orthodoxy*.

33. Salés, "Androprimacy"; Leonora Neville, *Byzantine Gender* (Leeds: Arc Humanities Press, 2019); Damien Casey, "The Spiritual Valency of Gender in Byzantine Society," in *Questions of Gender in Byzantine Society*, ed. Bronwen Neil and Lynda Garland (London: Ashgate, 2013), 167–82.

34. For detailed analysis of this, see my articles, "Innovating 'Traditional' Women's Roles: Byzantine Insights for Orthodox Christian Gender Discourse," *Modern Theology* 36.3 (2020): 641–61; and "Beyond the Binary: Hymnographic Constructions of Eastern Gender Identities," *Journal of Religion* 97, no. 4 (2017): 524–46.

35. Gillian Cloke, *"This Female Man of God": Women and Spiritual Power in the Patristic Age, AD 350–450* (New York: Routledge, 1995).

36. Some saints in this category are Matrona, Eugenia, and Mary. Even though there are numerous historical and theological reasons to explore such figures as transgender, within Orthodox commemorations such saints are always commemorated as women—even as problematic as that may be.

37. Luce Irigaray, *Sexes and Genealogies*, trans. G. Gill (New York: Columbia University Press, 1993), 64; a constructive feminist theological critique of Irigaray's claim can be found in Susan Hekman, "Divine Women? Irigaray, God, and the Subject," *Feminist Theology* 27.2 (2019): 117–25.

38. On the cross-dressing hagiographic motif, see Betancourt, *Byzantine Intersectionality*; Rebecca Wiegel, "Reading Matrona: The Sixth Century Life of a Trans Saint" (PhD diss, University of Notre Dame, 2019), 89–120; Crystal Lubinsky, *Removing Masculine Layers to Reveal a Holy Womanhood: The Female Transvestite Monks of Late Antique Eastern Christianity* (Turnhout: Brepols, 2013); John Anson, "The Female Transvestite in Early Monasticism: The Origin and Development of a Motif," *Viator* 5 (1974): 1–32; Stavroula Constantinou, "Holy Actors and Actresses: Fools and Cross-Dressers as the Protagonists of Saints' Lives," in *The Ashgate Research Companion to Byzantine Hagiography*, vol. 2: *Genre and Contexts*, ed. Stephanos Efthymiadis (Burlington, VT: Ashgate, 2014), 343–62; Évelyne Patlagean, "L'histoire de la femme déguise en moine et l'évolution de la sainteté féminen à Byzance," *Studi Medievali* 17 (1976): 598–623; and Judith Herrin, "In Search of Byzantine Women: Three Avenues of Approach," in *Images of Women in Antiquity*, ed. Avril Cameron (Detroit: Croom Helm, 1983), 179. Herrin notes, "The monastic disguises adopted by women enabled them to simulate a holiness reserved by male ecclesiastical authorities to men only. To the church fathers, the very idea of a holy woman was a contradiction in terms which women could only get round by pretending to be men" (179).

39. For the gendering of monasticism, see Alice-Mary Talbot, "A Comparison of the Monastic Experience of Byzantine Men and Women," in *Greek Orthodox Theological Review* 30 (1985): 1–20.

40. *Holy Women of Byzantium*, 18. On Matrona's life more generally, see Eva Topping, "St. Matrona and Her Friends: Sisterhood in Byzantium," in ΚΑΘΗΓΗΤΡΙΑ: Essays Presented to Joan Hussey on Her 80th Birthday, ed. J. Chrysostomides (Camberley: Porphyrogenitus, 1988); and Khalifa Abubakr Bennasser, "Gender and Sanctity in Early Byzantine Monasticism: A Study of the Phenomenon of Female Ascetics in Male Monastic Habit with a Translation of the Life of St. Matrona" (PhD diss., Rutgers University, 1984).

41. Linn Tonstad, "Ambivalent Loves: Christian Theologies, Queer Theologies," *Literature and Theology* 31.4 (2017): 472–89, 477.

42. "St. Mary of Egypt," in *Holy Women of Byzantium*, 65–93, 76–77.

43. *The Life of Melania the Younger*, trans. Clark, 54.

44. *Christian Novels from the Menologion of Symeon Metaphrastes*, trans. Stratis Papaioannou (Cambridge, MA: Harvard University Press, 2017), 79–81.

45. Susan Ashbrook Harvey, "Women in Byzantine Hagiography," in *That Gentle Strength*, ed. L. Coon (Charlottesville: University of Virginia Press, 1990), 40.

46. See, e.g., Velimirovic, *The Prologue of Ohrid*; Hieromonk Makarios, ed., *The Synaxarion: The Lives of the Saints of the Orthodox Church*, 7 vols., trans. Christopher Hookway, Maria Rule, and Joanna Burton (Ormylia, Greece: Holy Convent of the Annunciation of Our Lady, 1998–2008). One example of saints' lives being read by women as informing their own religious lives is Melinda Johnson, ed., *Seven Holy Women: Conversations with Saints and Friends* (Chesterton, IN: Ancient Faith Publishing, 2020).

47. *The Protevangelium of James*, trans. Lily Vuong (Eugene, OR: Cascade Books, 2019), sec. 19–20.

48. See the term's usage in early Christian texts to refer to both aspects, in *A Patristic Greek Lexicon*, ed. G. W. H. Lampe (Oxford: Oxford University Press, 1961), s.v. "ἀδιαφθόρως," 35.

49. See the hymn to Mary known as the megalynarion, Ἄξιον ἐστίν ("It is truly meet").

50. Mary Daly, *Beyond God the Father* (London: Women's Press, 1986), 81.

51. Vuola, "Finnish Orthodox Women and the Virgin Mary." This type of question also relates to the divergence of the Orthodox position on the immaculate conception compared to Catholicism. For the latter, see the Western position, which is based to a large extent on patristic (both Greek and Latin) witnesses and is set out at length in Martin Jugie, *L'immaculée conception dans l'Écriture Sainte et dans la tradition orientale* (Rome, 1952); and Christiaan

Kappes, *The Immaculate Conception: Why Thomas Aquinas Denied, While John Duns Scotus, Gregory Palamas, and Mark Eugenicus Professed the Absolute Immaculate Existence of Mary* (New Bedford, MA: Academy of the Immaculate, 2014). Although there is no dogmatic stance among Orthodox, for one example of refuting the Catholic teaching, see Sergius Bulgakov, *The Burning Bush: On the Orthodox Veneration of the Mother of God*, trans. Thomas Allan Smith (Grand Rapids, MI: Eerdmans, 2009).

52. Numerous Orthodox hymns to the Theotokos laud her as "Higher than the heavens" and "More honorable than the Cherubim," etc.

53. Maria McDowell, "Seeing Gender: Orthodox Liturgy, Orthodox Personhood, Unorthodox Exclusion," *Journal of the Society of Christian Ethics* 33.2 (2013): 73–92.

54. Neville, *Byzantine Gender*.

55. The spiritual danger of lust associated with women (but also youthful men) as akin to the dangers of heretical doctrines. Silviu Lupașcu, "Saintly Sexlessness: Notes on the Apophthegmata Patrum," *Review of Ecumenical Studies* 8 (2016): 391–400. Arsenius, saying 28, in John Wortley, trans., *Give Me a Word: The Alphabetical Sayings of the Desert Fathers* (Yonkers, NY: St Vladimir's Seminary Press, 2014), 47–48.

56. On the social construction of gender and sex, see the foundational arguments in Butler, *Gender Trouble*.

57. Mary of Egypt, for example, is so transformed that she is unrecognizable as a woman in "Life of St. Mary of Egypt," in *Holy Women of Byzantium*, 76. On even when that transformation is perhaps violently erotic in its own way, see Virginia Burrus, "Word and Flesh: The Bodies and Sexuality of Ascetic Women in Christian Antiquity," *Journal of Feminist Studies in Religion* 10.1 (1994): 27–25. On the related connection between asceticism and disordered eating in transforming the body in saints' lives, see Caroline W. Bynum, *Holy Feast and Holy Fast: The Religious Significance of Food to Medieval Women* (Berkeley: University of California Press, 1987).

58. "St. Mary the Younger, "in *Holy Women of Byzantium*, 258; on mourning children in early Christianity, see Maria Doerfler, *Jephthah's Daughter, Sarah's Son: The Death of Children in Late Antiquity* (Oakland: University of California Press, 2019); Neville, *Byzantine Gender*, also considers the gendered valence of mourning.

59. For example, Melania the Younger offers her husband all of her money so that she can avoid marriage but nevertheless becomes pregnant. *The Life of Melania the Younger*, trans. Clark, 28. Maroula Perisanidi, "Should We Abstain? Spousal Equality in Twelfth-Century Byzantine Canon Law," *Gender and History* 28.2 (2016): 422–37.

60. Increasing opportunities for girls to be involved in liturgical service in front of the iconostasis seem to be more widespread—such as carrying candles, holding baskets for antidoron, or reading the epistle—but female altar servers serving alongside males even behind the iconostasis remains limited, except in some churches belonging to the Church of Antioch in Syria and of course most women's monasteries.

61. These expectations do not necessarily mean women lack agency in their choices to be modest or not. See the excellent study on modesty: Kate Wilkinson, *Women and Modesty in Late Antiquity* (Cambridge: Cambridge University Press, 2015).

62. Vassa Larin, "What is Ritual Im/Purity and Why?," *St Vladimir's Theological Quarterly* 52.3–4 (2008): 275–92.

63. 1 Corinthians 6:19–20.

64. John Moschos, *The Spiritual Meadow (Pratum Spirituale)*, trans. John Wortley (Collegeville, MN: Liturgical Press, 2008), 39.29–30.

65. Brenda Llewellyn Ihssen, *John Moschos' Spiritual Meadow: Authority and Autonomy at the End of the Antique World* (Aldershot: Ashgate, 2014), 143. Ihssen draws the conclusion, "In a few cases, as we saw, healing of women by male ascetics was also done without comment on the appropriate or inappropriateness of that interaction. As we also saw, women did not have a voice in particular tales to express whether or not they wanted healing" (143).

66. Thomas Arentzen and Mary B. Cunningham, eds., *The Reception of the Virgin in Byzantium: Marian Narratives in Texts and Images* (Cambridge: Cambridge University Press, 2019).

67. Leena Mari Peltomaa, *The Images of the Virgin Mary in the Akathistos Hymn* (Leiden: Brill, 2001).

68. Thomas Arentzen, *The Virgin in Song: Mary and the Poetry of Romanos the Melodist* (Philadelphia: University of Pennsylvania Press, 2017).

69. Alexander Riehle, "Authorship and Gender (and) Identity: Women's Writing in the Middle Byzantine Period," in *The Author in Middle Byzantine Literature: Modes, Functions, and Identities*, ed. Aglae Pizzone (Berlin: De Gruyter, 2014), 245–62.

70. See my "Beyond the Binary"; see also the stichera in the voice of the mourning Theotokos in *The Lenten Triodion*, trans. Mother Mary and Kallistos Ware (South Canaan, PA: St. Tikhon's Seminary Press, 2002), 612.

71. For what an Orthodox woman's theological reflection on maternity might look like, see Frost, *Maternal Body*.

72. "Life of St. Mary of Egypt," in *Holy Women of Byzantium*, 80. See, e.g., the account of a sainted Mary of Egypt who was much more modest, in

Moschos, *The Spiritual Meadow*, 179; Benedicta Ward, *Harlots of the Desert: A Study of Repentance in Early Monastic Sources*, Cistercian Studies Series (Kalamazoo, MI: Cistercian Publications, 1987) 28–32; Efthalia Makris Walsh, "The Ascetic Mother Mary of Egypt," *Greek Orthodox Theological Review* 34.1 (1989): 61; Betancourt, *Byzantine Intersectionality*, 1–5.

73. Mary of Egypt features prominently in the Lenten cycle, with the fifth Sunday dedicated to her commemoration, her life being read in full interspersed with the Canon of Repentance attributed to Andrew of Crete on the Thursday of the fourth week, and an April 1 fixed feast that typically falls during Lent. See *The Lenten Triodion*, trans. Mother Mary and Kallistos Ware, 370–463, for examples of this commemoration.

74. Neville, *Byzantine Gender*.

75. Alwis, *Narrating Martyrdom*, 180.

76. A fascinating analysis of the theological discourse surrounding Mary's consent can be found in Betancourt, *Byzantine Intersectionality*, 19–58.

77. George Ventouris and Despoina Athanasiadou-Ventouris "Saint Methodia of Kimolos," ed. John Sanidopoulos, https://www.johnsanidopoulos.com/2013/10/saint-methodia-of-kimolos-1908.html (accessed December 9, 2020).

78. See accounts of the lives of St. Xenia and Maria of Paris in Sergei Hackel, *Pearl of Great Price: The Life of Mother Maria Skobtsova, 1891–1945* (London: Darton, Longman, & Todd, 1981); and *The Life and Miracles of Blessed Xenia of St. Petersburg* (Jordanville, NY: Holy Trinity Monastery, 1997).

79. For this version of her apolytikion, see "Saints of Recent Decades: St. Maria of Paris," Antiochian Orthodox Christian Archdiocese of North America, http://ww1.antiochian.org/christianeducation/saints-recent-decades/st-maria-paris (accessed December 9, 2020).

80. For instance, the troparion used by the Russian Orthodox Church outside of Russia, St. Xenia Orthodox Church, "Blessed Xenia, a homeless wanderer of the city of St. Peter," https://www.stxenia.org/stxenia (accessed December 9, 2020).

81. See, e.g., Michael Plekon, *Saints as They Really Are: Voices of Holiness in Our Time* (Notre Dame, IN: University of Notre Dame Press, 2012).

82. Cathy Caridi, *Making Martyrs East and West* (Ithaca, NY: Cornell University Press, 2016). Caridi demonstrates that modern Russian Orthodox canonization practices depend on the recognition and commemoration of the saint by at least the local bishop.

83. There are of course women involved in local devotional movements that recognize saintliness of individuals that may then prompt formal liturgical canonization and recognition.

84. Manne, *Entitled*, 8. Manne observes, "I take sexism to be the theoretical and ideological branch of patriarchy: the beliefs, ideas, and assumptions that serve to rationalize and naturalize patriarchal norms and expectations—including a gendered division of labor, and men's dominance over women in areas of traditionally male power and authority" (8).

85. Linda Alcoff, "The Problem of Speaking for Others," *Cultural Critique* 20 (1991): 5–32, 10–11.

86. Such limitations in the traditional Christian focus driven by male monastics are highlighted by Soskice, *The Kindness of God*, 14–25, 23.

87. On rejection of the "add women" solution to an otherwise patriarchal Christian tradition, see Soskice, *The Kindness of God*, 104 ff.

## CHAPTER THREE

1. Evidenced by my own experience and in conversation with other Orthodox women scholars about reactions to their work. We have received threatening emails, calls to our priests or bishops demanding that they correct and rebuke us, requests that we leave the church if we want a progressive denomination, derogatory assumptions about our goals, public misrepresentations of our work online, and misogynistic comments about our families and appearance.

2. See, e.g., the foundational work by Delores Williams, *Sisters in the Wilderness: The Challenge of Womanist God-Talk* (New York: Orbis), 1993; Ada Maria Isasi-Diaz, "Christ in Mujerista Theology," in *Thinking of Christ*, ed. Tatha Wiley (London: Continuum, 2003), 157–76. See also the disparate views in Daphne Hampson, ed., *Swallowing a Fishbone? Feminist Theologians Debate Christianity* (London: SPCK Publishing, 1996); and the compelling discussion about vulnerability in Gabrielle Thomas, "The Status of Vulnerability in a Theology of the Christian Life: Gregory of Nyssa on the 'Wound of Love' in Conversation with Sarah Coakley," *Modern Theology* 38 (2022): 777–95.

3. G. E. H. Palmer, Philip Sherrard, and Kallistos Ware, eds., *The Philokalia: The Complete Text Compiled by St. Nikodimos of the Holy Mountain and St. Makarios of Corinth*, 5 vols. (London: Faber and Faber, 1979, 1981, 1984, 1995, 2023); John Wortley, ed., *The Anonymous Sayings of the Desert Fathers: A Select Edition and English Translation* (Cambridge: Cambridge University Press, 2013); John Wortley, trans., *Give Me a Word: The Alphabetical Sayings of the Desert Fathers* (Yonkers, NY: St Vladimir's Seminary Press, 2014); John Moschos, *The Spiritual Meadow*, trans. John Wortley (Collegeville, MN: Liturgical Press, 1992).

4. J. L. Zecher, "Tradition and Creativity in the Construction and Reading of the *Philokalia*," in *The Philokalia: A Classic Text of Orthodox Spirituality*, ed. Brock Bingaman and Bradley Nassif (Oxford: Oxford University Press, 2012), 123. Zecher rightly observes that "the *Philokalia* may be perceived as describing a tradition which, if not incorporating the totality of Orthodox spirituality, certainly represents its highest ambitions and most pregnant possibilities" (123).

5. Introduction to *The Philokalia: The Complete Text*, 1:1–18; Bingaman and Nassif, *The Philokalia*; Graham Gould, *Desert Fathers on Monastic Community* (Oxford: Oxford University Press, 1993); John Wortley, *An Introduction to the Desert Fathers* (Cambridge: Cambridge University Press, 2019).

6. Despite my focus on drawing attention to the ways that the values of the past continue to give license to behaviors and attitudes in the present for women in particular, it is important to note that the privileging of unmarried saints and the celibate ascetic life applies to men as well as women in the historical tradition of the church. See Kallistos Ware, "The Monk and the Married Christian: Some Comparisons in Early Monastic Sources," *Eastern Churches Review* 6.1 (1974): 72–83. See also the review essay by John Chryssavgis of *The Sacrament of Love: The Married Saints of the Church*, *Greek Orthodox Theological Review* 34.2 (1989):182–89.

7. See, e.g., the recommendation from the recently sainted Joseph the Hesychast that saints' lives serve to "warm up" and "restore," in *Monastic Wisdom: The Letters of Elder Joseph the Hesychast* (Florence, AZ: St. Anthony's Greek Orthodox Monastery, 1998), 85–86.

8. See, e.g., Nun Gavrilia, *Mother Gavrilia: The Ascetic of Love*, trans. Helen Anthony (Milwaukee, WI: Sea Salt Books, 2022); *Monastic Wisdom: The Letters of Elder Joseph the Hesychast*.

9. "Life of Mary the Younger," trans. Angeliki Laiou, in *Holy Women of Byzantium: Ten Saints' Lives in English Translation*, ed. Alice-Mary Talbot (Washington, DC: Dumbarton Oaks, 1996), 254.

10. Valerie Saiving, "The Human Situation: A Feminine View," *Journal of Religion* 40.2 (1960): 100–112.

11. Patricia Hill Collins, *Intersectionality: As Critical Social Theory* (Durham, NC: Duke University Press, 2019), 201.

12. For non-Orthodox feminist theological approaches that offer alternative views, see Karen O'Donnell and Katie Cross, *Feminist Trauma Theologies: Body, Scripture and Church in Critical Perspective* (London: SCM Press, 2020).

13. This is further compounded by other intersections of identity, such as race, ethnicity, and class.

14. "Life of St. Mary the Younger," 254.

15. "Life of St. Thomaïs of Lesbos," in *Holy Women of Byzantium*, 305–6.

16. See the creative rethinking of women's suffering as strategic sacrifice in Kathleen Gallagher Elkins, *Mary, Mother of Martyrs: How Motherhood Became Self-Sacrifice in Early Christianity* (London: Wipf & Stock, 2020).

17. For a study of feminism and liberation theology that attends to the intersectionality of women's lives, see Elina Vuola, *Limits of Liberation: Feminist Theology and the Ethics of Poverty and Reproduction* (New York: Bloomsbury, 2002).

18. Anna Mercedes, *Power For: Feminism and Christ's Self-Giving* (London: T&T Clark, 2011).

19. Mercedes, *Power For*, 135.

20. Mercedes, *Power For*, 135.

21. For a brief synopsis of St. Sophia and her daughters, along with their commemorative hymns, see "Martyr Sophia and Her Three Daughters at Rome," Orthodox Church in America, accessed April 1, 2024, https://www.oca.org/saints/lives/2017/09/17/102638-martyr-sophia-and-her-three-daughters-at-rome.

22. See, for instance, the general dismissal hymn for virgin-martyrs, which has the saint being commemorated say, "I love You, my Bridegroom, and in seeking You, I endure suffering." See "Virgin Martyr Apollonia—Troparion & Kontakion," Orthodox Church in America, accessed August 9, 2023, https://www.oca.org/saints/troparia/2023/02/09/149035-virgin-martyr-apollonia.

23. See Mercedes, *Power For*; Angel Narro, "Domestic Violence against Women as a Reason for Sanctification in Byzantine Hagiography," *Studie Philologica Valentina* 20 (2019): 111–40. See the related discussion in Heleen Zorgdrager, "Churches, Dignity, Gender: the Istanbul Convention as a Matter of Public Theology in Ukraine," *International Journal of Public Theology* 14 (2020): 296–318; Ally Moder, "Women, Personhood, and the Male God: A Feminist Critique of Patriarchal Concepts of God in View of Domestic Abuse," *Feminist Theology* 29 (2019): 85–103.

24. Kyra Limberakis, "Archon Symposium, on 'Female Diaconate,'" YouTube, May 31, 2019, https://www.youtube.com/watch?v=wbW0V04chSY. Limberakis provides similar disturbing accounts of pastoral abuse and sexual assault as evidence for why there should be female deacons. For a helpful theological reflection on sexual abuse in Christianity broadly, see Grace Ji-Sun Kim and Susan M. Shaw, *Surviving God: A New Vision of God through the Eyes of Sexual Abuse Survivors* (Minneapolis: Broadleaf Books, 2024).

25. Nadieszda Kizenko, "Beat Her When You Are Alone Together: Domestic Violence in the Russian Tradition, Past and Present," Public Orthodoxy,

February 13, 2017, https://publicorthodoxy.org/2017/02/13/russia-domestic-violence/.

26. "Life of St. Thomaïs of Lesbos," in *Holy Women of Byzantium*, 308. The hagiographer explains, Thomaïs "was adorned by insults as with expensive earrings, her beauty was enhanced by the beatings, <and> she was cheered by the mockeries."

27. A popular book that sparked greater consideration of everyday gender imbalance of emotional and domestic labor in the United States is Gemma Hartley, *Fed Up: Emotional Labor, Women, and the Way Forward* (New York: HarperCollins, 2018).

28. John Colobos, in *Give Me a Word*, 134.

29. Peter Damaskos, "Treasury of Divine Blessings," in *The Philokalia*, 3:85.

30. Theodora, in *Give Me a Word*, 128.

31. For example, the new women saints Olga Michael and Gavrilia Papagiannis worked with the poor, abused, and infirm.

32. Makarios of Egypt, "The Freedom of the Intellect," in *The Philokalia*, 3:343–44.

33. Aristotle Papanikolaou, "Person, *Kenosis* and Abuse: Hans Urs von Balthasar and Feminist Theologies in Conversation," *Modern Theology* 19 (2003): 41–65.

34. Sarah Coakley, "Kenosis and Subversion," in *Powers and Submissions* (New York: Wiley-Blackwell, 2002), 31.

35. Thomas, "The Status of Vulnerability in a Theology of Christian Life," 779.

36. See the rich discussion of gender and emotion in Byzantine texts in Leonora Neville, *Byzantine Gender* (Leeds: Arc Humanities Press, 2019); Stavroula Constantinou and Mati Meyer, eds., *Emotions and Gender in Byzantine Culture* (London: Palgrave Macmillan, 2019).

37. Even saints who lived life as men, such as Marinos, are commemorated as women in Orthodoxy liturgy.

38. "Life of St. Mary the Younger," 254.

39. See the observations about religious ideology and intimate partner violence in the context of Russian Orthodoxy in Elena Chernyak and Betty Barrett, "A Chicken Is Not a Bird, Is a Woman a Human Being? Intimate Partner Violence and the Russian Orthodox Church," *Currents* 10, no. 1 (2011), http://search.proquest.com.ezp-prod1.hul.harvard.edu/scholarly-journals/chicken-is-not-bird-woman-human-being-intimate/docview/1431991072/se-2; and how Greek Orthodox religious ideals might impact abuse and healing in Elisabeth Gassin, "Eastern Orthodox Christianity and Men's Violence against Women," in *Religion and Men's Violence against Women*, ed. Andy

Johnson (New York: Springer, 2015), 163–76. Anecdotally, I also know of many unfortunate accounts of women being told by priests, bishops, and monastic spiritual fathers to stay in unhealthy relationships, endure hardship, or not pursue educational, medical, or economic opportunities for personal development because their suffering was spiritually beneficial and part of being a good Orthodox wife, mother, daughter, etc.

40. See the *Divine Liturgy of John Chrysostom*.

41. "Life of St. Athanasia of Aegina," in *Holy Women of Byzantium*, 154. See the episode of Athanasia of Aegina, who after her death cannot be properly dressed for burial until her nuns invoke the virtue of obedience, saying, "O mistress, as when associating with us you possessed unwavering obedience, so now please obey us and put on this cheap tunic."

42. Mark the Ascetic, "On the Spiritual Law," in *The Philokalia*, 1:120.

43. Anonymous saying 290, in Wortley, *The Anonymous Sayings of the Desert Fathers*, 195.

44. Symeon the New Theologian, "Practical and Theological Texts," in *The Philokalia*, 4:33.

45. John Colobos 14.4, in *Give Me a Word*, 131.

46. "Life of St. Theodora of Thessaloniki," in *Holy Women of Byzantium*, 190.

47. "Life of St. Theodora of Thessaloniki," 190.

48. "Life of St. Theodora of Thessaloniki," 190.

49. Christopher Johnson, *The Globalization of Hesychasm and the Jesus Prayer: Contesting Contemplation* (London: Continuum, 2010).

50. See, e.g., Symeon the New Theologian, "Practical and Theological Texts," in *The Philokalia*, 4:28.

51. I allude here to the broad definition of feminism by bell hooks. See bell hooks, *Feminism Is for Everybody: Passionate Politics* (London: Pluto Press, 2000), 1.

52. John Colobos 20, in *Sayings of the Desert Fathers*, 90.

53. See, e.g., the assessment of one Orthodox priest that "feminism, in all its forms, both the praiseworthy and the less so, may be seen as the quest for power." Lawrence Farley, *Feminism and Tradition: Quiet Reflections on Ordination and Communion* (Crestwood, NY: St Vladimir's Seminary Press, 2012), 105. I note also that the title of this book suggests it offers a counterperspective to "loud" and demanding feminists.

54. "The Divine Liturgy of St. John Chrysostom," Greek Orthodox Archdiocese of America, accessed July 15, 2024, https://www.goarch.org/-/the-divine-liturgy-of-saint-john-chrysostom.

55. Mark the Ascetic, "On the Spiritual Law," in *The Philokalia*, 1:188.

56. Of course, modesty and even submission can be used subversively or to augment agency at times too. See Kate Wilkinson, *Women and Modesty in Late Antiquity* (Cambridge: Cambridge University Press, 2015).

57. See the reflections on culture, the female body, and theology, in Grace Ji-Sun Kim, *Invisible: Theology and The Experience of Asian-American Women* (Minneapolis: Fortress Press, 2021).

58. Symeon the New Theologian, Hymn 15, in *Divine Eros: Hymns of Saint Symeon the New Theologian*, trans. Daniel Griggs (Crestwood, NY: St Vladimir's Seminary Press, 2010), 81–91; Derek Krueger, "Divine Fantasy and the Erotic Imagination in the Hymns of Symeon the New Theologian," in *Dreams, Memory and Imagination in Byzantium*, ed. Bronwen Neil and Eva Anagnostou-Laoutides (Leiden: Brill, 2018), 315–41.

59. Hence the emphasis in modern Orthodox thought on personhood in ethics. See John Zizioulas, *Being as Communion: Studies in Personhood and the Church* (Crestwood, NY: St Vladimir's Seminary Press, 1985), 18.

60. John 10:34. On the historical development of theosis and its use across contexts, see Norman Russell, *The Doctrine of Deification in the Greek Patristic Tradition* (Oxford: Oxford University Press, 2005); Michael Christensen and Jeffery Wittung, eds., *Partakers of the Divine Nature: The History and Development of Deification in the Christian Traditions* (Grand Rapids, MI: Baker Academic, 2008). On how theosis compares to other models of salvation in Christian thought, see Veli-Matti Kärkkäinen, *One with God: Salvation as Deification and Justification* (Collegeville, MN: Liturgical Press, 2004).

61. Aristotle Papanikolaou, *Being with God: Trinity Apophaticism, and Divine-Human Communion* (Notre Dame, IN: University of Notre Dame Press, 2006); Norman Russell, *The Doctrine of Deification in the Greek Patristic Tradition* (Oxford: Oxford University Press, 2004).

62. Athanasius, *On the Incarnation*, trans. John Behr (Crestwood, NY: St Vladimir's Seminary Press, 2011), 166–67.

63. John Behr, "From Adam to Christ: From Male and Female to Being Human," in *Women and Ordination in the Orthodox Church: Explorations in Theology and Practice*, ed. Gabrielle Thomas and Elena Narinskaya (Eugene, OR: Wipf & Stock, 2020), 4.

64. Behr, "From Adam to Christ," 9.

65. See the related theological arguments in Nicholas Cabasilas, *The Life in Christ*, trans. Carmino deCatanzaro (Crestwood, NY: St Vladimir's Seminary Press, 1998), 81, 122, 128, 141–42. Cabasilas notes regarding the Eucharist, "As we partake of His human Body and Blood we receive God Himself into

our souls. It is thus God's Body and Blood which we receive, His soul, mind, and will, no less than those of His humanity" (122).

66. See my *God, Hierarchy, and Power: Orthodox Theologies of Authority from Byzantium* (New York: Fordham University Press, 2018).

67. 2 Corinthians 6:1; Georges Florovsky, *Collected Works*, vol. 10: *The Byzantine Ascetic and Spiritual Fathers* (Vadez, Germany: Buechervertriesbanstalt, 1987), 31. Florovsky observes that "God has freely willed a synergistic path of redemption in which man must spiritually participate."

68. Maximus, "First Century on Theology," in *The Philokalia*, 2:116.

69. Gregory of Nyssa, *The Life of Macrina*, in *Handmaids of the Lord: The Lives of Holy Women in Late Antiquity and the Early Middle Ages*, trans. Joan Petersen (Minneapolis, MN: Cistercian Publications, 1996), 51-52.

70. Heleen Zorgdrager, "Is *theosis* a Gendered Concept? Theological Pitfalls and Perspectives for an Inclusive Affirmation of Human Dignity," *Journal of Eastern Christian Studies* 71.3-4 (2019): 343-68.

71. Peter Damaskos, "Book 1 Treasury of Divine Knowledge," in *The Philokalia*, 3:76.

72. "Life of Blessed Elisabeth the Wonderworker," in *Holy Women of Byzantium*, 122. On the overturning of the fall through a woman, see also the Sticheron of Matins for the Feast of the Synaxis of the Theotokos that says, "O Virgin Theotokos, who hast given birth unto the Saviour, though hast overturned the ancient curse of Eve." *The Menaion*, vol. 4, trans. Holy Transfiguration Monastery (Boston: Holy Transfiguration Monastery, 2005), 227.

73. It is worth noting that even female saints who spent their lives living as men (ostensibly transgender saints) are commemorated in Orthodoxy as women saints, a denial perhaps of even the most determined attempts to live beyond their assigned gender. See Rebecca Wiegel, "Matrona's Lament: Reading Trans Narratives in Eastern Orthodox Traditions," in *Rethinking Gender in Orthodox Christianity*, ed. Ashley Purpura, Thomas Arentzen, and Susan Ashbrook Harvey (Eugene, OR: Pickwick Press, 2023), 51-69.

74. "Life, Conduct, and Passion of the Holy and Glorious Martyrs Galaktion and Episteme," in *Christian Novels from the Menologion of Symeon Metaphrastes*, trans. Stratis Papaioannou (Washington, DC: Dumbarton Oaks, 2017), 257.

75. Maximus, "First Century on Love," in *The Philokalia*, 2:64.

76. Maximus, "First Century on Love," 2:132.

77. Maximus Confessor, Ambiguum 41 (PG 91:1309A-1312A). See the related study of division in Maximus: Emma Brown Dewhurst, "The 'Divisions of Nature' in Maximus' Ambiguum 41?," *Studia Patristica* 75 (2017): 149-54.

78. Heleen Zorgdrager, "Reclaiming *theosis*: Orthodox Women Theologians on the Mystery of the Union with God," *Internationale kirchliche Zeitschrift* 104 (2014): 220–45, 242–43; original emphasis.

79. Zorgdrager, "Is *theosis* a Gendered Concept?"

80. Roland Betancourt, "The Virgin's Consent," in *Byzantine Intersectionality: Sexuality, Gender, and Race in the Middle Ages* (Princeton, NJ: Princeton University Press, 2020), 19–58.

81. Matthew 1:18-25.

82. Stephen Shoemaker, trans., *Life of the Virgin attributed to Maximus the Confessor* (New Haven, CT: Yale University Press, 2012). This *Life* is likely later and not actually written by the Confessor, but the account of ascetic Mary is notable nonetheless. See C. Simelidis, "Two Lives of the Virgin: John Geometres, Euthymios the Athonite, and Maximos the Confessor," *Dumbarton Oaks Papers* 74 (2020): 125–59.

83. I have written more on this theological approach to negotiating power and authority in *God, Hierarchy, and Power*.

84. Zorgdrager, "Is *theosis* a Gendered Concept?"; Norman Russell, *Fellow Workers with God: Orthodox Thinking on Theosis* (Crestwood, NY: St Vladimir's Seminary Press, 2009); Aristotle Papanikolaou, *The Mystical as Political: Democracy and Non-Radical Orthodoxy* (Notre Dame, IN: University of Notre Dame Press, 2012).

## CHAPTER FOUR

1. Kallistos Ware, "Orthodox Theology Today: Trends and Tasks," *International Journal for the Study of the Christian Church* 12 (2012): 105–21. Ware notes that an "apophatic anthropology" is needed to be developed to better understand the human person in the divine image (117).

2. See, e.g., the Kontakion for the Sunday of Orthodoxy, "The uncircumscribed Word of the Father became circumscribed taking flesh from thee, O Theotokos," found in *The Lenten Triodion*, trans. Kallistos Ware and Mother Maria (South Canaan, PA: St.Tikhon's Seminary Press, 2002), 306; and Germanus of Constantinople, *Homily on the Dormition*, in which he says, "Because God had become flesh, they [the apostles] showed genuine honor to his Mother, the one who endowed him with that flesh." *Wider Than Heaven: Eighth-Century Homilies on the Mother of God*, trans. Mary Cunningham (Crestwood, NY: St Vladimir's Seminary Press, 2008), 177.

3. Athanasius, *On the Incarnation*, trans. John Behr (Crestwood, NY: St Vladimir's Seminary Press, 2014), 67.

4. Cyril, *Epistle to Nestorius*, in *Patrologia Graeca*, ed. J. P. Minge (Paris, 1864), 77:105.

5. On the concept of bodily impurity and liturgical participation, see Matthew Streett, "What to Do with the Baby? The Historical Development of the Rite of Churching," *St Vladimir's Theological Quarterly* 56.1 (2012): 51–71; Vassa Larin, "What Is 'Ritual Impurity' and Why?," *St Vladimir's Theological Quarterly* 52 (2008): 275–92.

6. Symeon the New Theologian, "First Ethical Discourse," in *On the Mystical Life: The Ethical Discourses*, vol. 1: *The Church and the Last Things*, trans. Alexander Golitzin (Crestwood, NY: St Vladimir's Seminary Press, 1985), 57.

7. Symeon the New Theologian, "First Ethical Discourse," 60.

8. *Tome of St. Leo* (PL 74:756) and *The Definition of Faith*, both trans. Henry Percival, Nicene and Post-Nicene Fathers 14, ed. Philip Schaff and Henry Wace (New York: Christian Literature Co., 1890–1900), 255, 345–46.

9. Cyril of Alexandria, *On the Unity of Christ*, trans. John McGuckin (Crestwood, NY: St Vladimir's Seminary Press, 2015), 55. Cyril explains, "As God he wished to make that flesh which was held in the grip of sin and death evidently superior to sin and death. He made it his very own, and not soulless as some have said, but rather animated with a rational soul, and thus he restored flesh to what it was in the beginning. He did not consider it beneath him to follow a path congruous to this plan, and so he is said to have undergone a birth like ours, while all the while remaining what he was. He was born of a woman according to the flesh in a wondrous manner, for He is God by nature, as such invisible and incorporeal, and only in this way, in a form like our own, could he be made manifest to earthly creatures."

10. Theodore the Studite, *On the Holy Icons*, trans. Catharine Roth (Crestwood, NY: St Vladimir's Seminary Press, 1981), 97.

11. Cyril of Alexandria, *On the Unity of Christ*, trans. McGuckin, 64. Cyril notes, "The Only Begotten, therefore, was by nature unlike us, and then he is said to have been made like us when he became as we are, that is man. There was only one way however, that this could properly happen, and that was by a human birth, even though in his case it happened so marvelously since the one who became flesh was God. We must admit, of course, that the body which he united to himself was endowed with a rational soul, for the Word, who is God, would hardly neglect our finer part, the soul, and have regard only for the earthly body. Quite clearly in all wisdom he provided for both the soul and the body."

12. Maximus Confessor, "Ambiguum 42," in *On the Cosmic Mystery of Christ*, trans. Paul Blowers (Crestwood, NY: St Vladimir's Seminary Press, 2003), 89.

13. Maximus Confessor, "Ambiguum 7," in *On The Cosmic Mystery of Christ*, 52. Maximus explains, "That which is in our power, our free will, through which the power of corruption entered into us, will surrender voluntarily to God and will have mastery of itself because it had been taught to refrain from willing anything other than what God wills."

14. John of Damascus, *An Exact Exposition of the Orthodox Faith*, in *Saint John of Damascus: Writings*, trans. Frederich Chase, Fathers of the Church, vol. 37 (Jackson, MI: Ex Fontibus Co., 2012), 292–93.

15. See the case study on how women relate to Mary in powerful ways precisely because of Mary's exceptionality: Andreas Kalkun and Elina Vuola, "The Embodied Mother of God and the Identities of Orthodox Women in Finland and Setoland," *Religion & Gender* 7.1 (2017): 18–41.

16. Athanasius, *On the Incarnation*, trans. Behr, 67.

17. See, e.g., the empowered yet sanitized depictions of Mary in *Wider Than Heaven*.

18. However, Mary's significance for women and men and various cultural moments is certainly not uniform. See, e.g., Natalia Ermolaev, "Our Mother of Paris: The 'Creative Renewal' of Orthodox Mariology in the Russian Emigration, 1920s–1930s," in *Framing Mary: The Mother of God in Modern, Revolutionary, and Post-Soviet Russian Culture*, ed. Amy Singleton Adams and Vera Shevzov (Ithaca, NY: Cornell University Press, 2018), 187–208.

19. *The Protoevangelium of James*, trans. Lily Vuong (Eugene, OR: Cascade Books, 2018); John of Damascus, *An Exact Exposition of the Orthodox Faith*, 366. John notes about Mary that "this blessed one, who had been found worthy of gifts surpassing nature, did at the time of the Passion suffer the pangs which she had escaped at childbirth."

20. See the depiction of postpartum Mary being inspected by the midwife to affirm her still-present virginity, in *The Protoevangelium of James*, trans. Lily Vuong (Eugene, OR: Cascade Books, 2018), 20:1–2.

21. Genesis 3:16.

22. Carrie Frederick Frost provides an excellent set of maternal reflections on Orthodoxy and the experiences of motherhood in *Maternal Body: A Theology of Incarnation from the Christian East* (Mahwah, NJ: Paulist Press, 2019).

23. Cyril of Alexandria, *On the Unity of Christ*, trans. McGuckin.

24. Athanasius, *On the Incarnation*, trans. Behr, 85,167.

25. Aritstotle Papnikolaou, *Being with God: Trinity Apophaticism, and Divine-Human Communion* (Notre Dame, IN: University of Notre Dame Press, 2006); Norman Russell, *The Doctrine of Deification in the Greek Patristic Tradition* (Oxford: Oxford University Press, 2004).

26. John of Damascus, *Three Treatises on the Divine Images*, trans. Andrew Louth (Crestwood, NY: St Vladimir's Seminary Press, 2003), 35.

27. Gregory of Nazianzus, "Oration 29", trans. Lionel Wickham, in *St Gregory of Nazianzus: On God and Christ: The Five Theological Orations and Two Letters to Cledonius* (Crestwood, NY: St Vladimir's Seminary Press, 2002), 86.).

28. Maximus Confessor, "Ambiguum 60," trans. Nicholas Constas, in *On Difficulties in the Church Fathers: The Ambigua*, vol. 2 (Cambridge, MA: Harvard University Press, 2014), 265.

29. See the explanations and defense of the title "Theotokos" in Cyril of Alexandria, *On the Unity of Christ*, trans. McGuckin.

30. John of Damascus, *On the Orthodox Faith*, trans. Chase, 295.

31. Maximus the Confessor, "Ambiguum 42," trans. Blowers, 83.

32. See, e.g., the Doxastikon of the Nativity Vespers attributed to John the Monk: "Paradise is opened unto us; the serpent is destroyed: for woman, whom he had formerly beguiled in Paradise, he hath now seen become the Mother of the Creator. . . . The instrument of sin that had brought death upon all flesh, is become the first-fruit of salvation for the whole world through the Theotokos." *The Menaion*, vol. 4, trans. Holy Transfiguration Monastery (Boston: Holy Transfiguration Monastery, 2005), 217.

33. Athanasius, *On the Incarnation*, trans. Behr, 82.

34. Cyril of Alexandria, *On the Unity of Christ*, trans. McGuckin, 101.

35. The Orthodox icon of the harrowing of hell comes to mind, depicting the resurrected Christ pulling both Adam and Eve up from the bonds of death.

36. Gregory Nazianzus, *Epistle 101*, trans. Lionel Wickham, in *On God and Christ* (Crestwood, NY: St Vladimir›s Seminary Press, 2002), 158.

37. Maximus the Confessor, *Ad Thalassium 22*, in *On the Cosmic Mystery of Christ*, trans. Blowers, 116, 139.

38. 1 Corinthians 15:21–22.

39. John of Damascus, *On the Divine Images*, trans. Louth, 29–30.

40. Several notable examples are Bissera Pentcheva, *The Sensual Icon: Space, Ritual, and the Senses in Byzantium* (University Park: Pennsylvania State University Press, 2010); Pavel Florensky, *Iconostasis*, trans. Donald Sheehan and Olga Andrejev (Crestwood, NY: St Vladimir's Seminary Press, 2000); Paul Evdokimov, *The Art of the Icon: A Theology of Beauty*, trans. Steven Bigham (Redondo Beach, CA: Oakwood Publications, 1990); Charles Barber, *Figure and Likeness: On the Limits of Representation in Byzantine Iconoclasm* (Princeton, NJ: Princeton University Press, 2002); Leonid Ouspensky and Vladimir Lossky,

*The Meaning of Icons*, trans. G. E. H. Palmer and Evgeniia Kadloubovsky (Crestwood, NY: St Vladimir's Seminary Press, 1999).

41. See the theological insights on the icon and its participative ability to reveal divinity, in Florensky, *Iconostasis*, esp. 70–98.

42. *Decree of the Holy Great, Ecumenical Synod, the Second of Nicaea*, trans. Percival, 550.

43. John of Damascus, *On the Divine Images*, trans. Louth, 86.

44. Theodore the Studite, *On the Holy Icons*, trans. Roth, 83–84.

45. Theodore the Studite, *On the Holy Icons*, trans. Roth, 90.

46. Apolytikion of St. Nicholas, in *Menaion*, 4:34.

47. For instance, the commemoration of St. Christopher the "dog-headed" in iconography, the hymnographic denial of the pseudonymity of Dionysius the Areopagite, and the conflation of the many lives of Mary of Egypt into the ornate version of Sophronius. The value of venerating (and even creating) fictitious saints for the believer, however, is not diminished and should be explored further elsewhere.

48. Theodore the Studite, *On the Holy Icons*, trans. Roth, 23.

49. Theodore the Studite, *On the Holy Icons*, trans. Roth, 95.

50. John of Damascus, *On Divine Images*, trans. Louth, 115.

51. Genesis 1:26-31. The next chapter expands on this concept of human iconicity.

52. Theodore the Studite, *On the Holy Images*, trans. Roth, 104.

53. John of Damascus, *On the Divine Images*, trans. Louth, 68.

54. For John of Damascus's explanation of the role of icons to inspire virtue and educate, see John of Damascus, *On Divine Images*, trans. Louth, 91.

55. Jean Gouillard, "Le Synodikon de l'Orthodoxie: Édition et commentaire," *Travaux et mémoires* 2 (1967): 45–46. Related discussion and translated excerpts can be found in Andrew Louth, "Orthodoxy and Its Discontents: 843–1438," *International Journal of Orthodox Theology* 10.1 (2019): 62–71.

56. See the patriarchally endorsed social document, *For the Life of the World: Toward a Social Ethos of the Orthodox Church*, ed. David Bentley Hart and John Chryssavgis (Greek Orthodox Archdiocese of America, 2020), https://www.goarch.org/social-ethos.

57. See the theology of "otherness" that warrants encounter rather than assertive determination, in Ashley Marie Purpura, "Knowing in Theosis: A Byzantine Mystical Theological Approach," in *Faith, Reason, and Theosis*, ed. George Demacopoulos and Aristotle Papanikolaou (New York: Fordham University Press, 2023), 231–50.

58. John Zizioulas, *Communion and Otherness: Further Studies in Personhood and the Church*, ed. Paul McPartlan (New York: T&T Clark, 2006), 112; original emphasis.

59. It is in solidarity with Catholic feminist theological predecessors that I move from critique to suggesting alternatives within the tradition and its theology, such as outlined in Susan Abraham, "Justice as the Mark of Catholic Feminist Ecclesiology," in *Frontiers in Catholic Feminist Theology* (Minneapolis: Fortress Press, 2009), 206–8.

## CHAPTER FIVE

1. See Aristotle Papanikolaou, *Being With God: Trinity, Apophaticism, and Divine-Human Communion* (Notre Dame, IN: University of Notre Dame Press, 2006).

2. See one example of how the "mind of the fathers" is negotiated and understood in the prominent neo-patristic writings of Georges Florovsky, in *The Patristic Witness of Georges Florovsky: Essential Theological Writings*, ed. Brandon Gallaher and Paul Ladouceur (London: T&T Clark, 2019).

3. For the classic Orthodox argument that forms of worship should reflect belief, see Alexander Schmemann, *Introduction to Liturgical Theology* (Crestwood, NY: St Vladimir's Seminary Press, 1966).

4. Here I refer to a present experienced liturgically as explored in Christina M. Gschwandtner, *Welcoming Finitude: Toward a Phenomenology of Orthodox Liturgy* (New York: Fordham University Press, 2019), 42–43.

5. David Bentley Hart, *Tradition and Apocalypse: An Essay on the Future of Christian Belief* (Grand Rapids, MI: Baker Academic, 2022).

6. Hart, *Tradition and Apocalypse*, 188; 1 John 4:16.

7. See, e.g., the construction of Mary in the Life of Mary of Egypt attributed to Sophronios, "St. Mary of Egypt," trans. Maria Kouli, in *Holy Women of Byzantium: Ten Saints' Lives in English Translation*, ed. Alice-Mary Talbot (Washington, DC: Dumbarton Oaks, 1996), 65–93, 76–77. See one example of how the "mind of the fathers" is negotiated and understood in the prominent neo-patristic writings of Georges Florovsky, in Gallaher and Ladouceur, *The Patristic Witness of Georges Florovsky*.

8. Catherine LaCugna, ed., *Freeing Theology: The Essentials of Theology in Feminist Perspective* (New York: HarperCollins, 1993), 3.

9. Here I have in mind not only the problematic commemorative language of women saints but also practices that address women in rites related

to childbirth, marriage, and menstrual taboos that are still perpetuated (often among women) with regard to receiving communion.

10. For the necessity of change coming gradually from within Orthodoxy, see Ina Merdjanova, *Women and Religiosity in Orthodox Christianity* (New York: Fordham University Press, 2021), 11.

11. bell hooks, *Understanding Patriarchy* (Louisville, KY: Louisville Anarchist Federation, 2010), 3.

12. Sarah Ahmed, *Complaint* (Durham, NC: Duke University Press, 2023), 139, 100.

13. Kate Manne, *Entitled: How Male Privilege Hurts Women* (New York: Crown, 2020), 8–9; Ibram Kendi, *How to Be an Antiracist* (New York: Random House, 2019); Stephen Brookfield and Mary Hess, *Becoming a White Antiracist* (Sterling, VA: Stylus Publications, 2021).

14. The words of the provocative punk hymn by Pussy Riot, calling on "Mary to become a feminist," seem apt here. See the discussion of this liturgical appeal in Nicholas Denysenko, "An Appeal to Mary: An Analysis of Pussy Riot's Punk Performance in Moscow," *Journal of the American Academy of Religion* 81.4 (2013): 1061–92; Vera Shevzov, "Women on the Fault Lines of Faith: Pussy Riot and the Insider/Outsider Challenge to Post-Soviet Orthodoxy," *Religion and Gender* 4.2 (2014): 121–44; Tara Tuttle, "Deranged Vaginas: Pussy Riot's Feminist Hermeneutics," *Journal of Religion and Popular Culture* 28.2–3 (2016): doi:10.3138/jrpc.28.2-3.2738.

15. Eva Catafygiotu Topping, "Reflections of an Orthodox Feminist," in *Holy Mothers of Orthodoxy: Women and the Church* (Minneapolis: Light and Life Publishing, 1987), 3.

16. For a study of such productive "penthos," see Hannah Hunt's *Joy-Bearing Grief: Tears of Contrition in the Writings of the Early Syrian and Byzantine Fathers* (Leiden: Brill, 2004).

17. Audre Lorde, "The Master's Tools Will Never Dismantle the Master's House," in *Sister Outsider: Essays and Speeches* (New York: Penguin Random House, 2007), 100–103.

18. See the debate in feminist theology about a usable past, in Marcella Althaus-Reid and Lisa Isherwood, eds., *Controversies in Feminist Theology* (London: SCM Press, 2007), 59.

19. I find it helpful to think about women in Orthodox tradition by also considering the ways reclaiming women in philosophy is explored via the writings of Luce Irigaray, in Sarah Tyson, "Reclamation from Absence? Luce Irigaray and Women in the History of Philosophy," *Hypatia* 28.3 (2013): 483–98.

20. John of Damascus, *Three Treatises on the Divine Images*, trans. Andrew Louth (Crestwood, NY: St Vladimir's Seminary Press, 2003), 19–58.

21. It is worth mentioning that there is no comparable women's mystical tradition in Orthodoxy to the robust writings we have from women in the medieval West.

22. "The Holy Anaphora," in *The Divine Liturgy of Saint John Chrysostom*, Greek Orthodox Archdiocese of America, accessed April 3, 2024, https://www.goarch.org/-/the-divine-liturgy-of-saint-john-chrysostom.

23. For an assessment of recent feminist engagements with kenosis that include Orthodox perspectives, see Anne Selak, "Orthodoxy, Orthopraxis, and Orthopathy: Evaluating the Feminist Kenosis Debate," *Modern Theology* 33.4 (2017): 529–48.

24. Ashley Marie Purpura, *God, Hierarchy, and Power: Theologies of Spiritual Authority from Byzantium* (New York: Fordham University Press, 2018), 132–56.

25. Jeannine Hill Fletcher, "Christology between Identity and Difference: On Behalf of a World in Need," in *Frontiers in Catholic Feminist Theology*, ed. Susan Abraham and Elena Procario-Foley (Minneapolis: Fortress Press, 2009), 87–91. Fletcher, for instance, describes kenosis in terms of "self-giving love in the pattern of a breast-feeding mother" (87).

26. See, e.g., the theology of descent and elevating the fallen reflected in the hymns of Pascha, particularly the Exapostilarion and the Kontakion in *The Pentecostarion*, trans. Holy Transfiguration Monastery (Boston: Holy Transfiguration Monastery, 2014), 19, 17.

27. See Purpura, "Thearchical Power in Theory and Practice," in *God, Hierarchy, and Power*, 132–56.

28. On kenosis of patriarchy, see Elizabeth Johnson, *She Who Is: The Mystery of God in Feminist Theological Discourse* (New York: Crossroad, 2002), 161; Rosemary Radford Ruether, *Sexism and God-Talk: Toward a Feminist Theology* (Boston: Beacon Press, 1983), 137; and for kenosis in feminist theology more broadly, see Annie Selak, "Orthodoxy, Orthopraxis, and Orthopathy: Evaluating the Feminist Kenosis Debate," *Modern Theology* 33.4 (2017): 529–48.

29. Johnson, *She Who Is*, 161; Ruether, *Sexism and God-Talk*, 137; on the very real issues of domestic violence and abuse with theologies of patriarchy, see Ally Moder, "Women, Personhood, and the male God: A Feminist Critique of Patriarchal Concepts of God in View of Domestic Abuse," *Feminist Theology* 28.1 (2019): 85–103.

30. Various hymns of Christ's passion and nativity emphasize extreme condescension in order to bring about human salvation. See the fifteenth

antiphon of Holy Friday, in *The Lenten Triodion*, trans. Mother Mary and Kallistos Ware (South Canaan, PA: St. Tikhon's Seminary Press, 2002), 587; and the similar antiphon in the sixth tone for the ninth hour of the Nativity, in *The Festal Menaion*, trans. Mother Mary and Kallistos Ware (South Canaan, PA: St. Tikhon's Seminary Press, 1998), 245.

31. In this way the tradition of patriarchy could be viewed as living. As Hart writes in *Tradition and Apocalypse* in reference to tradition more broadly, "No tradition is fully alive except one that anticipates and even wills its own overthrow in a fuller revelation of its own inner truth" (154).

32. Cyril of Alexandria observes the importance of Christ being the "express image" of the Father, which means also that the Son "humbled himself to the point of self-emptying for the salvation and life of all." *Cyril of Alexandria Select Letters*, trans. Lionel Wickham (Oxford: Oxford University Press, 1983), 107.

33. See, e.g., the second hymn for the Aposticha for Matins of Holy Monday, "O Lord, teaching Thy disciples to think perfect thoughts, Thou hast said to them: 'Be not like the Gentiles, who exercise dominion over those who are less strong. But it shall not be so among you, My disciples, for I of mine own will am poor. Let him, then, who is first among you be the minister of all. Let the ruler be as the ruled, and let the first be as the last. For I Myself have come to minister to Adam in his poverty, and to give my life as a ransom for the many who cry aloud to Me: Glory to Thee.'" In *The Lenten Triodion*, 515–16.

34. Maximus the Confessor, "Ad Thalassium 22," in *On the Cosmic Mystery of Jesus Christ*, trans. Paul Blowers and Robert Louis Wilken (Crestwood, NY: St Vladimir's Seminary Press, 2003), 116.

35. Maria Skobtsova, "The Mysticism of Human Communion," in *Mother Maria Skobtsova: Essential Writings*, trans. Richard Pevear and Larissa Volokhonsky (Maryknoll, NY: Orbis Books, 2003), 83.

36. See also the related brief overview of otherness and communion in John Zizioulas, *Communion and Otherness*, ed. Paul McPartlan (London: T&T Clark, 2006), 9–10.

37. See Purpura, *God, Hierarchy, and Power*.

38. Cyril of Alexandria, *On the Unity of Christ*, trans. John Anthony McGuckin (Crestwood, NY: St Vladimir's Seminary Press, 1995), 101. Cyril notes that in Christ is revealed "the strange and rare paradox" of "divine glory in human abasement."

39. Zizioulas, *Communion and Otherness*, 86. Zizioulas's arguments are theologically compelling and consistent with the arguments I set forth in this chapter. However, it is worth noting that from a feminist perspective, Zizioulas's consideration and theological reconstruction of kenosis and otherness

does not sufficiently engage with the human realities of disparities of power and positionality that render some people marginalized. The present chapter and the one following acknowledge these differences.

40. Purpura, *God, Hierarchy, and Power*, 157.

41. See a similar argument regarding the need for theology to reject binary bifurcations and the conception of an ideal "man" to participate in the field: Willie James Jennings, "Against the Finished Man," *Modern Theology* 37.4 (2021): 1054–65.

42. Nancy Hirschmann, *The Subject of Liberty: Toward a Feminist Theory of Freedom* (Princeton, NJ: Princeton University Press, 2003), 205. Hirschmann offers a feminist reminder that can be applied in this context: "Changing contexts and increasing freedom for women and other nondominant groups requires increasing their ability to participate in the process of social construction."

43. See the overall argument of Athanasius, *On the Incarnation*, trans. John Behr (Crestwood, NY: St Vladimir's Seminary Press, 2011).

44. Zizioulas, *Communion and Otherness*, 91.

45. See the debate in feminist theology about a usable past, in Marcella Althaus-Reid and Lisa Isherwood, eds., *Controversies in Feminist Theology* (London: SCM Press, 2007), 59.

46. Grace Jantzen, *Becoming Divine: Towards a Feminist Philosophy of Religion* (Bloomington: Indiana University Press, 1999), 205.

47. Zizioulas, *Communion and Otherness*, 9–10. Zizioulas notes, "One person is no person, this freedom is not freedom *from* the other but freedom for the other. Freedom thus becomes identical with *love*. God is love because he is Trinity. We can love only if we are persons, that is, if we allow the other to be truly other, and yet to be in communion with us. If we love the other not only in spite of his or her being different from us but *because* he or she is different from us, or rather *other* than ourselves, we live in freedom as love and in love as freedom" (original emphasis).

48. E.g., Matthew 37–40 clearly identifies good actions toward others as actions toward the Lord.

49. John 13:34–35.

50. Skobstova, "The Mysticism of Human Communion," 75–83. For an introduction to her life, see Paul Ladouceur, "Quelques enigmes de la biographie de saint Maria de Paris," *Contacts* 60.224 (2008): 445–93; and a more hagiographic retelling of her life, Sergei Hackel, *Pearl of Great Price: The Life of Mother Maria Skobtsova, 1891-1945* (Crestwood, NY: St Vladimir's Seminary Press, 1981).

51. Skobtsova, "The Mysticism of Human Communion," 79.
52. Skobtsova, "The Mysticism of Human Communion," 79.
53. Skobtsova, "The Mysticism of Human Communion," 80, 84.
54. See theological applications of her life and thought, in Petre Maican, "Vulnerability and Solidarity: An Improbable Connection," *Journal of Disability and Religion* 25.1 (2021): 55–67; Katerina Bauerova, "The Play of the Semiotic and the Symbolic: The Authenticity of the Life of Mother Maria Skobtsova," *Feminist Theology* 22.3 (2014): 290–301.
55. I explore the use of gender in hymns about saints in "Beyond the Binary: Hymnographic Constructions of Eastern Orthodox Gender Identities," *Journal of Religion* 97.4 (2017): 524–46.
56. Sarah Coakley is particularly noteworthy here for prompting a type of contemplative aspect as a grounding for systematic theology: see her *God, Sexuality, and the Self: An Essay "On the Trinity"* (Cambridge: Cambridge University Press, 2014). See also Catherine Keller, "The Apophasis of Gender: A Fourfold Unsaying of Feminist Theology," *Journal of the American Academy of Religion* 76.4 (2008): 905–33; Chris Boesel and Catherine Keller, eds., *Apophatic Bodies: Negative Theology, Incarnation, and Relationality* (New York: Fordham University Press, 2011). Apophatic theology is regarded as central to most Orthodox theology; see, e.g., Papanikolaou, *Being with God*.
57. See Ashley Marie Purpura, "Innovating 'Traditional' Women's Roles: Byzantine Insights for Orthodox Christian Gender Discourse," *Modern Theology* 36.3 (2020): 641–61.
58. Catherine Keller, "The Apophasis of Gender: A Fourfold Unsaying of Feminist Theology," *Journal of the American Academy of Religion* 76.4 (2008): 905–33; and for related discussion on apophasis and masculinity, see Brian McGrath Davis, "Apophatic Theology and Masculinities," *CrossCurrents* 61.4 (2011): 502–14; Elizabeth Stuart, "Sacramental Flesh," in *Queer Theology*, ed. George Loughlin (New York: Wiley, 2009), 69.
59. See also Purpura, "Innovating 'Traditional' Women's Roles"; Brandy Daniels, *Ekstasis* as (Beyond?) *Jouissance*: Sex, Queerness, and Apophaticism in the Eastern Orthodox Tradition," *Theology and Sexuality* 20.2 (2014): 89–107; Ann-Marie Priest, "Woman as God, God as Woman: Mysticism, Negative Theology, and Luce Irigaray," *Journal of Religion* 83.1 (2003): 1–23; Sigridur Gudmarsdottir, "Feminist Theology and the Sensible Unsaying of Mysticism," in *Apophatic Bodies*, ed. Chris Boesel and Catherine Keller (New York: Fordham University Press, 2009), 273–85.
60. Hart, *Tradition and Apocalypse*, 183.
61. *The Divine Liturgy of John Chrysostom*.

62. Zizioulas, *Communion and Otherness*, 112.

63. For instance, the affirmations of Orthodoxy in the first Sunday of Lent need not also be connected to the condemnation of historical "heretics." For an example of the ecumenical problems such commemorations cause, see Ephraim Lash, "Byzantine Hymns of Hate," in *Byzantine Orthodoxies* (London: Routledge, 2006), 151–64.

64. Jean Gouillard, "Le Synodikon de l'Orthodoxie: Édition et commentaire," *Travaux et mémoires* 2 (1967): 1–313; Paul Magdalino, "Orthodoxy and Byzantine Cultural Identity," in *Orthodoxy and Heresy in Byzantium*, ed. Antonio Rigo and Pavel Ermilov (Rome: Università degli sti di Roma "Tor Vergata," 2010), 21, 32; Karin Krause, *Divine Inspiration in Byzantium: Notions of Authenticity in Art and Theology* (Cambridge: Cambridge University Press, 2022), 357. See also Vera Shevzov, "Resistance and Accommodation: The Rite of Orthodoxy in Modern Russia," in *Religion and Identity in Russia and the Soviet Union: A Festschrift for Paul Bushkovitch*, ed. Nikolaos Chrissidis, Cathy Potter, David Schimmelpenninck van der Oye, and Jennifer Spock (Bloomington, IN: Slavica Publishers, 2011), 165–89.

65. For instance, some of the views of John Chrysostom about women's categorical subordination to men in his ninth homily on 1 Timothy in *Nicene and Post-Nicene Fathers*, ed. Philip Schaff, 1st ser., vol. 13. (Buffalo, NY: Christian Literature Publishing Co., 1889).

66. Hart, *Tradition and Apocalypse*, 180.

67. On the need for apophatic unsaying, see the theologically influential writings by (Pseudo-)Dionysius the Areopagite, esp. "The Divine Names" and "The Mystical Theology," in *Pseudo-Dionysius: The Complete Works*, trans. Colm Luibheid (New York: Paulist Press, 1987), 47–143.

68. There is an Orthodox liturgical practice for the week following Pascha to leave the doors to the altar open as a testament to Christ's harrowing of hell.

69. See my article on nondominative "knowing": "Knowing in Theosis: A Byzantine Mystical Theological Approach," in *Faith, Reason, and Theosis*, ed. George Demacopoulos and Aristotle Papanikolaou (New York: Fordham University Press, 2023), 232–50.

70. Gregory Palamas is probably the most prominent figure associated with defending hesychast claims and practices. However, other sainted figures such as Symeon the New Theologian, Seraphim of Sarov, and Silouan the Athonite have recorded detailed accounts of experiencing God in this way. See Gregory Palamas, *The Triads*, trans. Nicholas Gendle (Mahwah, NJ: Paulist Press, 1983); *Symeon the New Theologian: The Discourses*, trans. Carmino

DeCatanzaro (Mahwah, NJ: Paulist Press, 1980); Seraphim of Sarov, *The Aim of Christian Life: The Conversation of St Seraphim of Sarov with N. A. Motovilov*, trans. John Phillips (Cambridge: Saints Alive Press, 2010). In contrast to "Western" mysticism, Orthodoxy does not have a tradition of women visionaries who write of their own experiences (although sainted women having visions is recorded in hagiography—Mary of Egypt, for example).

71. Palamas, *The Triads*, 100.

72. Nicholas Cabasilas, *The Life in Christ*, trans. Carmino DeCatanzaro (Crestwood, NY: St Vladimir's Seminary Press, 1998).

73. Skobtsova, "The Mysticism of Human Communion."

74. Zizioulas, *Communion and Otherness*, 13–98.

75. A helpful overview of hesychasm can be found in Christopher D. L. Johnson, *Globalization of Hesychasm and the Jesus Prayer: Contesting Contemplation* (London: Continuum, 2010).

76. See, e.g., the modes of prayer described in Gregory Palamas's *Triads* but also variously indicated in the *Philokalia* and by such authors as Symeon the New Theologian (*Discourses*) and numerous modern Athonite elders.

77. Symeon the New Theologian, "Discourse XVI," in *The Discourses*, 202–3.

78. Cabasilas, *The Life in Christ*.

79. Betty Friedan, *The Feminine Mystique* (New York: Norton, 1963). It is important to note the ways that Friedan's depiction of women, restricted through an androcentric idealization of them as feminine, does not consider racial, economic, sexual, etc., diversity among women.

80. Skobstova, "The Mysticism of Human Communion," 75–83.

81. See Palamas, *The Triads*, 49–51.

82. Palamas, *The Triads*, 111. Palamas explains, "Those who love the good thus transform this power, and do not put it to death; they do not enclose it immovable in themselves, but activate it towards love of God and their neighbors."

83. See the description of the experience of the divine light, in Symeon the New Theologian, *The Discourses*, 198–203.

84. See the related discussion in Zizioulas, *Communion and Otherness*, 74–98.

85. Zizioulas, *Communion and Otherness*, 74. Zizioulas notes that "love as *eros* hypostasizes beings, that is, makes them exist as particular, by incorporating them into a unique (a uniquely loved) *hypostasis*."

86. Orthodox theologians might benefit from thinking alongside such transformative hope and person-centered gender theology as described

in Pamela Lightsey, "Transforming Until Thy Kin(g)dom Come," in *Our Lives Matter: A Womanist Queer Theology* (London: Wipf & Stock, 2015), 67–77.

87. Zizioulas, *Communion and Otherness*, 286–307. Zizioulas concludes based on Chalcedonian Christology that "the Church as the body of Christ points to a mysticism of communion and relationship through which one is so united with the 'other' (God and our fellow man) as to form one indivisible unity through which otherness emerges clearly, and the partners of the relationship are distinct and particular not as individuals but as persons" (307).

88. Catherine LaCugna, *God for Us: The Trinity and Christian Life* (New York: HarperCollins, 1991), 1, 15; original emphasis.

89. Skobtsova, "The Mysticism of Human Communion," 78–79.

90. Palamas, *The Triads*, 100.

91. Purpura, "Knowing in Theosis," 232–50.

92. See the description of "other" via Levinas, in Zizioulas, *Communion and Otherness*, 49–52, yet this is somewhat disjointed from the way one might consider to be "other" that is not gift but marginalization.

93. Maria Skobtsova, "Types of Religious Life," in *Mother Maria Skobtsova*, 182.

94. See, e.g., the overview in Linn Tonstad, *Queer Theology: Beyond Apologetics* (Eugene, OR: Cascade Books, 2018).

95. Perhaps this might be a way to respond to the critique of inclusion given in Linn Tonstad, "The Limits of Inclusion: Queer Theology and Its Others," *Theology & Sexuality* 21.1 (2015): 1–19.

96. James Allison, "The Gay Thing: Following the Still Small Voice," in *Queer Theology: Rethinking the Western Body*, ed. Gerard Loughlin (Malden, MA: Blackwell, 2007), 50–62.

97. Daphne Hampson, ed., *Swallowing a Fishbone? Feminist Theologians Debate Christianity* (London: SPCK, 1996); Linn Tonstad, *God and Difference: The Trinity, Sexuality, and the Transformation of Finitude* (New York: Routledge, 2016); Margaret Kamitsuka, *Feminist Theology and the Challenge of Difference* (Oxford: Oxford University Press, 2007).

98. Further examples of these debates being addressed and described can be found in Serene Jones, "Women's Nature," in *Feminist Theory and Christian Theology: Cartographies of Grace* (Minneapolis: Fortress Press, 2000), 22–48; Marcella Althaus-Reid and Lisa Isherwood, eds., *Controversies in Feminist Theology* (London: SCM Press, 2007). On theological approaches to intersectionality, see Grace Ji-Sun Kim and Susan Shaw, *Intersectional Theology: An Introductory Guide* (Minneapolis: Fortress Press, 2018).

## CHAPTER SIX

1. Eleni Kasselouri-Hatzivassiliadi, Fulata Mbano Moyo, and Aikaterini Pekridou, eds., *Many Women Were Also There . . . : The Participation of Orthodox Women in the Ecumenical Movement* (Geneva: World Council of Churches, 2010), 126.

2. Marcella Althaus-Reid and Lisa Isherwood, eds., *Controversies in Feminist Theology* (London: SCM Press, 2007), 59.

3. The "Doxastikon of Pascha," in *The Pentecostarion*, trans. Holy Transfiguration Monastery (Brookline, MA: Holy Transfiguration Monastery Press, 2014), 20.

4. See, e.g., Alice-Mary Talbot, ed., *Byzantine Defenders of Images* (Washington, DC: Dumbarton Oaks, 1998).

5. Genesis 1:27; David Bentley Hart and John Chryssavgis, eds., *For the Life of the World: Toward a Social Ethos of the Orthodox Church* (Brookline, MA: Holy Cross Orthodox Press, 2020), 1.

6. Bissera Pentcheva, *The Sensual Icon: Space, Ritual, and the Senses in Byzantium* (Philadelphia: Pennsylvania State University Press, 2010); Leonid Ouspensky and Vladimir Lossky, *The Meaning of Icons* (Crestwood, NY: St Vladimir's Seminary Press, 1999); Pavel Florensky, *Iconostasis*, trans. Donald Sheehan and Olga Andrejev (Crestwood, NY: St Vladimir's Seminary Press, 2000).

7. *The Acts of the Second Council of Nicaea (787)*, trans. Richard Price (Liverpool: Liverpool University Press, 2020), 565.

8. Leonid Ouspensky, *Theology of the Icon* (Crestwood, NY: St Vladimir's Seminary Press, 1992), 503.

9. Maria Skobstova, "The Mysticism of Human Communion," in *Mother Maria Skobtsova: Essential Writings*, trans. Richard Pevear and Larissa Volokhonsky (Maryknoll, NY: Orbis Books, 2003), 80.

10. Skobtsova, "The Mysticism of Human Communion," 80.

11. See the brief description of "living icons" in Michael Plekon, *Living Icons: Persons of Faith in the Eastern Church* (Notre Dame, IN: University of Notre Dame Press, 2002), 19.

12. One could also substitute "iconophile" (lover of icons) here, but I prefer "iconodule" (one who serves icons) because, at least to me, it connotes action more than emotion, an aspect that is important to applying the concept to the icons within. However, I hope the reader understands love in an active sense as well and then can use either term interchangeably.

13. Tsakaridou, *Icons in Time Persons in Eternity*, 16.

14. See the related discussion in John Zizioulas, *Communion and Otherness*, ed. Paul McPartlan (London: T&T Clark, 2006), 165–68.

15. Genesis 1:26.

16. Florensky, *Iconostasis*, 67.

17. For examples, see Karin Krause, *Divine Inspiration in Byzantium: Notions of Authenticity in Art and Theology* (Cambridge: Cambridge University Press, 2022), 232–45.

18. See the discussion of theosis as "Christification," which implies a union without confusion, in Philip Kariatlis, "Deification as Christification and Human Becoming," in *Faith, Reason, and Theosis*, ed. Aristotle Papanikolaou and George Demacopoulos (New York: Fordham University Press, 2023), 72–92.

19. "Life of St. Theodosia of Constantinople," trans. Nicholas Constas, in Talbot, *Byzantine Defenders of Images*, 6; see also the "Life of St. Theodora the Empress," in the same volume. For a discussion complicating the destruction of the Chalke icon and imperial involvement in it, see Marie-France Auzépy, "La destruction de l'icône du Christ de la Chalcé par Léon III: Propagande ou réalité?," *Byzantion* 40 (1990): 445–90. For further discussion of imperial women and their influence, see Judith Herrin, *Women in Purple: Rulers of Medieval Byzantium* (Princeton, NJ: Princeton University Press, 2001).

20. Genesis 1:26–31.

21. Beth Allison Barr, *The Making of Biblical Womanhood: How the Subjugation of Women Became Gospel Truth* (Grand Rapids, MI: Brazos Press, 2021), 212.

22. See Talbot, *Byzantine Defenders of Images*; John of Damascus, *Three Treatises on the Divine Images*, trans. Andrew Louth (Crestwood, NY: St Vladimir's Seminary Press, 2003); Theodore the Studite, *On the Holy Icons*, trans. Catharine Roth (Crestwood, NY: St Vladimir's Seminary Press, 2001).

23. Vladimir Lossky, *In the Image and Likeness of God*, ed. John Erickson and Thomas Bird (Crestwood, NY: St Vladimir's Seminary Press, 1974), 137.

24. See also Athanasius, *On the Incarnation*, trans. John Behr (Crestwood, NY: St Vladimir's Seminary Press, 2011), 77–85. Athanasius figures God almost as an iconographer. About the renewal of the divine image in humanity in the incarnation, he says, "For as when a figure painted on wood has been soiled by dirt from outside, it is necessary for him whose figure it is to come again, so that the image can be renewed on the same material—because of his portrait even the material on which it is painted is not cast aside, but the portrait is reinscribed on it. In the same way the all holy Son of the Father, being the Image of the Father, came to our place to renew the human being made according to himself" (79).

25. Genesis 1:27; 1 Corinthians 6:19.

26. See, e.g., Jesus as the fulfillment of the prophetic overcoming of oppression, infirmity, poverty, and captivity, in Luke 4:16–22.

27. There are well-known prosomia hymns that begin with the phrasing, "O paradoxical mystery" (Ὢ τοῦ παραδόξου θαύματος), as well as the fifteenth antiphon of Holy Friday (*The Lenten Triodion*, trans. Mother Mary and Kallistos Ware [South Canaan, PA: St. Tikhon's Seminary Press, 2002], 587), that celebrate divine condescension.

28. See, e.g., hymns from nearly every service included in *The Pentecostarion*.

29. This depiction of Mary is celebrated in the megalynarion for the Divine Liturgy of St. Basil the Great, "All Creation Rejoices in Thee."

30. See, e.g., the depiction in John Geometres, *Life of the Virgin Mary*, trans. Maximos Constas and Christos Simelidis (Cambridge, MA: Harvard University Press, 2023).

31. This section draws heavily from my article, "Innovating 'Traditional' Women's Roles: Byzantine Insights for Orthodox Christian Gender Discourse," *Modern Theology* 36.3 (2020): 641–61.

32. I use the masculine pronouns for this female-born saint out of respect for the saint's chosen life as a male monk. As I mentioned previously, however, Orthodox commemoration still numbers such saints as women.

33. "The Life of St. Mary/Marinos," trans. Nicholas Constas, in *Holy Women of Byzantium*, ed. Alice-Mary Talbot (Washington, DC: Dumbarton Oaks, 1996), 1–12. I have adopted masculine pronouns in referring to the saint in this passage because at this point in the saint's hagiography the saint verbally self-identifies as a man, although, as previously mentioned, the Orthodox Church commemorates the saint as a woman.

34. See the multiple hagiographic retellings of Mary of Egypt, with their narrative retellings described, in Alexander Kazhdan and Nancy Patterson Ševčenko, "Mary of Egypt," in *The Oxford Dictionary of Byzantium* (Oxford: Oxford University Press, 1991), https://www-oxfordreference-com.ezp-prod1.hul.harvard.edu/view/10.1093/acref/9780195046526.001.0001/acref-9780195046526-e-3375.

35. Patricia Cox Miller, "Is There a Harlot in This Text? Hagiography and the Grotesque," *Journal of Medieval and Early Modern Studies* 33.3 (2003): 419–35; Selamawit Mecca, "An Unusual Prostitute Heroine: the Ethiopic Version of the Hagiography of St. Mary of Egypt," *Ekklesiastikos Pharos* 94.1 (2012): 333–53; Ulla Tervahauta, "What Happened to Mary? Women Named Mary in the *Meadow* of John Moschus," *Women and Knowledge in Early Christianity* 144 (2017): 154–72.

36. Nil 8, in *Give Me a Word: The Alphabetical Sayings of the Desert Fathers*, trans. John Wortley (Yonkers, NY: St Vladimir's Seminary Press, 2014), 212.

37. Matoes 3, in *The Sayings of the Desert Fathers: The Alphabetical Collection*, trans. Benedicta Ward (Collegeville, MN: Liturgical Press, 1975), 143.

38. John 14:6.

39. Apolytikion of St. Catherine, in *The Menaion*, vol. 3: *The Month of November* (Boston: Holy Transfiguration Monastery, 2005), 187.

40. See the discussion of the widespread influence of these examples in Stephanie Cobb and Andrew Jacobs, eds., *The Passion of Perpetua and Felicitas in Late Antiquity* (Oakland: University of California Press, 2021); Stephen Davis, *The Cult of St Thecla: A Tradition of Women's Piety in Late Antiquity* (Oxford: Oxford University Press, 2001); Christine Walsh, *The Cult of St Katherine of Alexandria in Early Medieval Europe* (London: Routledge Press, 2017).

41. A number of Byzantine authors recount this scene; see Leo Grammaticus (Bonn ed., 1842), 213–14; Theodosius Melitenus (T. Tafel ed., 1859), 147; Georgius Monachus (Bonn ed., 1838), 789–90, Ps.-Symeon, 624–25.

42. Diane Touliatos-Banker, "Women Composers of Medieval Byzantine Chant," *College Music Symposium* 24.1 (1984): 62–80; Kurt Sherry, *Kassia the Nun in Context* (Piscataway, NJ: Gorgias Press, 2013); Anna M. Silvas, "Kassia the Nun," in *Byzantine Women: Varieties of Experience 800–1200*, ed Lynda Garland (Burlington, VT: Ashgate, 2006); Susan Ashbrook Harvey, *Women's Voices Bearing Witness: Biblical Memory in Ancient Orthodox Liturgy*, Orthodoxy in America Annual Lecture (New York: Fordham University Press, 2009), 18; Marc Lauxtermann, "Three Biographical Notes," *Byzantinische Zeitschrift* 91 (1998): 391–97; Eva Catafygiotu Topping, "The Psalmist, St. Luke and Kassia the Nun," *Byzantine Studies* 9 (1982): 199–219; and *Kassia: The Legend, the Woman, and Her Work*, ed. Antonía Tripolitis (New York: Garland, 1992).

43. *Christian Novels from the Menologion of Symeon Metaphrastes*, trans. Stratis Papaioannou (Cambridge, MA: Harvard University Press, 2017), 73, 75–79. Pelagia of Antioch, for one, threatens the bishop to baptize her immediately, and after struggling physically with the bishop, refusing to let go of his feet, the narrator explains that "before her spiritual baptism, there was another purification, the more arduous baptism of tears" (73).

44. This slightly adapted section on Kassia originally appeared in my article, "Innovating 'Traditional' Women's Roles."

45. See, e.g., the interpretive imagining in Byzantium around Mary, in Mary Cunningham, *The Virgin Mary in Byzantium c. 400–1000 CE: Hymns, Homilies, and Hagiographies* (Cambridge: Cambridge University Press, 2022).

46. There are several popular books about women saints that offer reflection points for modern laywomen in this way; see Melinda Johnson, ed., *Seven Holy Women: Conversations with Saints and Friends* (Chesterton, IN: Ancient Faith Publishing, 2020); Kyriaki Karidoyanes-FitzGerald, ed., *Encountering Women of Faith*, 3 vols. (Brookline, MA: Holy Cross Press, 2005, 2011, 2019).

47. The themes of joy, liberation, and universality are emphasized liturgically in the hymns for Pascha. See *The Pentecostarion*, 15–24.

48. See John Chrysostom's "Catechetical Homily," in *The Pentecostarion*, 20–21. In addition to the undoing of the power of death, Chrysostom mentions other concerns that might keep individuals from celebrating Pascha, including anxiety about their own unworthiness, poverty, unkindness, sinfulness, and fear of death, and shows they are all to be overcome in the joy of the resurrection.

49. Athanasius, *On the Incarnation*, 113.

50. The Paschal Catechetical Homily of John Chrysostom prescribed to be read on Pascha highlights this universality of celebration. *The Pentecostarion*, 20–21.

51. See the description of the myrrh-bearing women in the Hypakoe in fourth tone for the Resurrection, in *The Pentecostarion*, 16. Scriptural accounts of women receiving first the news of the resurrection include Matthew 28:1–10; Mark 16:1–8 and 9–14; Luke 24:1–44; and John 20:1–29.

52. Topping, *Holy Mothers of Orthodoxy*, 69; capitalization in the original.

53. Doxastikon for Pascha, in *The Pentecostarion*, 20. The hymn reads, "It is the day of Resurrection; let us be radiant for the festival and let us embrace one another. Let us say, O brethren, even to those that hate us: Let us forgive all things on the Resurrection; and thus let us cry: Christ is risen from the dead, by death hath He trampled down death, and on those in the grave hath He bestowed life."

54. The Orthodox icon of the "Harrowing of Hell" is particularly apt in depicting this liberation.

55. Third hymn for the Paschal Hours, in *The Pentecostarion*, 21.

56. See, e.g., the Exapostilarion of the myrrh bearers, in *The Pentecostarion*, 75. The hymn includes Christ saying, "Hasten ye quickly and proclaim the gladsome tidings to My friends; for I have willed that joy shine forth thence upon all My creation from whence there first came forth sorrow."

57. See, e.g., the instructions given in one of the Stichera of Pascha, in *The Pentecostarion*, 20. The hymns say, "Today Christ hath shone forth from the tomb as from a bridal chamber, and hath filled the women with joy, saying: Proclaim it unto the Apostles" and also "Come from that scene, O women,

bearers of good tidings, and say to Sion: Receive from us the tidings of joy, of the Resurrection of Christ. Exalt, dance, and be glad, O Jerusalem, for thou has seen Christ the King as a bridegroom come forth from the tomb."

58. Chimamanda Ngozi Adichie, "The Danger of a Single Story," TED-Global, July 2009, https://www.ted.com/talks/chimamanda_ngozi_adichie_the _danger_of_a_single_story?language=en.

## CONCLUSION

1. There has been increasing interest in highlighting Orthodox women's voices and issues of gender, although some would reject an identification with "feminism." See, e.g., Eleni Kasselouri-Hatzivassiliadi, Fulata Mbano Moyo, and Aikaterini Pekridou, eds., *Many Women Were Also There* . . . : *The Participation of Orthodox Women in the Ecumenical Movement* (Geneva: World Council of Churches Publications, 2010); Ina Merdjanova, ed., *Women and Religiosity in Orthodox Christianity* (New York: Fordham University Press, 2021); Carrie Frederick Frost, *Maternal Body: A Theology of Incarnation from the Christian East* (Mahweh, NJ: Paulist Press, 2019); Carrie Frederick Frost, ed., *The Reception of the Holy and Great Council: Reflections of Orthodox Christian Women* (New York: Greek Orthodox Archdiocese Department of Inter-Orthodox, Ecumenical, and Interfaith Affairs, 2018); Valerie Karras, "Patristic Views on the Ontology of Gender," in *Personhood: Orthodox Christianity and the Connection between Body, Mind, and Soul*, ed. John Chirban (Westport, CT: Bergin & Garvey, 1996), 113–19; Eleni Kasselouri-Hatzivassiliadi, "Orthodox Women and Theological Education," *Ecumenical Review* (2014): 471–76; Nonna Harrison, "Orthodoxy and Feminism," *St. Nina Quarterly* 2.2 (2009), accessed March 11, 2016, http://www.stnina.org/node/262; Elisabeth Behr-Sigel, *The Ministry of Women in the Church*, trans. Steven Bigham (Crestwood, NY: St Vladimir's Seminary Press, 1990); Maria McDowell, "Seeing Gender: Orthodox Liturgy, Orthodox Personhood, Unorthodox Exclusion," *Journal of the Society of Christian Ethics* 33.2 (2013): 77; Leonie Liveris, *Ancient Taboos and Gender Prejudice: Challenges for Orthodox Women and the Church* (Burlington, VT: Ashgate, 2005); Paul Evdokimov, *Woman and the Salvation of the World: A Christian Anthropology on the Charisms of Women*, trans. Anthony Gythiel (Crestwood, NY: St Vladimir's Seminary Press, 1994); John Behr, "A Note on the 'Ontology of Gender,'" *St Vladimir's Theological Quarterly* 42.3–4 (1998): 363–72; Thomas Hopko, *Women and the Priesthood* (Crestwood, NY: St Vladimir's Seminary Press, 1999); Timothy Patitsas, "The Marriage of Priests: Towards an Orthodox Christian Theology of Gender," *St Vladimir's Theological*

*Quarterly* 51.1 (2007): 71–105; Maria McDowell, "Seeing Gender: Orthodox Liturgy, Orthodox Personhood, Unorthodox Exclusion," *Journal of the Society of Christian Ethics* 33.2 (2013): 73–92; Helena Kupari and Elina Vuola, eds., *Orthodox Christianity and Gender: Dynamics of Tradition, Culture and Lived Practice* (London: Routledge, 2019); Heleen Zorgdrager, "Is *theosis* a Gendered Concept? Theological Pitfalls and Perspectives for an Inclusive Affirmation of Human Dignity," *Journal of Eastern Christian Studies* 71.3–4 (2019): 343–68; Kateřina Bauerová, "Motherhood as a Space for the Other: A Dialogue between Mother Maria Skobtsova and Hélène Cixous," *Feminist Theology* 26.2 (2018): 133–46.

2. One example is the use of Elizabeth Schüssler Fiorenza in the biblical hermeneutics of Eleni Kasselouri-Hatzivassiliadi. I will note also the excellent and theologically compelling work for women of the Orthodox theologian and scholar Carrie Frederick Frost.

3. See, e.g., Merdjanova, *Women and Religiosity in Orthodoxy Christianity*; Nadieszda Kizenko, *Good for the Souls: A History of Confession in the Russian Empire* (Oxford: Oxford University Press, 2021), 143–94.

# INDEX

**A**
Ahmed, Sarah, 7–8, 12, 55, 143, 153
akolouthias, 85
*Ancient Taboos and Gender Prejudices* (Liveris), 15
androcentric control, of women's bodies, 83–85
androcentrism, 3, 20, 21, 22, 65, 150–51
 anti-patriarchal, 143
 critiques of, 201
 effects of, 193
 historical, 118, 193
 patriarchal (*see* patriarchal androcentrism)
 privileged, 60, 73, 126, 194
 problematic impact of, 203
 reinforces religious leadership of men, 2
 transformation, need of, 145
androprimacy, 65
Antioch, Church of, 234n60
anti-patriarchal androcentrism, 143
apophasis, 22, 118, 146, 152–57
 cataphasis and, 140
 issues related to gender, applying to, 165
 of kenosis of patriarchy, 164
 of presumed limits, 141
 recognizing God, 155
apophatic theology, 20, 154, 253n56
Aristotle, 49

Arsenius, Abba, 78–79
asceticism, 75, 76, 79, 80, 113, 131
ascetic virtues, 91–92, 94
Athanasius, 46, 49, 120, 123, 125, 128, 186
Athanasopoulou-Kypriou, Spyridoula, 170
authority, 147, 180, 183
 ecclesial, 67, 126, 149
 male, 86, 182
 patriarchal, 56, 87
 religious, 26
 spiritual, 146
 subversion of, 85, 183–84
 universal, 47
 of woman, 81
 *See also* power

**B**
Barr, Beth Allison, 176
Bauerová, Kateřina, 16
Beauvoir, Simone de, 10, 63
Behr, John, 107
Behr-Sigel, Elisabeth, 15, 49, 51, 54, 72, 111
Bennett, Judith, 5
Bible, 43–44
 feminist approaches to, 219n54
 New Testament, 44, 219n59
 Old Testament, 43
bodily impurity, 244n5

Body of Christ, 42, 49, 99, 135, 142, 148, 186, 193, 200
Bulgakov, Sergius, 30, 41
Butler, Judith, 10, 63

C
Cabasilas, Nicholas, 158
Catholic feminist theology, 17, 32
Christ. *See* Jesus Christ
Christianity, 8, 32, 57, 136
  feminism in, 10, 141
  muscular, 218n44
  premodern, 11
Chrysostom, John, 45, 46, 51, 254n65
*Church and the Second Sex, The* (Daly), 32
Cixous, Hélène, 16
clerical hierarchy, 38, 53
Climacus, John, 46
Coakley, Sarah, 18, 100
Collins, Patricia Hill, 94
Colobos, Abba John, 98, 102–3, 105
commemoration/commemorative tradition, 52, 62, 63, 88, 122, 138, 172, 179, 186–87, 202
  construction of women, 166
  men and masculinity in, 64
  of saintly women, 63, 153, 172
  of Virgin Mary, 81–82
Copeland, Shawn, 18
Crenshaw, Kimberlé, 11
cultural identity, 9
Cyril of Alexandria, 46, 120, 125, 128, 251n32

D
Damascus, John of. *See* John of Damascus
Daly, Mary, 32, 42
dehumanization, 21, 42, 61, 142, 143, 165, 175, 176

deification, 18, 52, 99, 107, 111, 125–29, 137, 144, 162, 199, 215n8
Dionysius the Areopagite, 247n47
disobedience, 101, 103, 179, 183
  of earthly powers, 114
  righteous, 104, 172
  *See also* obedience
divine feminine, 41
divine-human communion, 18, 26, 111, 148
  goal of, 149
  mysticism of, 171–72
  paradoxical logic of, 139
  tradition and, 140
divine-human unity, 23, 85, 134, 137, 170, 171, 193, 195, 197–99
  Christological emphasis on, 161
  confession of, 23, 32, 82, 144, 152, 164, 171, 182
  incarnational imperative of, 117
  participants in, 190
  possibilities of, 32
  for women, 82
divine knowledge, 161
divine light, 22, 144, 163
  faith in seeing, 158
  vision of, 157, 159, 160
divine Logos, 31, 41, 42, 120
divine love, 98, 101, 114, 126, 144
divine power, 57, 73–74, 149, 153, 178, 182
divine suffering, 99–100
Divine Word, 72

E
ecclesial authority, 67, 126, 149
ecclesiastical hierarchy, 67, 149
Emmelia of Caesarea, 110
Epistle, 43
equality, 2–5, 9, 15, 184
  empty claim of, 68–72
  gender (*see* gender equality)

before God, 13
spiritual, 13
essentialism, 40, 63, 69, 72, 106, 161, 163, 186
exclusion, 2, 35, 36, 55, 58

**F**
faith
  fullness of, 135–36
  in seeing divine light, 158
  true, 154
female saints, 74, 183, 184, 231n36
  commemoration in Orthodox Church, 63, 153, 172
  historical hagiographies of, 69
  living as men, 242n73
  within Orthodox hagiography, 63
feminism, 9–21, 24, 92, 141
  under communism, 10
  disruption of tradition, 180–81
feminist theology, 17, 26, 29, 32, 106, 146, 166, 170–72, 177, 199, 202
Fiorenza, Elisabeth Schüssler, 17
Frost, Carrie Frederick, 7, 205n2

**G**
Garcia, Manon, 14, 38
gender-based abuses, 55, 118
gender-based disparities, 45
gender-based exclusion, 2, 35, 36, 55, 58
gender-based hostility, 13, 39
gender-based inequality, 2, 30, 32, 35, 36, 63, 70
gender-based negation, 77–78
gender-based oppression, 67
gender-based violence, 118
gender constructions, 3, 4, 26, 85, 163
gendered tropes, 85–89
gender equality, 2, 20, 51, 58, 65, 68, 166
  human, 49
  issues of, 7, 9
  religious, 69

religious patriarchy support, 37
  spiritual values and, 91–115
  value of, 16
gender-exclusive patriarchy, 150
gender hierarchy, 23, 56, 73, 107, 115, 183
  feminism, 180–81
  instituted, 92
  Jesus Christ and, 147
  patriarchal, 75
  reinforced, 92
  religious system and, 20
  social, 51, 87
  and spiritual hierarchy, 110
  women in, 100
gender inclusivity, 24, 29
Gilligan, Carol, 14
God
  activity in humanity, 162
  communion with, 3, 99, 104, 126, 152, 179, 182, 190, 197
  encounter with, 157–67
  equality before, 13
  gendered language for, 216n17
  icon of, 149, 171–72, 174, 176
  image of, 57, 59, 106, 108, 133, 134, 135, 137, 152, 162, 173, 174, 177, 190, 216n17
  individuality as, 178
  meeting in other, 151–52
  Orthodox beliefs about, 197
  reality of, 157
  as Trinity, 161–62
Gregory of Nazianzus, 51, 126
Gregory of Nyssa, 50, 51, 100, 108
Gregory Palamas, 46, 49, 158, 254n70

**H**
hagiography, 33, 45, 50, 62, 63, 69, 86, 95, 154, 179, 184
  gender tensions in, 71
  of Horaiozele of Constantinople, 70
  Mary the Younger, 70

hagiography (*cont.*)
  tropes about women in, 156
  use of gender in, 153
Harrison, Nonna Verna, 15
Hart, David Bentley, 139–40, 154, 156
Harvey, Susan Ashbrook, 40, 61, 76
Herbel, Oliver, 30
hesychasm, 157–67
hierarchy
  clerical, 38, 53
  divine participation and humanity, 107
  ecclesiastical, 67, 149
  gender (*see* gender hierarchy)
  institutional, 54
  ordained, 55, 92
  ordered, 184
  spiritual, 103, 110, 115, 147
Hilkert, Mary Catherine, 17
Hirschmann, Nancy, 14, 36
Holy and Great Council, 1–2, 55, 205n3
Holy Spirit, 30, 47, 82, 113, 119, 166
  living temples of, 177
  Pentecost of, 31
  in Syriac Orthodox tradition, 40
  theology and, 31
  tradition and witness of, 135–38
  true faith and, 154
  women's bodies and, 80, 84
holy subversion, 104, 178–85
  hagiographic depictions of, 181
  in sources and practices, 44
Horaiozele of Constantinople, 70
humility, 19, 93, 131, 152–57
  in divine imitation, 102
  Orthodox tradition and values, 106, 156, 157
  penitential, 83
  spiritual values, 22, 32, 171
  subordinating, 105–6
hymns, 2, 11, 25, 43, 52, 56, 58, 82, 86, 128, 178, 182, 233n52

I
icon
  of Christ, 175, 176, 186
  of God, 149, 171–72, 174, 176
  of Mary, 36
  Orthodox, 246n35
  of saint, 131
  of the Theotokos, 58
iconodule, 257n12
iconodule commitment, 172–78
iconophile, 257n12
icon veneration, 129–34
  goal of, 130–31
  Orthodox theology and, 173, 177
  theological justification for, 138
idealism, 70, 151, 174
identities, 5, 10–12
  cultural, 9
  intersectional reflection on, 24
  as Orthodox Christian, 6–7
  religious, 6, 34
incarnation, 119–25
incarnational reality, 171
  confessing, 123–24
  diverse aspects of, 201
  of human existence, 22
  Orthodox obligation and, 161
  of Orthodox women, 25
inclusion, 24, 31, 122, 165
inequality, 70, 92, 94, 118
  acknowledging, 19
  embedded, 203
  fundamental, 111
  gender-based, 2, 30, 32, 35, 36, 63, 70
  ignoring, 101
  sacred traditions of, 202
Irigaray, Luce, 12, 74
Isaac of Nineveh, 46

J
Jantzen, Grace, 151

Jesus Christ, 114, 121, 147, 185–90
  body of, 42, 49, 99, 135, 142, 148, 186, 193, 200
  divine-human revelation in, 30
  divine Logos as, 31, 41
  icon of, 175, 176, 186
  risen, 187
  saving work of, acknowledging, 125–26
  *See also* God
John of Damascus, 46, 49, 52, 123, 126, 127, 129, 131, 133, 145, 247n54
Johnson, Elisabeth, 18
Jones, Serene, 17

## K
Karidoyanes-FitzGerald, Kyriaki, 7
Karras, Valerie, 15, 31
Kasselouri-Hatzivassiliadi, Eleni, 15
Kassia, 47, 58, 82, 182–83
kataphasis, 136
Kendi, Ibrahim, 143
kenosis, 96, 100, 143
  as Christological imitation, 146
  feminist engagements with, 250n23
  as kenotic love, 112
  of patriarchy, 146–51, 164–65
  self-sacrificing, 111
kenotic patriarchy, 147–48
knowledge
  divine, 161
  of God, 125, 140
  relational, 154, 161
  of women, 37
Kyrill, Patriarch, 208n25

## L
LaCugna, Catherine, 141, 161–62
*Life of Melania the Younger*, 71–72
Liveris, Leonie, 15
Logos, 31, 41, 42, 120
Lorde, Audre, 11, 144

Lossky, Vladimir, 177
Lot-Borodine, Myrrha, 15, 111

## M
Makarios of Egypt, 99
manliness, 80, 110, 131
Manne, Kate, 13, 39, 66, 67, 143
Maria of Paris. *See* Skobtsova, Maria
Marinos, 180–81
Mark the Ascetic, 101, 105
Mary Magdalene, 4, 53
Mary of Egypt, 33, 75–76, 82–83, 181, 233n57, 235n73
Mary the Theotokos, 42, 58, 77, 126, 183
Mary the Younger, 69, 70, 73, 79, 94, 95
masculinity, 75
  divine, 41
  limited representation of, 64
  liturgical privileging of, 40–42
  *See also* patriarchy
Matoes, Abba, 181–82
Maximus the Confessor, 46, 49, 108, 111, 122, 126, 127, 128
McVey, Kathleen, 40
Melania the Younger, 71–72, 73, 233n59
Mercedes, Anna, 96
Metaphrastes, Symeon, 75
Methodia of Kimolos, 85
misogyny, 13, 36, 39, 135, 141, 143, 155, 203
Moschus, John, 81
myrrh-bearing women, 23, 186–88

## N
negation, of women, 72-78
New Testament, 44, 219n59

## O
obedience, 101–5, 114, 115
  in divine imitation, 102
  gendered, 80
  righteous, 104

obedience (*cont.*)
  self-sacrificial, 92
  of Theodora, 103
  tropes of valorized, 183
  values of, 112–13
  *See also* disobedience
Old Testament, 43
openness, 22, 163, 166, 196, 202
  to gender, 161
  queer theological categorical, 165
  to reality of God, 157
  to revelation, 154
  vulnerability as, 100
ordained hierarchy, 55, 92
Orthodox believers, 3, 36, 64, 130
  listening to women, 189
  Paschal proclamation and, 189
  sainted figures and, 45
Orthodox engagement
  with feminist theology and gender theory, 199
  reframing, theological justification for, 156
  of women, 128
Orthodox spirituality, 45, 102–3, 138, 144, 145
  commemorative tradition, 179
  teaching of, 91, 101, 102, 169
  texts and, 96
  understanding of, 165
  values, 22, 171
Orthodox theology, 8, 189, 199
  addressing gender, 196
  argument for equality, 92
  deification in, 215n8
  feminist theological development and, 17–18
  Holy Spirit, 31
  icon veneration and, 173
  Paschal commitments for, 194
  of past, 166
  patriarchal androcentrism for, 24
  patriarchalism and, 201
  problem for women, 25–26
  teachings and tradition of, 30–31, 92
Orthodox tradition, 2–4, 20, 23, 26, 30–34, 194, 199, 205n1
  of apophasis, 22
  construction of womanhood, 11
  examining, 12
  historical, 70
  holy subversion, 178–85
  iconodule commitment, 172–78
  idealization of voluntary suffering, 180
  natural bodies of women in, 80
  Orthodox feminist theological approach to, modeling, 170–72
  Orthodox theology and, 30–31
  Paschal proclamation, 185–91
  patriarchal, 14, 35, 142–46, 196–97
  public performance of womanly identities, controlling, 82–83
  reflection on, 171
  sources of, 8, 194
*orthopraxia*, 7
otherness, 158
Ouspensky, Leonid, 173

P
Palamas, Gregory. *See* Gregory Palamas
Papanikolaou, Aristotle, 100
partial patriarchal woman, 63–68
Paschal proclamation, 185–91
  claiming of power, rejecting, 188
  Orthodox believers and, 189
*Passion of Tatiana*, 84
patriarchal androcentrism, 4, 6, 17, 24, 29, 32, 61, 117–18, 130, 139–67, 191, 195, 201
  affirming, 135
  of Christianity, 32, 57, 136
  as culture, 38

dominance of, 144
historical constraints of, 5
normative, 20, 62
problems associated with, 169
reinforced, 72
rejecting, resources for, 144
witness of Holy Spirit, 135
patriarchal bargain, 6
patriarchalism, 142, 163
androcentric, 22, 134, 220n65
existing structures of, 201
patriarchal privilege, 22, 42, 59, 188
betraying, 20, 138
in church, 60
embrace kenosis, 149
in Orthodox tradition, 19, 60, 159
reframing of, 164
unavoidable, 29
patriarchal woman, 61–89, 191
patriarchy, 7, 12, 16, 21, 166, 203
accounts of women, patristic, 50–51
addressing, 34–39
conciliar dominance, 47–48
as culture, 38
impact on church, 8
internalized historical, 44–46
interpretations of gender, patristic, 48–50
kenosis of, 146–51
liturgical privileging of masculinity, 40–42
patristic (and patriarchal) Mary, 51–53
in patristic tradition, 46–47
pervasive tradition of, 32
priestly, partiality of, 53–57
religious, 35, 37, 39
in scriptural tradition, 43–44
social-psychological construction of, 14

tradition for women, 34
*See also* masculinity
Pelagia of Antioch, 75
Peter of Damascus, 98, 109
Pentecost, 178
of Holy Spirit, 31
personhood, 22, 71, 82, 138
free self-giving, 70
Orthodox theology on, 161, 241n59
suffering and, 96
*Philokalia*, 93
*phronema*, 33
Plato, 49
power, 185
divine, 57, 73–74, 149, 153, 178, 182
gender-based, 67
thearchical, 146–47
*See also* authority

R
redemption, 125–29
reflective believers, 156
righteous disobedience, 104, 172
Rizk-Asdourian, Donna, 67
Romanos the Melodist, 82
Ruether, Rosemary Radford, 16, 72, 148, 164
Russian Orthodox Church, 9

S
Saiving, Valerie, 94
sanctification, 94–101
Sarah, Amma, 71, 222n80
self-deprecation, 105, 106, 175, 181, 184
self-preservation, 115, 186
honoring, 196
as spiritual virtue, 177
silent schism, 7
sinfulness, 31, 100, 106, 137, 180, 181
hesychasm and, 160
of humanity, 199

sinfulness (*cont.*)
    sexual, 82
    spiritual, 98
    spiritual-beneficial model of, 83
Skobtsova, Maria (of Paris), 15, 16, 85–86, 111, 149, 151–52, 158, 159, 163, 171, 173, 175
Snyder, Naomi, 14
Solov'ev, Vladimir, 41
sophiology, 41–42, 218n47
Soskice, Janet Martin, 40
spiritual equality, 13, 21, 48, 59
spiritual hierarchy, 103, 110, 115, 147
*Spiritual Meadow* (Moschus), 81
spiritual present, 45
spiritual values, 20
    humility, 32
    Mary as paragon of, 112–15
    Orthodox, 22
Spivak, Gayatri Chakravorty, 12
Stefaniw, Blossom, 37
subordination, 101–5
subversion
    of authority, 85, 183–84
    of gender, 182
    holy, 44, 104, 178–85
    of oppressive or abusive situations, 182, 184
    self-claimed, 180
suffering, 93–101
    and sanctification, 94–101
    subordinate, 93
    valorization of, 92
Symeon the New Theologian, 40, 46, 102, 106, 120, 159
*synaxaria*, 76
Syncletica, Amma, 222n80
Syriac Orthodox traditions, 40

T
thearchical power, 146–47

Theodora, Amma, 98, 222n80
Theodora of Thessaloniki, 103, 175
Theodore the Studite, 46, 122, 129, 131, 132, 133
*theosis*. *See* deification
Thomas, Gabrielle, 100
Tonstad, Linn, 41, 74
Topping, Eva Catafygiotu, 15, 29, 32, 53, 187
Tsakaridou, Cornelia, 174
Tsalampouni, Aikaterini, 15

V
veneration, 129–34, 137–38, 173–74, 177. *See also* icon veneration
virtues, 78, 94, 102, 113
    ascetic, 91–92
    preeminent, 175
    of self-giving, 115
    spiritual, self-preservation as, 177
vulnerability, 100

W
women, 7, 23, 33, 91, 191, 236n1
    bodies of, 80, 83–85
    challenge of scholarship, 228n5
    empty claim of equality, 68–72
    holiness of, 71, 73, 87
    as inherently problematic, 78–80
    myrrh-bearing, 23, 186–88
    negation of womanhood as holy, 72–78
    as objects in relation to men, 81–82
    in Orthodox Church, 7, 9, 226n115
    overidealizing, 77
    partial patriarchal, 63–68
    patriarchal control of, 57–60
    "patriarchalness" for, 36
    patristic accounts of, 50–51
    realization of being fully human, 106–12

religious participation, 55
in sources of tradition, 62
*See also* female saints; feminism
Word of God, 148

X
Xenia of St. Petersburg, 85–86, 235n80

Z
Zizioulas, John, 135, 149, 150, 151, 158
Zorgdrager, Heleen, 111

ASHLEY MARIE PURPURA is an associate professor
of religion in the School of Interdisciplinary Studies
at Purdue University. She is the author of *God, Hierarchy,
and Power: Orthodox Theologies of Authority from Byzantium*,
and co-editor of *Orthodox Tradition and Human Sexuality*
and *Rethinking Gender in Orthodox Christianity*.

www.ingramcontent.com/pod-product-compliance
Lightning Source LLC
Chambersburg PA
CBHW072143160425
25272CB00004B/72